Praise for French Wine For Dummies

"The best way to sift through this informative tome is to pour yourself a big glass of Haut Brion, sit back, and enjoy. Whether you are an avid collector or wine novice, this book offers an extensive resource in an accessible format."

— Charlie Trotter, Acclaimed Chef and Award-Winning Restaurant Owner and Author

"Helping people to love wine is worthy of encouragement. Congratulations to Mary Ewing-Mulligan and Ed McCarthy for your book about one of the greatest treasures of France: the vineyards. This book is an invitation to discover the bountiful wine regions, each different from one another, and is an homage to the beauty and uniqueness of the delicious wines they produce. I am convinced that your readers will enjoy reading this book, and I am sure they will enjoy tasting the wines you praise. I propose a toast: to the joy of reading and to your good health! (Santé)"

— Georges Duboeuf, Les Vins Georges Duboeuf

"The diversity of French wine is one of its attractions, but it can seem perplexing . . . until you pick up this marvelous guide. The route is well-marked, easy-to-follow, and the destinations are delicious."

— Kermit Lynch, Wine Merchant and Author of *Adventures on the Wine Route*

"In *French Wine For Dummies,* Ed McCarthy and Mary Ewing-Mulligan lead us by the hand down the road of adventure to discover the wines of France that they know so well. We can follow them like trusted friends while they decipher the mystery and help us discover the pure enjoyment and attainability of these wines. In their relaxed, wise, and mischievous way, they show us the joy and pleasure of drinking French wine."

— Prince Alain de Polignac, Winemaker, Champagne Pommery

"This is an extraordinarily-detailed, yet easy-to-understand look at the world of French wine written from a loving perspective. Full of useful information as well as down-to-earth facts, I found myself pondering just which French wines I wanted to drink as I read the book."
— Todd Hess, Wine Director, Sam's Wines & Spirits

"Through its long history, France has produced the most fascinating and subtle array of wines. Wine novices understandably need help with the complexity of choices. To those who have no time to spend hours studying wines and visiting France, Mary Ewing-Mulligan and Ed McCarthy have succeeded in providing intelligent and crystal-clear guidance. As a Burgundian, I am very thankful to them."
— Bertrand DeVillard, President of Antonin Rodet and Wine-Grower in Burgundy

"Ed McCarthy and Mary Ewing-Mulligan are well-informed wine experts, and this is an original, accurate, and essential book for anyone willing to learn about French wine. There are discriminating palates behind their knowledge, and that their knowledge comes with such good taste is excellent for us!"
— Jacques Lardière, Technical Director, Maison Louis Jadot

"If you 'nose' little about wine, it is time for you to tickle your tastebuds by reading this wonderful book. Our two experienced globetrotters, Mary and Ed, will help you discover the world of wine. They are sure to open your mind to many new exciting sensations. An incredible experience for everyone, whether you like red, rosé, or white. This will add sparkle to your enjoyment of wine."
— Frédéric Jaboulet, Co-Proprietor, Paul Jaboulet-Ainé winery

French Wine
FOR
DUMMIES®

by Ed McCarthy and
Mary Ewing-Mulligan MW

WILEY

John Wiley & Sons, Inc.

French Wine For Dummies®

Published by
John Wiley & Sons, Inc.
111 River Street
Hoboken, NJ 07030
www.wiley.com

Copyright © 2001 by John Wiley & Sons, Inc., Hoboken, New Jersey

No part of this publication may be reproduced, stored in a retrieval system, or transmitted in any form or by any means, electronic, mechanical, photocopying, recording, scanning, or otherwise, except as permitted under Sections 107 or 108 of the 1976 United States Copyright Act, without either the prior written permission of the Publisher, or authorization through payment of the appropriate per-copy fee to the Copyright Clearance Center, 222 Rosewood Drive, Danvers, MA 01923, 978-750-8400, fax 978-750-4744. Requests to the Publisher for permission should be addressed to the Permissions Department, John Wiley & Sons, Inc., 111 River Street, Hoboken, NJ 07030, 201-748-6011, fax 201-748-6008, or online at http://www.wiley.com/go/permissions.

Trademarks: Wiley, the John Wiley & Sons logo, For Dummies, the Dummies Man logo, A Reference for the Rest of Us!, The Dummies Way, Dummies Daily, The Fun and Easy way, Dummies.com and related trade dress are trademarks or registered trademarks of John Wiley & Sons, Inc., in the United States and other countries, and may not be used without written permission. All other trademarks are the property of their respective owners. John Wiley & Sons, Inc., is not associated with any product or vendor mentioned in this book.

For general information on our other products and services or to obtain technical support, please contact our Customer Care Department within the U.S. at 877-762-2974, outside the U.S. at 317-572-3993, or fax 317-572-4002.

Wiley publishes in a variety of print and electronic formats and by print-on-demand. Some material included with standard print versions of this book may not be included in e-books or in print-on-demand. If this book refers to media such as a CD or DVD that is not included in the version you purchased, you may download this material at http://booksupport.wiley.com. For more information about Wiley products, visit www.wiley.com.

Library of Congress Cataloging-in-Publication Data:

Library of Congress Control Number: 00-112165

ISBN 978-0-7645-5354-7 (pbk); ISBN 978-1-118-06958-5 (ebk); ISBN 978-1-118-07126-7 (ebk)

20 19 18 17 16 15 14 13 12 11

1O/QV/QZ/QS/IN

About the Authors

Ed McCarthy and **Mary Ewing-Mulligan** are two wine lovers who met at an Italian wine tasting in New York City's Chinatown in 1981. Two years later, they formally merged their wine cellars and wine libraries when they married. They've since co-authored seven wine books, taught hundreds of wine classes together, run five marathons, and raised ten cats. Along the way, they've amassed more than half a century of professional wine experience between them.

Mary grew up in Pennsylvania, and graduated from the University of Pennsylvania, where she majored in English literature. Ed, a New Yorker, graduated from City University of NY with a Master's degree in psychology. He taught high school English in another life, while working part time in wine shops to satisfy his passion for wine and to subsidize his growing wine cellar. That cellar is especially heavy in his favorite wines — Bordeaux, Barolo, and Champagne.

Mary has spent half her professional career as owner and president of International Wine Center in New York. She teaches classes at the Center — mainly for wine professionals — as well as at a local university. She is a wine columnist for the *NY Daily News* and contributes to various other publications. In 1993, Mary became America's first woman Master of Wine (MW) after five years of independent study. There are only 233 Masters of Wine in the world, including 18 in America.

In 1999, Ed took a solo gig as author of *Champagne For Dummies*, about his favorite wine. He shares a wine column with Mary in *Nation's Restaurant News*, and he also writes for *Wine Enthusiast Magazine* and *Underground Wine Journal*. He and Mary are both accredited as Certified Wine Educators (CWE).

When they're not writing or teaching, Mary and Ed maintain a busy schedule of continuing education, by visiting the wine regions of the world, judging at professional wine competitions, and tasting as many new wines as possible. They admit to leading thoroughly unbalanced lives in which their only non-wine pursuits are jogging, and picnicking in the Alps — when they find the time. At home, they wind down to the tunes of Bob Dylan and Neil Young, in the company of their feline roommates, Léoville, Pinot, Brunello, Dolcetto, Clicquot, and Black & Whitey.

Dedication

We dedicate this book to the two people who taught us the most about French wine, Alexis Bespaloff and Bernie Fradin.

Authors' Acknowledgments

We've enjoyed a long love affair with France and French wines, which has fueled our enthusiasm for this book. For this, we thank all the French wine producers who have been so warm and hospitable to us over the years. You are in a wonderful profession, bringing such joy to the world with your great wines!

We thank the creative genius, CEO John Kilcullen — who's been known to enjoy a good glass or two of French wine — for making the *For Dummies* books the phenomenal success that they are. We sincerely thank Publisher Jennifer R. Feldman for giving us the "green light" on *French Wine For Dummies*. And thanks to Senior Editor Linda Ingroia — you have the ingenious skill of being sweet and tough at the same time! Really special thanks to our project editor Mary Goodwin; it was so nice working with you again. You're so even-tempered, and have such patience with us.

We were blessed to have French wine expert Jean-Louis Carbonnier as our technical reviewer. No mistake slips through your hands — even if that can be exasperating! Thanks to Steve Ettlinger, our agent, who brought us to Hungry Minds, Inc., in the first place.

We're grateful for the support of our colleagues at International Wine Center, Linda Lawry and May Matta-Alliah, who sustained our absence while we wrote this book. Finally, to Elise McCarthy, E.J. McCarthy, and his wife Bernadette, and to Cindy McCarthy Tomarchio and her husband, David, thanks for your continual encouragement and support.

Publisher's Acknowledgments

We're proud of this book; please send us your comments through our online registration form located at www.dummies.com/register.

Some of the people who helped bring this book to market include the following:

Acquisitions, Editorial, and Media Development

Project Editor: Mary Goodwin

Senior Editor: Linda Ingroia

Assistant Acquisitions Editor: Erin Connell

Editorial Coordinator: Michelle Hacker

Technical Editor: Jean-Louis Carbonnier

Editorial Manager: Pam Mourouzis

Editorial Assistant: Carol Strickland

Cover Photos: © iStock/beatrice preve

Composition Services

Project Coordinator: Dale White

Layout and Graphics: Joyce Haughey, Jackie Nicholas, Jill Piscitelli, Jacque Schneider, Julie Trippetti

Proofreaders: Laura Albert, Corey Bowen, Andy Hollandbeck, Susan Moritz

Indexer: Aptara

Publishing and Editorial for Consumer Dummies

Kathleen Nebenhaus, Vice President and Executive Publisher

Kristin Ferguson-Wagstaffe, Product Development Director

Ensley Eikenburg, Associate Publisher, Travel

Kelly Regan, Editorial Director, Travel

Publishing for Technology Dummies

Andy Cummings, Vice President and Publisher

Composition Services

Debbie Stailey, Director of Composition Services

Contents at a Glance

Table of Contents

Introduction

*E*ver since we wrote *Wine For Dummies* in 1995, we've wanted to write *French Wine For Dummies*. In trying to make the broad topic of wine more understandable, so that regular people (not just wine geeks, like us) could enjoy wine with greater appreciation and less apprehension, we realized that French wines particularly begged for clarification.

If you're one of the more than half a million who purchased *Wine For Dummies* (thank you!), you've already discovered something about French wines from that book. *French Wine For Dummies* tells you the rest of the story. We take a detailed look at every important aspect of French wines, and we cover every French wine region — not just the main ones.

We believe that wine drinkers like you can use *French Wine For Dummies* for two reasons:

- ✔ French wines are a vast and confusing field — especially for people who don't speak French, who are accustomed to seeing wines named after grape varieties (which most French wines aren't), and who live an ocean away from the regions where French wines grow. This book breaks down these barriers for you.

- ✔ The image of French wine is so prestigious that many people believe they need to know about France's wines, despite the difficulty inherent in mastering them (see the preceding bullet). Having this book as your ally will give you confidence around French wines and eliminate whatever intimidation the wines' prestigious image might evoke.

But, beyond giving you a book that you can use, our goal in writing *French Wine For Dummies* involved another issue: We love French wines, and we want you to love them, too. We hope that by clearing away the confusion, we can incline you to experiment with French wines, so that you can discover a few types that you really enjoy. If you become fascinated enough with the subject that you get on a plane and visit Bordeaux, or Burgundy, or Alsace, all the better!

Why do we love French wines (and want you to try them)? For one thing, their variety and their range of expression — the seductiveness of a red Burgundy, the power of a Cornas, the agelessness of a great red Bordeaux. For another thing, their food-friendliness. Their unparalleled quality (in the case of some wines) and their surprising value (in the case of others). And the discovery of them: After decades of drinking French wines, we're still discovering new wines ourselves.

We're big fans of French wines, but we're not apologists for them. France makes as many ordinary wines as any other country — or maybe more, considering how much wine France makes. But the top wines are incomparable, and even the affordable wines are totally unique.

With the knowledge you gain from *French Wine For Dummies,* you'll navigate a new wine world, the universe of French wines — which, for us, includes many of the best wines in existence. To enjoy wine without discovering the wines of France would be a real pity, in our book.

How to Use This Book

Know nothing about French wines? Start reading *French Wine For Dummies* at the beginning; you'll find that it lays out the building blocks of French wine knowledge in a logical, clear way.

Just want to know the highlights — the top wines, from the top regions, for example? Or want to read about a particular type of wine you've just seen for the first time? Turn to the part or the chapter that applies to your interest at the moment. (You can also scan the Table of Contents or check the Index if you are looking for information about a particular topic.) The following sections describe the type of information in each part of the book.

(For basic information about wine, such as how it's made, or how to taste it, pick up a copy of *Wine For Dummies,* 2nd Edition, published by Hungry Minds.)

Part 1: Why France Is the Home of Great Wines

The first two chapters explain the reasons for France's dominant position in the wine world, and provide an overview of the many styles of French wine. Chapter 3 explains how the French name their wines, and the meaning of an abbreviation we use throughout the book, AOC (Hint: It has to do with France's system of wine laws). To understand the French wine label, take a look at Chapter 3.

Part 11: France's High-Profile Wine Regions

In Part II we explore France's most important wine regions — with a special emphasis on its red wines: Bordeaux, Burgundy, Beaujolais, and the Rhône Valley. While we're at it, we dedicate a separate chapter, Chapter 5, to Bordeaux's value red wines, and another, Chapter 6, to its white wines and dessert wines. (Bordeaux is so major that we could have written a book on Bordeaux alone.)

Part 111: France's Other Wine Regions

We begin with a pop! — with a discussion of the world's greatest sparkling wine, Champagne. Then we look at France's two most important predominantly white wine regions, Alsace and the Loire Valley. We also cover the up-and-coming regions of Languedoc-Rousillon, Provence, and Southwest France (a conglomeration of small districts), plus a couple of France's little-known regions.

Part 1V: The Part of Tens

The fun part is writing what we call the "Part of Tens." Here we give you answers to ten common questions about French wines, and we expose ten popular myths concerning French wines.

Part V: Appendixes

One of the main reasons people shy away from French wine is that they're not sure how to pronounce the names of the wines. We address that issue with our pronunciation guide in this part. In addition, we provide important classifications of Bordeaux wines, plus Burgundy's *grands crus,* and end with a vintage chart of French wines.

Icons Used in This Book

We're not trying to turn you into a winemaker or a French legislator, but some technical issues are important for understanding French wines — depending on how deeply you want to understand them, of course.

Advice and information that will make you a wiser French wine drinker and buyer is marked by this bull's-eye so that you won't miss it.

When you see this sign, you'll know that you're in the territory of a common misunderstanding about French wine. We alert you to help prevent confusion, or help you avoid a common mistake.

Some issues in wine are so fundamental that they bear repeating. Just so you don't think we repeated ourselves without realizing it, we'll mark the repetitions with this symbol.

Wine snobs practice all sorts of affectations designed to make other wine drinkers feel inferior. A comment such as "We *are* drinking classified growth Bordeaux tonight, aren't we?" can throw you for a loop. But you won't be intimidated by snobbery once you recognize it.

To our tastes, the wines we mark with this icon are bargains because we like them, and their price is low compared to other wines of similar type, style, or quality. You can also interpret this logo as a badge of genuineness, as in "This Chablis is the real deal."

Unfortunately, some of the finest, most intriguing, most delicious wines are made in very small quantities, and you can't always get your hands on a bottle, even if you're willing to pay their price. We mark such wines with this icon, and we hope that your search proves fruitful.

Part I

Why France Is the Home of Great Wines

In this part . . .

Have you ever wondered what France did to deserve such a stellar reputation in the wine world? The three chapters in this part explain what's behind the hoopla and the hype — France's very real natural assets for making great wine, and making so much wine.

One of these assets is the cumulative experience of French winemakers over the centuries. (When it comes to wine, the French invented *savoir faire*.) Another is the excellent grape varieties that call France home. You'll read about both those issues here, along with one of the less celebrated realities of French wines: the laws that govern wine names and labels. Even if you can't quite come to grips with the bureaucracy of the labels, at least you'll discover what all the words mean.

Chapter 1

France, Superstar

● ●

In This Chapter

▶ Experience counts when it comes to making wine

▶ France's winemaking legacy

▶ France's lucky coincidence of climate and soil

▶ Wines are grown, not made

● ●

Some people are just born with certain talents. Some countries are just born with certain gifts. In the case of France, the ability to grow wine grapes and make good wine is hardwired into the land and the people who live there. That's why France is not only the greatest wine producing country on Earth, but also the greatest wine culture.

France has been the leader of the winemaking world for centuries. France is number one not only in wine production (in many years) but also in wine consumption. In the quality department, the most critically-acclaimed, most treasured red wines, white wines, sparkling wines, *and* sweet wines all come from France. The country's renown is such that winemakers from all over the world find inspiration and motivation in French wines.

In the Beginning . . .

The French have the Greeks and Romans to thank for getting them started as a wine producing land. As we remember so well from our Latin classes, Julius Caesar conquered Gaul in 51 B.C.; what the teacher didn't tell us, of course, was that the Roman troops almost certainly brought grapevine cuttings with them, and planted them in what is now France.

The region of Provence, in southern France, was already a Roman province in the second century B.C. And long before that, in 600 B.C., the southern French city of Marseilles *(mar say)* was a Greek colony, most likely complete with vineyards.

By the 200's A.D., the areas known today as Bordeaux and Burgundy were producing wine, and by the 500's, grape growing and winemaking were common all over France.

Over the centuries, some wine regions of France became more important than others. Historically, the popularity of a region's wines had as much to do with politics and with proximity to waterways, for transportation of the wine, as it did with the quality of the wines themselves.

As one example, the wines of the Bordeaux region, in western France, benefited enormously from the fact that most of western France was part of England in the 12th century — making those wines less expensive to British wine drinkers than other French wines. That the city of Bordeaux is a major port didn't hurt, either. English demand spurred Bordeaux wine production in the 14th century, and Dutch enthusiasm for the wines helped bring Bordeaux to supremacy during the 17th and 18th centuries. Other wine regions of France progressed at a different pace, according to their own circumstances.

Everything hasn't necessarily been wine and roses for French winemakers, though. Three major fungal scourges (powdery mildew, downy mildew, and black rot) devastated their vineyards in the mid to late 19th century. And the phylloxera louse — an insect that eats vine roots — almost wiped out the entire species of wine grapes during the same period. But French wine rebounded. Today the wines of France are better than at any time in their history.

Natural Talents

France's thousands of years of winemaking experience count for a lot. But the fact is, France had a couple of other things going for her since Day One: climates extremely suitable for growing high quality wine grapes; and the right types of soils in the right climates.

France is large by European standards — it's the largest ~try in western Europe — but compared to countries such as the United States or Australia, it isn't really such a big place. (All of France could fit easily into Texas, for example, with plenty of room to spare.) And yet, France has a strong diversity of soil types and climates. Each of France's major wine regions has different growing conditions for its grapes. (Figure 1-1 depicts France's wine regions.)

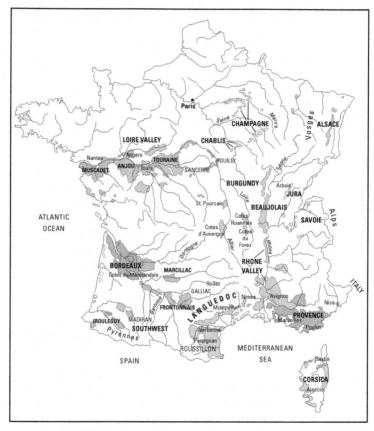

Figure 1-1: France's wine regions.

Climate ups and downs

Because French wines are so acclaimed, wine people tend to credit France with having an ideal location for grape growing and winemaking. The 45th parallel, which runs through the regions of Bordeaux and the Rhône Valley, has taken on mythical connotations as the It position for fine wine production.

In reality, though, a lot of seriously good wine comes from places that occupy a much more southerly position than France does — such as all of Spain and Portugal, California, and most of Italy (not to mention, in the southern hemisphere, Chile, Argentina, Australia, New Zealand, and South Africa!). Furthermore, plenty of France's wine regions are even more northerly than Bordeaux; Champagne and Alsace, for example, are situated about as north as wine grapes can viably grow. From a global perspective, France would seem to be out of the mainstream of wine production, latitude-wise.

But latitude doesn't tell the whole story. France has ideal climates for growing wine grapes thanks to where the country happens to be situated relative to the rest of Europe, and thanks to the lay of the land within France's borders:

✔ Water surrounds France on three sides: the Atlantic Ocean on the west, the English Channel on the north, and the Mediterranean Sea along part of the country's southern border. These bodies of water influence the climate of the land nearby. In particular, winds passing over the Atlantic's Gulf Stream carry moisture and warm air to western France, providing a climate that's more suitable for grape growing than France's northerly position might suggest.

✔ The Massif Central, a high plateau in south central France, blocks the Atlantic's maritime influence about halfway across the country — and creates a particular climate in eastern France (hot but relatively short summers, and cold winters) that's distinctly different from the damp, temperate climate in the west. Farther east, France is landlocked and mountainous, with the mighty Alps Mountains separating France from Italy and Switzerland.

✔ The Mediterranean Sea creates yet another climate pattern in southern France: warm, dry, long summers and mild, rainy winters.

According to the way experts categorize climates, in fact, France boasts all three of the major climates for grape growing and wine production:

   ✔ The maritime climate (in the Bordeaux region and elsewhere in western France)

   ✔ The continental climate (in the regions of Alsace and Burgundy)

   ✔ The Mediterranean climate (in the southern Rhône Valley region and in southern France)

These different climates each favor the cultivation of different grape varieties and the production of different types of wine.

Old dirt

The variation in soil types within France has to do with the geological origins of the European continent — the melting of polar ice caps, the drying of seas, the decomposition of rocks, and so forth. We know of two books devoted entirely to the subsoils and the soils of France's wine regions: That's how complex the soils are.

Different wine regions of France have markedly different soils; for example:

   ✔ Gravel in the western part of Bordeaux

   ✔ Chalky soil in Champagne, in the northeast

   ✔ Granite in Beaujolais, in the southeast

   ✔ Large stones in the Châteauneuf-du-Pape district of the southern Rhône Valley

And even within individual wine regions, the soil varies quite a lot. The difference between western Bordeaux and eastern Bordeaux is one classic example: Different soils in each area favor different grape varieties. Within the region of Alsace, the soils change literally from one hillside to the next, and within Burgundy, soils change between vineyards separated from each other by the width of a cow path. (See Chapters 4, 11, and 7 respectively for more information on Bordeaux, Alsace, and Burgundy.)

None of this is to say that French dirt is any better than any other country's dirt, though. What's important about France's soils is that they are the right soils in the right climates for the right grape varieties. Where the climate is rainy (as in Bordeaux), for example, the soil provides good drainage. Where there's an impressionable grape variety, such as Pinot Noir, the soil varies from patch to patch (as in Burgundy) to create compellingly individual wines. And so forth.

Time passages

France's climate and soil are natural endowments, but choosing the right grape variety for each climate and soil is a human challenge. Which brings us back to those thousands of years of experience that the French have in growing grapes and making wines: Through centuries of trial and error, they've managed to discover which grape varieties do best where.

For most of France's history, wine grapes grew all over the country; transportation being difficult, each community had to produce its own wine in order to have any. That all changed in the 19th century, when the double whammy of vineyard devastation (via fungal diseases and the phylloxera bug) and better transportation (railroads) put many areas out of the grape growing business. The French wine regions that exist today are the survivors, the fittest — the regions whose climate, soil, and grape varieties make wines worth making.

French Wine-Think

We picture the French as sensualists, romantics, and lovers. When it comes to wine, they're also quite humble. Sure, most French people believe that French wines are the greatest wines anywhere — but they don't take personal credit for that greatness.

The French believe that their wines are so exceptional because their land is blessed. They attribute every nuance in a wine to the particular place where the grapes grow — to the rain that falls or refrains from falling; the sun that shines down on the vineyard; the wind that warms or cools the air; and the soil that holds the rain or drains it, that reflects the sun's heat back onto the grapes, or contains just the right minerals.

The French have a single word for the whole package of natural, interactive forces that affect the grapevine and its fruit: *terroir* (pronounced *ter wahr*). *Terroir* encompasses:

- ✔ The soil and subsoil of a vineyard, including its mineral content, fertility, and drainage
- ✔ How the vineyard is situated, on a slope, for example, or near a river
- ✔ The climate of the wine region, including sun, heat, wind, rain, and humidity
- ✔ The grape variety or varieties that grow in the vineyard

Every wine comes from a unique *terroir,* and — in the Gallic way of looking at wine — is what it is because of its *terroir.*

Of course, every French wine also has a winemaker who turns the fruit of the vineyard into wine. And there's no arguing with the fact that what the winemaker does — such as fermenting the grape juice at a certain temperature or aging a wine in a particular type of oak barrel — can affect the quality and style of the wine. For the most part, however, French winemakers perceive their responsibility as bringing out in the wine what the *terroir* put into the grapes. (And because of the long history of each region, the winemakers have a pretty good idea of what that is.)

The title that most French winemakers use — *vigneron* — suggests what they consider their role to be. The word means winegrower, not winemaker. Their wines grow from their vineyards, rather than being "made" in their wineries.

The concept of *terroir* is so fundamental to French wine that it even dictates how the wines are named: The overwhelming majority of French wines carry the name of the place where the grapes grow, because the place (rather than just the grape variety) is what makes the wines the way they are. Depending on the wine, the place might be any of the following:

- ✔ A large wine region
- ✔ A district within a region
- ✔ Even a single vineyard

Chapter 3 elaborates on the names of French wines.

A lesson in humility

We'd heard about *terroir,* and how important the French regard it, many times. But the message came alive for us several years ago, when we enjoyed a lunch in Bordeaux with five of that region's top winemakers. One of them was Paul Pontallier, the enormously gifted winemaker of Château Margaux, an elite, First Growth property. (Chapter 4 describes what a First Growth is.) Pontallier is credited with bringing Château Margaux back to top form in 1978 after years of below-par performance, but to our surprise, he was not the least bit boastful about the turnaround. He described himself as the current custodian of the glorious Château Margaux *terroir* — a *terroir* that existed long before he came onto the scene, and that will go on long after him. His wish was merely that history look favorably on the Pontallier era, and judge that he upheld the potential of the *terroir.*

In France, even the greatest winemakers give Nature most of the credit. *Terroir* rules!

Chapter 2

French Wine Today

*W*hat credentials does a country need in order to call itself the most important wine country in the world? A large production? Lots of different types of wines? Critical acclaim for its wines? When it comes to French wines, all we can say is check, check, and check. Regardless of how you measure wine stature, France has it.

We're Number One

France produces more wine than any other country — except when Italy does. (The two countries are neck and neck.) The amount varies from one year to the next, according to the weather. Generally speaking, France makes about 1.5 billion gallons of wine each year.

How much wine is that? Well, it's enough to fill about 8 billion standard, 750 ml wine bottles each year. Looking at the number another way, it's about 30 percent of all the wine produced in the entire world each year, and more than twice as California makes. Looking at it another way, it's a heckuva lot of wine.

The Variety of French Wine

We'll be the first to admit that in wine, quantity doesn't necessarily equate with quality. In fact, the opposite is often true: The smaller the quantity produced, the more concentrated and higher-quality a wine will be. Luckily for the reputation of French wines, the huge quantity produced each year comprises hundreds of different types of wine.

Variety, in fact, is the rule for French wines:

- ✔ French wines are white, red, and pink.
- ✔ French wines are still (non-bubbly) wines and bubbly wines; dry wines, semi-dry wines, and sweet wines.
- ✔ French wines sell for less than $8 a bottle and for several thousand dollars a bottle.
- ✔ French wines are simple wines for enjoying while they're young, and serious wines that aren't at their best until they age for a few decades.
- ✔ French wines are hand-crafted artisan wines made by small family wineries and mass-production wines made by large corporations.

The colors of France

France produces more red wine than white or rosé (pink) wine. Precise figures are hard to come by, but we do know this: In 1999, 28 percent of the wine produced in France was white. Most of the remaining 72 percent was, most likely, overwhelmingly red.

Rosé wines are made throughout France, and some of them are quite special, but they represent just a tiny part of the country's production.

Dry, sweet, and bubbly

French wines are predominantly dry, non-sparkling wines. Sparkling wines represent less than 10 percent of France's production. Champagne itself — the major sparkling wine of France (and the world) — accounted for about 5.5 percent of French wine production in 1999. Many other regions also make sparkling wine, but in significantly smaller quantity than Champagne. (See Chapter 10 for more information on Champagne.)

Almost every region of France makes some type of sweet, dessert wine, but no one region specializes in it. The quantity varies quite a lot from year to year because sweet wine production often depends on specific weather patterns that don't visit a region predictably each year.

Quantity aside, France makes outstanding sweet wines. Sauternes, which is probably the world's most revered type of sweet wine, carries the banner — but not without protest from the legendary sweet wines of the Loire Valley, such as Coteaux du Layon. Sweet wines from southern France, southwestern France, and the region of Alsace are also noteworthy.

Collectable to highly affordable

French wine authorities apparently never heard the expression, "You can't be all things to all people." Or maybe, by the time that way of thinking evolved, the nature of French wines was already a *fait accompli*. However it happened, France has managed to satisfy wine drinkers across all price and ageability spectrums: from Château Lafite-Rothschild to Beaujolais Nouveau.

France's finest wines enjoy the highest reputation of any wines anywhere, period. The best wines of the Champagne, Bordeaux, Burgundy, and Rhône regions dominate the cellars of the world's most celebrated wine collectors, as well as the auctions where rare wines are bought and sold. Bottles of mature wines from these regions can cost thousands of dollars each, depending on the wine and the vintage — that's how desirable these wines are.

But France makes plenty of mid-range and inexpensive wines, too. In just about any good wine shop in the U.S., you can find wines from southern France that sell for as little as $6 a bottle — good, everyday wines for casual enjoyment. Between the least expensive and the most precious French offerings are the majority of French wines — high quality wines that cost from about $15 to $35 and are suitable either for drinking young or for aging a few years.

Regional characters

In 1961, when he was president of France, Charles de Gaulle remarked, "How can you be expected to govern a country that has 246 kinds of cheese?"

The reason France has so many cheeses (now estimated at over 700 types) is the same as the reason that France has so many wines: regional particularities. Wineries in different parts of France cultivate different grape varieties and make their wines in different ways. Even when two regions grow the same grape variety, their wines usually turn out to be distinctly different, because of *terroir* differences, or different winemaking traditions. The Sauvignon Blanc grape variety provides a good example of how the same grape makes different wines:

- ✔ In the Loire Valley, it makes crisp, un-oaked wines with well-concentrated, minerally flavors.

- ✔ In the Bordeaux region, winemakers frequently blend Sauvignon Blanc wine with Sémillon, making a fleshier, longer lasting wine with more subtle flavors; often, they use oak barrels, which give the wine a smoky or toasty character.

- ✔ In the south of France, Sauvignon Blanc wines have riper fruit flavors than those from either the Loire or Bordeaux.

Wine critics who sample thousands of wines each year complain about the "cookie cutter" wine phenomenon — that so many wines lately taste pretty much the same. We've voiced that criticism ourselves, but generally not about French wines. Regional individuality is inbred among the French. That might make governing the country a challenge, but it makes drinking the wines an adventure.

The Grapes of France

Practically all the most famous grape varieties in the world are French varieties, meaning that they either originated in France or became famous through their expression in French wines. (Chapter 4 of *Wine For Dummies* explains grape varieties and how they differ.)

Which varieties are they? Name a variety, and chances are, it's French. Chardonnay? Yep. Merlot? Yes. Sauvignon Blanc? Right again. Cabernet Sauvignon, Pinot Noir, or Syrah? *Oui,* all three. (In fact, only two of France's top grape varieties are not technically French. Riesling is a German variety, and Grenache originated in Spain, where it's called Garnacha.)

Over the centuries, different grape varieties have acclimated to certain regions of France. In some regions, winemakers make blended wines, from several grape varieties; in other regions, the wines derive from a single variety. Table 2-1 names the major white grape varieties of France, and indicates in which of France's wine regions each grape is important. Table 2-2 does the same for France's major red grapes. Several of our previous books — *Wine For Dummies, Red Wine For Dummies,* and *White Wine For Dummies* — describe the major French varieties and the types of wines made from them. In Chapters 4 through 14 of this book, we describe the wines made from these varieties in each region of France.

Table 2-1   France's Major White Grape Varieties

Grape Variety	*Region(s) Where Important*
Chardonnay	Burgundy; Champagne; Languedoc
Chenin Blanc	Loire Valley
Sauvignon Blanc	Bordeaux; Loire Valley; southwestern France; Languedoc
Gewurztraminer	Alsace
Pinot Gris	Alsace
Pinot Blanc	Alsace
Marsanne	Rhône Valley
Muscadet	Loire Valley
Riesling	Alsace
Sémillon	Bordeaux; Southwest France
Viognier	Rhône Valley; Languedoc

Table 2-2	France's Major Red Grape Varieties
Grape Variety	*Region(s) Where Important*
Cabernet Sauvignon	Bordeaux; Southwest France; Languedoc
Cabernet Franc	Loire Valley; Bordeaux; Southwest France
Carignan	Rhône Valley; Southern France
Cinsault	Rhône Valley; Southern France
Gamay	Beaujolais
Grenache	Rhône Valley; Southern France
Merlot	Bordeaux; Southwest France; Languedoc
Malbec	Southwest France; Bordeaux
Mourvèdre	Rhône Valley; Southern France
Pinot Noir	Burgundy; Champagne
Syrah	Rhône Valley; Southern France

Wine lovers often use a certain shorthand in talking about French grapes:

- ✔ **"Bordeaux varieties" (generally used in reference to red varieties):** Cabernet Sauvignon, Merlot, and Cabernet France, principally; Malbec and Petit Verdot are two minor red varieties of Bordeaux

- ✔ **"Red Rhône varieties":** Syrah, Grenache, Cinsault, and Mourvèdre

- ✔ **"White Rhône varieties":** Marsanne, Roussanne, Grenache Blanc, and Viognier

The wines of Bordeaux, the South of France, and the Rhône Valley (the larger, Southern Rhône, at least) are blends, made from several grape varieties in varying proportions. When winemakers from other parts of the world use these varieties together, they sometimes describe their wines as being "Bordeaux blends" or "Rhône blends," a more convenient lingo than naming all the varieties used.

Chapter 3

Wine Laws and Labels

● ●

In This Chapter

▶ The logic behind French wine names

▶ The long arm of the (wine) law

▶ What AOC means

▶ Words that appear on French labels

● ●

*W*hat's in a name? A tremendous amount of information, if the name happens to belong to a French wine. In fact, the names of French wines transmit so much hidden information that they're rather like codes. (And until you become familiar with them, they can be as frustrating as codes.)

Once you crack the beautiful logic that lies behind France's system for naming wines, however, you can de-code almost any French wine label and understand just what that wine in your hand is.

France's Wine Laws: The Opposite of Laissez-Faire

The first step toward understanding French wine names and labels is to realize that, in France, the government controls how wines may be named, and every wine name is a reflection of French wine law. In theory, you could learn all sorts of information about any French wine just by looking up its name in the French laws. That information would include the general vineyard territory for that wine, which grape varieties could possibly be in that wine, and so forth.

If you were to research several wine names, you'd discover that most of them are the names of places — the vineyard area where the grapes for the wines grow. Vineyard location is the organizational principle behind French wine law and the basis for naming French wines.

In Chapter 1, we discuss *terroir,* the French word for the set of natural conditions that any one vineyard (or wine region) has — the unique combination of climate, soil, altitude, slope, and so forth, in any one location. *Terroir* is not a self-serving concept that the French invented, but a reality that they experienced and witnessed over the centuries:

- Different vineyards produce different wines.
- The locale where the grapes grow affects the quality and style of the wine.

Naturally, then, *terroir* became the basis of French wine law, and the system for naming French wines.

Privileged versus ordinary locales

Not all *terroirs* are equal in the eyes of the French wine law. Some vineyards are very privileged locations, and other vineyards lie in more ordinary territory. The status of the locale determines, to a large extent, the price and the prestige of the wine grown there.

Two basic categories of wine zones exist in France:

- Classic wine areas
- Newer grape growing and winemaking areas

Every vineyard in France lies within one type of wine zone or the other — or sometimes, both. Where classic zones and newer areas overlap, a winemaker can use either area's name for the wine, provided that he follows the rules governing the production of the wine whose name he uses.

These rules are stricter for vineyards in the classic areas, and more flexible in the newer areas. For example, winemakers in a classic zone have less choice of what grape variety to plant. But wines from the classic areas are generally more prestigious.

Small is beautiful

Where territories overlap, a winemaker generally chooses the name that represents the smallest, most specific *terroir* for which the vineyard is eligible. This is true for several reasons:

- ✔ The smaller area is more exclusive; fewer people can have vineyards there, and use that name for their wine.

- ✔ Wines from smaller *terroirs* generally command a higher price than wines named after larger areas.

- ✔ Wines from smaller areas are generally perceived to be of higher quality.

(An exception to this rule can occur when the name of the larger area is better known and more marketable than the name of the smaller area.)

AOC, VDQS, and Vin de Pays

French words on the labels of French wines indicate whether a wine comes from a classic region or a newer wine area:

- ✔ Wines from classic regions carry the words *"Appellation . . . Contrôlée" (ahp pel laht zee ohn con troh lay)* on the label, in small print under the name of the wine. Between the two words is the name of the place that's the wine official name. (Figure 3-1 shows the label of a wine from a classic area.)

- ✔ Wines from lesser classic regions carry the words *"Vin Délimité de Qualité Supérieure" (van dee lim ee tay deh kal ee tay su per ee ehr)* on the label, below the name of the wine.

- ✔ Wines from newer regions carry the words *"Vin de pays de . . ." (van de pay ee deh)* on their labels. The official name of the area appears at the end of this phrase. (Figure 3-2 illustrates such a label.)

Figure 3-1: The words *Appellation . . . Contrôlée* on this label indicate that the wine comes from one of France's classic wine regions.

Appellation Contrôlée translates as "regulated name." Sometimes, in reading about French wines, you might see the phrase *Appellation d'Origine Contrôlée;* it translates as "regulated place name." The two phrases are used interchangeably, and mean the same thing, but the shorter version usually appears on wine labels. People who talk about wine a lot use the abbreviations "AC" or "AOC" for these phrases.

Vin Délimité de Qualité Supérieure translates as "demarcated wine of superior quality." The abbreviation "VDQS" applies to these wines. *Vin de pays* translates as "country wine."

At the bottom of the quality ladder is another category, *vins de table (van de tah bleh),* table wines. These very inexpensive wines carry no geographic name other than "France"; they're not vintage dated and never carry the name of a grape variety on their labels. (This use of the term "table wine" is distinctly different from the meaning of this phrase in the U.S.; refer to Chapters 1 and 9 of *Wine For Dummies* for more information on "table wines.")

Are AOC wines better than country wines?

When you buy a bottle of AOC wine, chances are it will cost more than a bottle of *vin de pays,* or country wine, because it has a higher pedigree. But is it worth the difference in price?

Which type of wine has higher quality depends entirely on what the two wines are; some AOC wines are mediocre, and some country wines are very good — but many AOC wines are far superior to most country wines.

The difference between AOC wines and country wines is one of winemaking mentality and style. In particular, country wines are often varietal wines; that is, they're labeled with the name of the grape variety that makes the wine. (They still have a place-name, too, but it's in smaller print.) They're made to express the characteristics of that grape rather than the region where the grape grows (which, frankly, can be quite large and not very distinctive). France's country wines are good values if you want a varietal wine, or if you want a simple French wine that's a bit fruitier than the classic French wines, generally speaking.

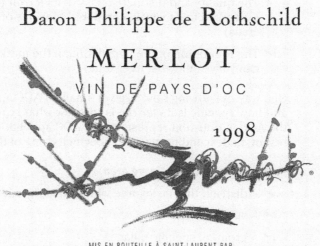

Baron Philippe de Rothschild

MERLOT

VIN DE PAYS D'OC

1998

MIS EN BOUTEILLE À SAINT-LAURENT PAR
BARON PHILIPPE DE ROTHSCHILD, S.A.-NÉGOCIANTS À PAUILLAC-GIRONDE-FRANCE
ALC.12.5% BY VOL. RED TABLE WINE-PRODUCE OF FRANCE-750 ML
A

Figure 3-2: The words *Vin de pays* on this label indicate that the wine comes from a newer French wine region.

France's overall system of wine laws is called its *AOC laws,* after the name of the highest wine category. These laws went into effect beginning in 1935. Most other European wine-producing countries have used France's AOC laws as a model for their own wine laws.

Currently, France has more than 340 AOC-level wines (the highest level), comprising about 40 percent of the country's wine production. VDQS wines number ten; these are wines from locales that hope to earn AOC status in the future. *Vin de pays* areas number about 140; this relatively new category became effective only in 1979.

Degrees of pedigree within the AOC ranks

AOC is the highest status that a French wine zone can aspire to have, legally speaking. But practically speaking, some AOC zones are more prestigious than others. This extra prestige derives from the following:

- The size of the locale (small is better)

- The quality and distinctiveness of its *terroir* (as expressed in its wines, compared to wines of neighboring areas)

- The reputation of the appellation in the market (which can vary somewhat over time)

One way of knowing how large or small an AOC appellation is, and how specific is its *terroir,* is to know what type of territory the AOC in question represents. An AOC appellation can represent, in descending size and specificity, any of the following:

- A region (a fairly large area)

- A district, that is, an area within the larger region

- A sub-district

- A group of specific villages

- A single village (also called a *commune)*

- A single vineyard (the smallest and most specific *terroir)*

Unfortunately, you can't generally deduce the nature of the AOC territory from the wine's label. The word "villages" as part of the wine name, such as "Mâcon-Villages" (pronounced *mah con vil lahj),* means that the wine comes from a smaller area than a similar wine without the "villages" appendage on its name. (It comes from a group of specific villages rather than from a larger district.) But most of the time, the label holds no clues. (That's where Chapters 4 to 14 come in handy.)

Other than that "villages" example, in fact, we can't think of a single clue that's universally applicable throughout France. We're tempted to say that the words *grand cru* (meaning "great growth") always indicate the highest appellations in those regions that use that term, such as Burgundy or Alsace — but then we remember St.-Emilion, in the Bordeaux region, where *grand cru classé* (classified great growth) bests *grand cru.* (And *premier grand cru classé,* or first classified great growth, bests *grand cru classé.*) In terms of clarity for the buyer, the system is a mess, let's face it.

The reason that France's appellations lack any sort of uniformity is that the system is decentralized. There's a central governing body, of course; this organization is the INAO. (It almost always goes by the name "INAO" because its full name — *Institut National des Appellations d'Origine,* or National Institute of Appellations of Origin — is a mouthful.) The INAO rules with a firm hand. But the process of creating an appellation begins with the local grape growers who want their area recognized as an AOC area, and they get to name the area. Because local customs differ from one area to the next (remember those 246 cheeses?), the wine names don't follow any single pattern.

One fairly reliable standard for determining the precision of the *terroir* of an AOC wine is price. French wineries always charge more for wines from more prestigious appellations than they do for their lesser AOC wines, and this price differential carries down to the shelf price of the wine. Also, French wines are so well known that most knowledgeable people working in wine shops can help you distinguish between, say, a region-wide AOC and a single-village AOC name. (They can also tell you whether a wine with a technically higher appellation is actually better wine than another wine with a less specific appellation; that depends on the producers of each wine.)

The French Wine Label

Labels of AOC wines have one significant difference from those of country wines:

- For AOC wines, the place name is the primary name of the wine.

- For country wines, a grape name is usually the primary name of the wine, with the place name in smaller print.

The notable exception to this rule is the region of Alsace, where AOC wines are named for their grape variety, followed by the AOC name, Alsace. You could argue that another exception is Muscadet, because that word is used as a synonym for Mélon de Bourgogne, the grape that makes Muscadet wines.

Here are other words or expressions that you may see on French wine labels, and their meanings:

- *Millésime* (pronounced *mill eh seem*), meaning vintage year, the year the grapes were harvested.

- *Mis en bouteille au château* (pronounced *mees ahn boo tay oh sha toh*), which means bottled at the château — or *au domaine*, at the winery; it's equivalent to the term "estate bottled."

- *Vieilles vignes* (pronounced *vee ay veen*), meaning old vines; this term is unregulated, but it suggests a superior wine because old vines produce fewer grapes and hence a more concentrated wine.

- *Réserve*, translated as reserve, an unregulated term.

- *Premier cru* (pronounced *prem y'ay crew*), literally meaning "first growth" but more correctly, "first growth vineyard"; this term is used in certain regions to denote superior vineyards that have special AC status.

- *Grand cru (grahn crew)*, meaning great growth or great growth vineyard; like *premier cru*, this term is used only in certain regions, where it applies to the very best vineyards.

- *Supérieure, (soo pehr ee ehr)* superior; this word appears as part of some AOC names, and it usually connotes a wine with a slightly higher alcohol level than the non-superior version of the same wine.

Part II
France's High-Profile Wine Regions

In this part . . .

These six chapters are truly the heart of this book. Like a stylized heart, they're red: They cover France's most prestigious regions for red wine, namely Bordeaux, Burgundy, Beaujolais, and the Rhône. (One of these regions — Burgundy — is also famous for white wine, and another — Bordeaux — is also renowned for dessert and white wine, but red wine is the lifeblood of all four areas.)

Proving the enormous diversity of French wines, these four regions each specialize in profoundly different styles of wine made from completely different grape varieties than are used in the other three regions. We explore the unique personalities of these wines region by region, name the top producers, and give you tips on enjoying the wines.

By the time you've finished reading the chapters in this part, you'll have made the acquaintance of France's most important red wines. If you happen to *sip* your way through the pages, all the better. Your heart will thank you.

Chapter 4

Elite Red Wines of Bordeaux

*B*efore we ever tasted our first Bordeaux wine (many years ago — don't ask how many), we knew that Bordeaux wines must be special, because whenever anyone uttered the word "Bordeaux," it was with a tone of awe and respect. Back then, we didn't know that a Bordeaux could be a dry or sweet white wine as well as a dry red wine. We just knew that Bordeaux had some mystique about it.

At first, we found Bordeaux confusing, what with all its districts, sub-districts, and villages — not to mention the classifications of specific properties, and the different types of classifications in different districts! But gradually, we figured it all out.

Now, thousands of Bordeaux wines later, we're the ones holding Bordeaux in awe. The wines met the test of time for us. Of all the different kinds of wines we've enjoyed, the largest percentage of truly great wines have been red Bordeaux wines. Hands down. No contest. Yes, there is something special about Bordeaux.

We devote three chapters to Bordeaux. We introduce the region in this chapter, and discuss Bordeaux's "Red Wine Elite."

The Bordeaux Advantage

The Bordeaux wine region lies in the southern part of western France, on the Atlantic coast (see Figure 4-1). The Gironde Estuary and its two major rivers, the Dordogne and the Garonne, run through the heart of the region. Almost all of Bordeaux's great wine estates are near the Gironde or one of its tributaries. The city of Bordeaux, France's fourth largest city, lies in the center of the region.

The Bordeaux area has a maritime climate, with damp springtimes, rather hot, fairly dry summers, rather mild winters, and quite a bit of rain during autumn and winter. When rain does occur in the fall, it often spells trouble for the vintage: Too much rain can turn a promising grape crop into a mediocre one.

Bordeaux's landscape is rather flat in most places, and the soil is quite infertile. Not much else but grapes can grow there. In fact, the Bordeaux wine region — with the exception of the historic town of St.-Emilion — is plain looking. You don't go there for its natural beauty.

But the Bordeaux region is a place worth visiting in the eyes of wine lovers, because it's the home of more sought-after and expensive wines than any other region in the world. How has Bordeaux become the world's most prestigious and most renowned wine region? First of all, the Bordelais, as the natives of Bordeaux are called, have experience on their side; wine has been made in this region for about 2,000 years. But it's more than that. Other wine regions in Europe have been producing wine just as long and even longer, but they have not attained Bordeaux's renown.

Bordeaux's superiority derives from the region's very special *terroir,* its unique combination of climate and soil. It's also due to the fact that, throughout the centuries, the Bordelais have figured out which grape varieties grow best in their locale. And that the varieties that thrive there happen to be among the greatest varieties in the world.

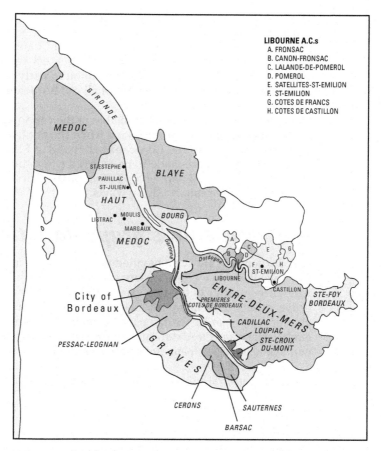

Figure 4-1: Bordeaux is a complex region, with many districts.

Bordeaux the red

Bordeaux's reputation as a great wine region rests on its most superb reds, legendary and long-lived wines made by historic wine estates (called *châteaux*), which can improve for several decades. Seventy-five to 80 percent of Bordeaux's wines are red. (Most of the rest is dry white, and 2 or 3 percent is stunning dessert wine.)

The greatest, most age-worthy red Bordeaux wines start at $30 a bottle retail, and can go up to about $800 a bottle and more for rare wines such as a newly-released Château Pétrus — with older, fine vintages of the greatest and rarest wines even more expensive. But the famous, costly wines make up only about 2 to 3 percent of all red Bordeaux.

Many fine Bordeaux reds are available in the $18 to $30 range; these wines are perfect for drinking when they're five to ten years old. And lots of red Bordeaux sell for $8 to $18; these inexpensive wines are made to be enjoyed when they're released at the age of two, on up to five or six years of age. (See Chapter 5 for info on these wines.)

Red Bordeaux's grape varieties

Red Bordeaux is always a blended wine. It's made from two to five so-called *black* grape varieties — with most wines made from three or four of the five varieties. The percentage of each grape variety used in a particular red Bordeaux wine can change from year to year, depending on the climate, and how each variety has fared during the growing season. The percentage also varies from one estate to another.

The five grape varieties of red Bordeaux are the following:

- ✔ Cabernet Sauvignon *(cab er nay so vee n'yohn)*
- ✔ Merlot *(mer loh)*
- ✔ Cabernet Franc *(cab er nay frahn)*
- ✔ Petit Verdot *(peh tee vair doe)*
- ✔ Malbec *(mahl bec)*

Either Cabernet Sauvignon or Merlot is the dominant variety in practically all red Bordeaux wines; Cabernet Franc is the third most-utilized variety, followed by Petite Verdot and Malbec. (Actually, Malbec has been rapidly disappearing from most Bordeaux wines, because it has not been growing well in the region.)

Red Bordeaux can be quite a different wine depending on whether Cabernet Sauvignon or Merlot is the dominant grape variety, as we discuss in the following sections.

The High-Rent Districts

The Bordeaux region is quite large, encompassing more than a quarter of a million acres of vineyards, and it produces about 660 million bottles annually (about 10 percent of France's wine, but more than 25 percent of its AOC wine). Naturally, climate and soil vary across this large area. Four major districts, each with its own particular *terroir,* exist within the region, along with several minor districts.

The four major districts are the following:

- **Haut-Médoc,** pronounced *oh meh dock* (the southern — and most important — part of the Médoc peninsula, which occupies the western bank of the Gironde)

- **Graves/Pessac-Léognan,** pronounced *grahv/peh sack lay oh nyahn* (Pessac-Léognan, the area south of the Médoc, and south of and around the city of Bordeaux, was part of the Graves district until 1987, when it became a separate district; in terms of elite red wines, it is far more important than the Graves district, but we mention both names for historical reasons)

- **St.-Emilion** (*sant em eel yon*), east of the city of Bordeaux

- **Pomerol** *(pohm eh roll),* east of the city of Bordeaux

Wines with the Haut-Médoc, St.-Emilion, or Pomerol appellations must be red; Graves or Pessac-Léognan wines may be red or white.

Because of certain similarities in the wines, and for historical reasons, these four major districts for red Bordeaux are often grouped as two entities, which are often known as the *Left Bank* and the *Right Bank.*

The Médoc peninsula and Graves/Pessac-Léognan make up the Left Bank, because they're situated on the left, or western side, of the Gironde and Garonne as they flow to the sea (see Figure 4-1). St.-Emilion and Pomerol are Right Bank districts.

Wines from these four districts, quality-wise, represent the top of the pyramid for red Bordeaux. At the base of the pyramid are the thousands of inexpensive Bordeaux wines made from grapes grown throughout the region, which are entitled to the simple regional appellation, Bordeaux AOC (or Bordeaux AC). In the middle are Bordeaux from lesser districts, which we discuss in Chapter 5.

The Left Bank style

Our own very favorite red Bordeaux wines come from the Left Bank of Bordeaux, especially from the Haut-Médoc and Pessac-Léognan.

The soil on the Left Bank is primarily gravelly, with excellent drainage. Although the area is relatively flat, mounds or terraces of gravel, left by a retreating sea thousands of years ago, exist throughout the Left Bank. Cabernet Sauvignon, which does very well in gravelly soil, is the predominant red grape variety of the Left Bank. A typical Bordeaux from the Haut-Médoc or Pessac-Léognan usually has 60 to 65 percent Cabernet Sauvignon in its blend, with about 25 to 30 percent Merlot.

Generally speaking, the red Bordeaux wines from the Left Bank are quite tannic and austere when they are young (see Chapter 2 in *Wine For Dummies* for an explanation of "tannic"), and they have a pronounced black currant aroma and flavor. With age, they develop complex secondary aromas and flavors, such as stewed fruit, leather, earth, and tobacco; their colors lighten and flavors soften, as the tannin begins to drop out of the wine. (See the sidebar, "Experiencing a great, mature, red Bordeaux," later in this chapter, for more about mature Bordeaux wines.)

These wines need ten years or more to come into their own, and the best of them are capable of developing further for decades. The most common mistake regarding Left Bank Bordeaux wines is drinking them when they're less than ten years old: They can taste harsh and bitter at this age, and then you wonder what all the fuss is about red Bordeaux.

The Villages of the Haut-Médoc

Of the four major districts in Bordeaux, the Haut-Médoc historically has been the most important one during the last two centuries. It is here that many of the most famous Bordeaux wines are made.

The Haut-Médoc encompasses four villages that rank among the aristocracy of wine names. As you drive north from the city of Bordeaux, taking the road marked "D 2" (also known as the "Route des Châteaux"), you go through these four villages, passing many wine estates on either side of the road. The four villages are regarded so highly in Bordeaux that, together with two less-renowned villages, they are each official AOC appellations, reflecting a *terroir* more specific than the Haut-Médoc at large. Only red wines may carry the names of these villages on their labels.

The four famous Haut-Médoc wine communes (the term "commune" is synonymous with "village" in French), from south to north, are the following:

- **Margaux** *(mahr go)*
- **St.-Julien** *(san jhoo lee ehn)*
- **Pauillac** *(poy yac)*
- **St.-Estèphe** *(sant eh steff)*

The two other communes in the Haut-Médoc which have their own AOCs are

- **Listrac** *(lee strahk)*
- **Moulis** *(moo lees)*

The names of these six villages are an official part of the names of the wines made within these communes. For example, underneath the name of the wine, let's say, "Château Latour," are the words, "Appellation Pauillac Contrôlée." Any wines from the Haut-Médoc which do not come from vineyards within these six communes carry the broader appellation, "Appellation Haut-Médoc Contrôlée."

Each of the four major communes of the Haut-Médoc produces wines of a distinct style, which experienced tasters can identify without knowing the wine's provenance. Table 4-1 describes the different characteristics of the four major communes' wines.

Table 4-1	The Haut-Médoc's Big Four Wine Villages
Village	**Typical Style of Its Wines**
Margaux	Fragrant aroma; elegant, medium-bodied, supple wines with complex flavors; a typical Margaux wine is Château Palmer. Also home to Château Margaux, one of Bordeaux's most famous wines.
St.-Julien	Flavorful, rich, medium- to full-bodied wines; subtle, balanced, and consistent; a typical St.-Julien wine is Château Ducru-Beaucaillou.
Pauillac	Black currant and cedar aromas; powerful, firm, rich, tannic, full-bodied, concentrated wines that are very long-lived; home of three famous Bordeaux: Châteaux Lafite-Rothschild, Latour, and Mouton-Rothschild; a typical Pauillac wine is Château Pichon-Lalande.
St.-Estèphe	Dark-colored, austere, full-bodied, tannic, acidic, earthy wines; very long-lived, needing time to evolve; a typical St.-Estèphe wine is Château Montrose.

The Right Bank style

The vineyards of Bordeaux's Right Bank lie east of the city of Bordeaux and the Gironde Estuary, and north of the Dordogne River (see Figure 4-1). The two major sub-regions of Bordeaux on the Right Bank are the following:

- St.-Emilion, southeast of the port of Libourne
- Pomerol, northeast of Libourne

Because the Right Bank is farther from the ocean, the soil contains less gravel; it tends to be a mixture of clay, silt, sand, and limestone. In this *terroir,* the Merlot grape variety flourishes, and is clearly the Right Bank's dominant grape variety. (Actually, Merlot is the most-planted grape variety in the entire Bordeaux region.)

Cabernet Franc, which ripens faster than Cabernet Sauvignon, is the second-most important variety on the Right Bank. A typical St.-Emilion or Pomerol contains about 70 percent Merlot, with the reminder usually Cabernet Franc and Cabernet Sauvignon — but invariably more Cabernet Franc.

Right Bank Bordeaux reds, such as St.-Emilions and Pomerols, are a good choice for the novice red Bordeaux drinker because they are less tannic and austere, and more approachable, than Left Bank Bordeaux. This difference is particularly noticeable when the wines are young (less than ten years old). The reason for the different style is that the Merlot grape variety has considerably less tannin — and softer tannin — than does Cabernet Sauvignon, which dominates Left Bank Bordeaux. Also, the somewhat richer soil on the Right Bank contributes to a fruitier, softer profile for Right Bank Bordeaux. For this reason, we would drink a Pomerol or St.-Emilion that's less than ten years old, but we seldom drink a Left Bank Bordeaux that young.

Although Right Bank red Bordeaux wines are readier to drink sooner than Left Bank Bordeaux, the better examples of these wines can live for many decades — nearly as long as Left Bank Bordeaux, especially in good vintages. (See our vintage chart in Appendix C.)

Generally speaking, the wines of Pomerol are the most expensive Bordeaux wines and the most difficult to find — for the simple reason that these wines come from the smallest wine estates of any of the major Bordeaux sub-regions. For instance, the typical Haut-Médoc wine estate produces about 20,000 to 25,000 cases (12 bottles to a case) of wine annually, while the average Pomerol winery makes only 3,000 to 5,000 cases of wine a year.

Classified Information

Because so many Bordeaux wines are so renowned, down through the years many people have attempted to rank them, according to the wines' merit or quality. These rankings have become an important part of the region's lore.

Some of these classifications have been official, sanctioned by the Bordelais, and others have been unofficial, such as personal classifications from wine critics. Various districts of Bordeaux have undertaken official classifications of their wines, but at different times, using different categories to grade the wines. No one ranking or classification covers all the wines of Bordeaux. In this section, we cover the classifications that apply to Bordeaux's finest wines; in Chapter 5 we discuss another classification that's applicable to less expensive red Bordeaux wines.

The 1855 Classification

No classification of Bordeaux wines has created more of an impact than the "1855 Classification of the Great Growths of the Gironde." Here's how this legendary classification came about.

The 1855 Exposition in Paris was going to have a special guest — Queen Victoria of England. Since the Brits had always been partial to Bordeaux (and, in fact, owned this region at one time, then called Aquitaine), the organizers of the Exposition asked the Bordeaux Chamber of Commerce to develop the ultimate classification of great Bordeaux wines. The Chamber of Commerce in turn asked the *négociants* of Bordeaux — the merchants who bought and sold Bordeaux wine — to devise the list. The *négociants* based their classification on the prices that the wines commanded at that time, as well as the wines' track records over the past 100 years. They came up with a ranked list of 61 red Bordeaux wines (as well as a list of dessert wines, which we discuss in Chapter 6).

These 61 wines became known as "Classified Growths" or, in French, *"Grands Crus Classés"* wines (a *cru* in Bordeaux refers to a wine estate). At that time, the Haut-Médoc sub-region dominated the Bordeaux wine trade, and so 60 of the 61 wines were Haut-Médoc wines; one was from the Graves (the part now known as Pessac-Léognan). All of the Right Bank wines were shut out of the famous 1855 ranking.

The 1855 Classification divided the 61 classified growths into five categories, or classes, according to quality. The "first growths" ranked at the top, followed by the "second growths," and so forth.

At the time, the first growth category contained only four wines, but one wine was subsequently added to that rank. These five top wines are

- ✔ Château Lafite-Rothschild

- ✔ Château Latour

- ✔ Château Margaux

- ✔ Château Haut Brion (Graves)

- ✔ Château Mouton-Rothschild (elevated from a Second Growth in 1973)

The remaining categories encompass 56 wines, including

- ✔ 14 Second Growths

- ✔ 14 Third Growths

- ✔ 10 Fourth Growths

- ✔ 18 Fifth Growths

(For a listing of all 61 wines, refer to Appendix B.)

The 61 classified growths, which account for about 25 percent of the wine production in the Médoc peninsula, have enjoyed more prestige than most other Bordeaux wines over the years. Today, 13,000 wine producers (8,000 of which are wine estates) exist in Bordeaux, but only 61 wines have been blessed or "ordained" by this most renowned of all wine classifications.

The 1855 Classification has remained remarkably accurate. Naturally, a few of the classified wines have declined in quality over the past century and a half, and some wines not classified at that time have improved. Also, some Bordeaux wines of today that weren't around in 1855 might be worthy of inclusion. But for the most part, the classification has held up well.

Because of the politics involved, no changes in the classification have been made since 1855 — with one exception (see the sidebar, "Mouton-Rothschild — highly promotable") — nor are any foreseen in the near future.

Mouton-Rothschild — highly promotable

In 1855, the Bordeaux merchants placed Château Mouton-Rothschild at the top of the list of Second Growths in their Bordeaux wine classification, excluding it from the elite ranks of First Growths. In keeping with the friendly rivalry that existed between two branches of the wealthy Rothschild family, the owners of Mouton-Rothschild were annoyed that their cousins' wine, Château Lafite-Rothschild, received First Growth recognition, while their wine did not. (Château Mouton-Rothschild has been regarded on a par with the First Growths at least since the 1920s, if not before, by many wine critics and consumers.)

In 1923, the late, colorful Baron Philippe de Rothschild took over the management of Château Mouton-Rothschild. He made improvements at Mouton and introduced several innovations that subsequently became the norm for Bordeaux, such as bottling his wine at his estate, rather than selling it by the barrel

to the merchants. (Estate-bottling enabled him to control the wine's quality, and also prevented possible fraud.) The Baron waged a 50-year crusade with the French government to have his wine upgraded to a First Growth. Finally, in 1973, the French Minister of Agriculture authorized the change; Château Mouton-Rothschild was declared a First Growth, and the Baron lived to see it happen. This is the only change ever made in the 1855 Classification.

The Baron's family crest then changed. Before 1973, it had read:

"First, I cannot be; second, I do not deign to be; Mouton, I am."

On his 1973 Château Mouton-Rothschild label, the Baron printed his new motto:

"First, I am; second, I was; Mouton does not change."

Does this story make you curious to taste Château Mouton-Rothschild, or what?

The Graves/Pessac-Léognan classification

Wine producers in the Graves district were not too pleased that only one of their red wines, Château Haut-Brion, was classified in 1855. But it took them almost 100 years to change the situation. Actually, until the Institut National des Appellations d'Origine (INAO; see Chapter 3) was founded in 1935, with regulatory power over all French wines, the apparatus to make any changes was not in place.

In 1953, the INAO officially rated the red wines of the Graves for the first time; the classification was revised in 1959, and this time included the dry white wines of the Graves. (The dessert wines from the Graves district, Sauternes and Barsac, had been part of the 1855 Classification.) The 1953 classification named 13 red Graves wines (all in what is now the Pessac-Léognan district), but did not rank them individually. All the area's top estates — such as Château Haut Brion, Château La Mission-Brion, Domaine de Chevalier, and Château Pape Clément — are classified growths, or *Crus Classés*. For a list of the 13 properties, refer to Appendix B.

The St.-Emilion classification

The 1855 Classification completely ignored the wines of the St.-Emilion sub-region, which are all red. Frankly, St.-Emilion wines were not very important commercially until the 20th century, even though they have a longer history than the Médoc wines.

In 1955, the INAO undertook a classification of these overlooked wines. In one important way, the St.-Emilion classification is superior to both the 1855 Classification and the Graves classification: It provides for revisions every decade. The St.-Emilion classification has been revised (some wines added, others dropped) in 1969, 1985, and 1996. (Okay, so they missed the 1970s.)

This classification names wines at three quality levels. From the best to the least, these quality levels are the following:

- **Premier Grand Cru Classé** (First Great Classified Growth)
- **Grand Cru Classé** (Great Classified Growth)
- **Grand Cru** (Great Growth)

On the bottom tier of the classification are some 200 wines which are entitled to the appellation, "St.-Emilion Grand Cru." This particular appellation is rather meaningless because many very ordinary wines are among the 200. (On the other hand, eight overachievers in this group make such good wine today that we list them later in this chapter among our favorite St.-Emilions.) Also, the "Grand Cru" designation is confusing because it sounds similar to the next-highest appellation, "St.-Emilion Grand Cru Classé."

The middle tier — with a total of 55 wines — singles out many very good wines, most of which are on a par with Fourth and Fifth Growths (Haut-Médoc wines) from the 1855 Classification, and some of which are even better. In fact, at least four wines with the appellation "St.-Emilion Grand Cru Classé" are now so good that we believe they deserve a promotion to the highest St.-Emilion classification in the near future. The four great "Grand Cru Classé" wines are the following:

- ✔ **Château Canon-La-Gaffelière**
- ✔ **Château Pavie Decesse**
- ✔ **Château Pavie Macquin**
- ✔ **Château Troplong-Mondot**

Experiencing a great, mature, red Bordeaux

Red Bordeaux wines go through a complete metamorphosis as they age. When they're young, they usually have deep cranberry color — some darker than others, depending on the wine and the vintage. They have all sorts of aromas, which could include black currants, spices, plums, cassis, and cedar. They are very dry in this youthful stage, and the tannins in the wine can sometimes mask the fruit flavors.

When red Bordeaux ages, the color turns garnet, first at its edge, and then throughout the wine. With more age, as the wine's tannin literally drops out as sediment, the color becomes distinctly lighter, taking on a light brownish-red hue. The wine develops a more complex bouquet and flavor, sometimes with hints of leather, tobacco, and/or stewed fruit. The wine tastes softer and sweeter, with a wonderful, lingering aftertaste. You are now tasting a mature Bordeaux — one of the great gustatory experiences. A hunk of hard cheese, such as Cheddar or Asiago, and some crusty bread, and you're all set!

Currently, 13 wines hold the highest St.-Emilion ranking, "Premier Grand Cru Classé." The INAO distinguishes two of the 13 wines by placing them in Category A of the Premiers Grands Crus Classés:

- ✔ **Château Ausone**
- ✔ **Château Cheval Blanc**

The other 11 Premier Grand Cru Classé wines are in Category B. The two Category A wines are equivalent in quality to the First Growths of the 1855 Classification, in our opinion, and the 11 wines in Category B are roughly comparable to Second and Third Growths of the 1855 Classification.

We list the 68 Premiers Grands Crus Classés and Grands Crus Classés wines in Appendix B.

Bordeaux's Best Reds

Sorry, we can't keep our spoons out of the soup. Even after all the official classifications, we still feel the need to give you our own personal list of the very best Bordeaux wines today.

Our top ten

Ten wines occupy our elite class of red Bordeaux. They include the five First Growths, one "super second" growth (all from the famous 1855 Classification), the two best St.-Emilion wines, and the two best Pomerols. We do not attempt to list these wines in any particular order of preference; they're all great, and each Bordeaux lover has his or her own favorites.

First Growth
Château Lafite-Rothschild
  (Pauillac, Haut-Médoc)
Château Latour (Pauillac,
  Haut-Médoc)
Château Margaux (Margaux,
  Haut-Médoc)
Château Haut Brion (Pessac-
  Léognan)
Château Mouton-Rothschild
  (Pauillac, Haut-Médoc)

Second Growth
Château Léoville-Las Cases,
  (St.-Julien, Haut-Médoc)

St.-Emilion
Château Ausone
Château Cheval Blanc

Pomerol
Château Pétrus
Château Lafleur

Unfortunately, all ten of these wines are very expensive, and a few (Ausone, Pétrus, and Lafleur) are very difficult to find. But since Bordeaux is a huge wine region, it offers scores of other great wines nearly as fine and considerably less costly than these ten elite wines. In the next two sections, we list some of the best red Bordeaux wines on the Left and Right Banks.

Great Haut-Médoc wines

Our favorite Haut-Médoc wines (after those named among our Top Ten) are all classified growths. We place them into our own unofficial "Class One" and "Class Two" categories, according to our perception of their quality. We list them in our rough order of preference, and include their village appellation and 1855 rank after the wine. All these wines sell in the $30 to $100 range (most are under $65).

Class One

Château Pichon-Longueville — Comtesse de Lalande, Pauillac (2nd Growth)*

Château Ducru-Beaucaillou, Saint-Julien (2nd Growth)

Château Palmer, Margaux (3rd Growth)

Château Pichon-Longueville Baron, Pauillac (2nd Growth)**

Château Gruaud-Larose, St.-Julien (2nd Growth)

Château Montrose, St.-Estèphe (2nd Growth)

Château Clerc-Milon, Pauillac (5th Growth)

Château Grand-Puy-Lacoste, Pauillac (5th Growth)

Château Léoville-Barton, St.-Julien (2nd Growth)

Château Lynch-Bages, Pauillac (5th Growth)

Château Duhart-Milon-Rothschild, Pauillac (4th Growth)

Château Léoville-Poyferré, St.-Julien (2nd Growth)

Château Kirwan, Margaux (3rd Growth)

Château Cos d'Estournel, St.-Estèphe (2nd Growth)

Château Malescot St.-Exupéry, Margaux (3rd Growth)

Château Lagrange, St.-Julien (3rd Growth)

Château Lafon-Rochet, St.-Estèphe (4th Growth)

Château Branaire-Ducru, St.-Julien (4th Growth)

Château Langoa-Barton, St.-Julien (3rd Growth)

Château Brane-Cantenac, Margaux (2nd Growth)

Château Rauzan-Ségla, Margaux (2nd Growth)

Class Two

Château d'Armailhac, Pauillac (5th Growth)

Château Haut-Batailley, Pauillac (5th Growth)

Château d'Issan, Margaux
(3rd Growth)
Château Dauzac, Margaux
(5th Growth)
Château Pontet-Canet,
Pauillac (5th Growth)
Château Calon-Ségur, St.-
Estèphe (3rd Growth)
Château du Tertre, Margaux
(5th Growth)
Château Giscours, Margaux
(3rd Growth)
Château Cos Labory, St.-
Estèphe (5th Growth)
Château Talbot, St.-Julien
(4th Growth)

Château Beychevelle, St.-
Julien (4th Growth)
Château Prieuré-Lichine,
Margaux (4th Growth)
Château Cantemerle, Haut-
Médoc (5th Growth)
Château de Camensac, Haut-
Médoc (5th Growth)
Château La Lagune, Haut-
Médoc (3rd Growth)
Château Ferrière, Margaux
(3rd Growth)
Château Grand-Puy-Ducasse,
Pauillac (5th Growth)
Château Haut-Bages-Libéral,
Pauillac (5th Growth)

*Commonly known as Château Pichon-Lalande
**Commonly known as Château Pichon-Baron

Top Pessac-Léognan wines

Most of our favorite Pessac-Léognan wines are also classified growths (in 1953 and 1959); only three of them are unclassified. Château Haut-Brion, which makes our Top Ten, isn't repeated here.

With the exception of Château La Mission-Haut Brion, which retails for over $100 — but which is really in a class by itself, quality-wise, in this group — all of these wines sell for $30 to $65 a bottle. We list them in our rough order of preference:

Château La Mission-Haut-
Brion
Château Pape-Clément
Château Malartic-Lagravière
Château Smith-Haut-Lafitte
Domaine de Chevalier
Château Les Carmes Haut-
Brion (unclassified)
Château La Tour-Haut-Brion

Château Larrivet–Haut-Brion
(unclassified)
Château La Louvière
(unclassified)
Château d'Olivier
Château Latour-Martillac
Château de Fieuzal
Château Haut-Bailly

Great second acts in Bordeaux

One of the big changes in Bordeaux during the last two decades is that most of the classified growths are now producing a "second" wine. These are wines made at the château from grapes grown in the château's vineyards, but, for whatever reason, not deemed suitable for the winery's "first wine" or *grand vin*.

A few of the truly superb Bordeaux properties, such as Château Lafite-Rothschild and Château Latour, have made a second wine for a long time, but now almost all of the great Bordeaux properties have joined the trend. (Not all of these wines are available in the U.S., however; some are sold only in France or other European countries.)

Second-label Bordeaux wines benefit both the producer and the consumer. The producer can make good use of second-quality grapes and/or wine (from vines that are too young, for example, or from part of the vineyard that's less ideal), thus assuring that his *grand vin* is of the highest quality. You then can buy a good wine from a great producer for a price that's about 20 to 50 percent the cost of the estate's primary wine. And you can get an idea of the château's style. Usually, the château name is incorporated into the second-label wine.

We don't have the space to list all of the second-label Bordeaux wines here, but we do single out five of the very best, which we list alphabetically:

Second Wine	Primary Wine	Appellation
Bahans-Haut-Brion	Château Haut-Brion	Pessac-Léognan
Carruades de Lafite	Château Lafite-Rothschild	Pauillac
Clos du Marquis	Château Léoville-Las Cases	St.-Julien
Les Forts de Latour	Château Latour	Pauillac
Pavillon de Château Margaux	Château Margaux	Margaux

The Best St.-Emilion Bordeaux

All of our favorite St.-Emilion wines were classified in the latest (1996) St.-Emilion classification. We omit the many new, very small-production St.-Emilion wines (those producing a few hundred cases or less annually) because these wines — often called "garage wines" since most of them do not have their own winery — are impossible to find, prohibitively expensive, and have no track record.

The two greatest St.-Emilion wines, Château Cheval Blanc and Château Ausone, are among our Top Ten elite wines mentioned earlier in this chapter. Otherwise, we list our favorites in our rough order of preference, and mention their official classification rank. (For an explanation of the classification, see "The St.-Emilion classification" section earlier in this chapter.) A few of these wines sell in the $20 to $30 price range, most are in the $30 to $60 range, and a few are in the $60 to $100 range.

We place these wines into our unofficial "Class One" and "Class Two" categories, according to our perception of their quality:

Class One

Château Pavie (Premier Grand Cru Classé)

Château Pavie-Macquin (Grand Cru Classé)

Château Canon-La-Gaffelière (Grand Cru Classé)

Château Pavie-Decesse (Grand Cru Classé)

Château Troplong-Mondot (Grand Cru Classé)

Château Beau-Séjour Bécot (Premier Grand Cru Classé)

Château Monbousquet (Grand Cru)

Château La Clusière (Grand Cru Classé)

Clos de l'Oratoire (Grand Cru Classé)

Château Figeac (Premier Grand Cru Classé)

Château Magdelaine (Premier Grand Cru Classé)

Château La Couspaude (Grand Cru Classé)

Château La Dominique (Grand Cru Classé)

Château Angélus (Premier Grand Cru Classé)

Château Le Tertre-Rôteboeuf (Grand Cru)

Château Grand-Mayné (Grand Cru Classé)

Clos Saint-Martin (Grand Cru Classé)

Château Les Grandes-Murailles (Grand Cru Classé)

Château Chauvin (Grand Cru Classé)

Château Beauséjour-Duffau-Lagarrosse (Premier Grand Cru Classé)

Clos Fourtet (Premier Grand Cru Classé)

Château La Gaffelière (Premier Grand Cru Classé)

Château Faugères (Grand Cru)

Château Larmande (Grand Cru Classé)

Château l'Arrosée (Grand Cru Classé)

Château Trottevieille (Premier Grand Cru Classé)

Château Destieux (Grand Cru)

Class Two

Château Grand-Pontet (Grand Cru Classé)

Château Berliquet (Grand Cru Classé)

Château La Fleur (Grand Cru)

Class Two (continued)

Château Laniote (Grand Cru Classé)

Château Grand Corbin (Grand Cru)

Château Dassault (Grand Cru Classé)

Château Franc-Mayné (Grand Cru Classé)

Château Couvent des Jacobins (Grand Cru Classé)

Château Haut-Corbin (Grand Cru Classé)

Château La Tour Figeac (Grand Cru Classé)

Château Larcis Ducasse (Grand Cru Classé)

Château Belair (Premier Grand Cru Classé)

Château Canon (Premier Grand Cru Classé)

Château Tertre Daugay (Grand Cru Classé)

Château Yon-Figeac (Grand Cru Classé)

Château Fleur Cardinale (Grand Cru)

Château Rocher Bellevue Figeac (Grand Cru)

Château Clos des Jacobins (Grand Cru Classé)

A Pomerol ranking (unofficial)

Even though the wines of the Pomerol sub-region — which, like St.-Emilion's, are all red — have never been officially classified, we've come up with our own ranking of these very wonderful wines.

We place the best Pomerol wines into Classes One, Two, and Three. Our Class One Pomerols deserve to be in a category apart; they're equivalent in quality to the First Growths of the 1855 ranking. Both are very expensive and very difficult to find. They are the renowned Château Pétrus *(peh troos)* and the little-known Château Lafleur.

Our Class Two Pomerols are roughly equivalent in quality to Second and Third Growths from the 1855 Classification, and our Class Three Pomerols are about the same in quality as Fourth and Fifth Growths from that ranking. We don't rank those few Pomerol estates making very small amounts of wine (500 cases or fewer), because their wines are practically impossible to find. We list the wines in our rough order of preference (along with the number of cases produced annually):

Class One

Château Pétrus (4,000)

Château Lafleur (1,000)

Class Two

Château Trotanoy (3,500)

Château L'Evangile (4,500)

Vieux-Château-Certan (6,500)

Château L'Eglise-Clinet
(2,500)
Château Clinet (3,000)
Château La Fleur Pétrus
(3,500)
Clos L'Eglise (2,500)
Château La Conseillante
(5,000)
Château Certan de May
(2,000)
Château La Tour à Pomerol
(3,500)
Château Nenin (12,000)
Château La Fleur de Gay
(1,200)

Class Three
Château Le Bon Pasteur
(3,500)
Château La Croix du Casse
(5,000)
Château Gazin (10,000)
Château Petit-Village (5,000)
Château La Grave à Pomerol
(3,500)
Château Rouget (6,500)
Château Le Gay (3,000)
Château Certan-Giraud*
(3,500)
Château La Croix de Gay
(6,000)

*Starting with the 1999 vintage, Château Certan-Giraud, which is under new ownership, will be known as Château Hosanna.

A few of our Class Three wines sell for $30 to $50 retail; many of the wines in Class Two retail for over $100 a bottle.

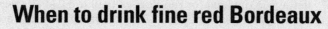

If you want to experience a great Pomerol — despite the price and scarcity — we suggest one of the wines at the top of our Class Two list, such as Château Trotanoy (*troh tahn wah)* or Vieux-Château-Certan (*v'yuh shah toe sair tan*).

When to drink fine red Bordeaux

Red Bordeaux wine is an extraordinary taste experience, in our judgment, *only when it has fully developed, and is mature.* That stage varies according to the vintage and the wine. Most better red Bordeaux wines are ready to drink between 10 to 20 years of age, and the best wines, from the best vintages, are mature enough between 20 and 40 years of age. In a few exceptional cases (as with the 1928 and 1945 Bordeaux vintages), the wines take even longer to mature. By consulting vintage charts (we have one in Appendix C of this book) or seeking the advice of wine experts, and factoring in your own preferences for more youthful or more mature wine, you can determine the optimum period for drinking your red Bordeaux. Naturally, these aging estimates refer to the elite Bordeaux wines we discuss in this chapter, not the inexpensive wines we discuss in Chapter 5, which you can drink much sooner.

Drinking Red Bordeaux

We seldom order the best red Bordeaux wines in restaurants because the young wines from the currently available vintages that dominate wine lists are far from ready to drink. (See the sidebar, "When to drink fine red Bordeaux," in this chapter, for maturity guidelines.) And when older vintages *are* available, their prices are usually very expensive. The best restaurant strategy is to drink inexpensive, readier-to-drink red Bordeaux — if they are available. Save the better, mature red Bordeaux for drinking at home or at your friends' homes.

Red Bordeaux is not the easiest wine to match with food. It goes best with simple cuts of red meat, lamb, or venison. It's also fine with hard cheeses, such as Cheddar or Comté, and good, crusty bread.

A fine Bordeaux needs decanting, whether it's young or mature. A young wine will benefit from the extra aeration (at least an hour) that decanting provides. A mature (ten years or older) Bordeaux has sediment, a harmless but disagreeable by-product, that's removed by careful decanting. Inexpensive Bordeaux wines do not need decanting.

Serve red Bordeaux at cool room temperatures — about 63°F to 66°F (18° to 19°C). A fine, large glass (not too wide) is best.

Vintages are very important in the Bordeaux region. The 1982 vintage is the best for red Bordeaux of the last 20 years — actually the best since 1961 — and almost all 1982s are ready to drink now. Other good vintages are the 1985, 1986, 1988, 1989, 1990, 1995, and 1996 (the last two are far from ready to drink). The promising 1998 will need many years to develop.

Visiting Bordeaux

Once you're hooked on Bordeaux, you might want to visit the "mecca" from which these great wines emanate. Fortunately, during the last 15 years, a number of fine inns and restaurants have opened in the Haut-Médoc and Graves/Pessac-Léognan. These districts had been in dire need of these establishments; in earlier days, the traveller had to stay in the city of Bordeaux and trek to the wine regions daily.

St.-Emilion, a picturesque town, has always attracted its share of tourists, and the hotel/restaurant scene has improved there, as well, lately. The Pomerol region, mainly farmland, with no village to speak of, has no accommodations or restaurants, nor does the nearby city of Libourne offer much. But the Pomerol region is close enough to St.-Emilion so that you can use that town as your base of operations when visiting wineries in Pomerol.

Haut-Médoc and Graves

A visit to the Bordeaux region should certainly include a stop at some of the magnificent châteaux in the Haut-Médoc; Château Margaux and Château Mouton-Rothschild (which has an interesting wine museum), especially, are not to be missed. Other châteaux worth visiting are Château Pichon-Longueville-Baron in Pauillac, with its new, modern winery, and the more traditional Château Palmer in Margaux. All of these châteaux are close to Route D 2, the road that winds its way through the four main villages of the Haut-Médoc. Call ahead for an appointment, and ask for a tasting — or else they might schedule just a tour for you.

In the Haut-Médoc, most of the better hotels and restaurants are in or near the villages of Margaux and Pauillac. Two fine hotel-restaurants in the Margaux area are both quite new. Pavillon de Margaux is a warm, comfortable inn with eight large rooms and a fine restaurant. The Relais de Margaux, a little over a mile north of Margaux, is located right in the middle of the vineyards, with a view of the Gironde. This is a luxurious inn with 28 rooms, three suites, and a very good restaurant. For additional dining, try the excellent Auberge de Savoie, in the village of Margaux, or Le Lion d'Or, in the commune of Arcins, just north of Margaux, on Route D 2.

In Pauillac, the place to stay is Château Cordeillan-Bages, close to Château Lynch-Bages *(lansh bahj),* a classified Pauillac wine estate, and, in fact, owned by Jean-Michel Cazes, the proprietor of Lynch-Bages. Cordeillan-Bages is a luxurious "Relais & Château" inn with one Michelin star, clearly one of the best hotels in the entire Bordeaux region. A new restaurant worth trying in the area, just outside of Pauillac, is Le St. Julien, a local favorite.

In the Pessac-Léognan district, which surrounds and includes the city of Bordeaux, one estate well worth a visit is the First Growth, Château Haut-Brion, located near Bordeaux.

The most exciting hotel-restaurant in the region is Les Sources de Caudalie, which is amidst the vineyards on the property of Château Smith-Haut-Lafitte, less than a half hour south of Bordeaux and just north of the village of Martillac. Les Sources de Caudalie, which just opened in the spring of 1999, is also a spa; it practices "Vinotherapy," which uses grapeseed oil to cleanse the skin and keep it youthful. Two restaurants are here, one serving low-calorie food, and the other serving haute cuisine and great wine. This dazzling hotel and spa is run by the daughter of Florence and Daniel Cathiard, the owners of Château Smith-Haut-Lafitte.

A trip to the southern Graves should certainly include a visit to the great Château d'Yquem *(dee kem),* in the village of Sauternes. (Read about this wine in Chapter 6.) Write far in advance for an appointment because Château d'Yquem is one of the most popular wine addresses in the world. The best restaurant in the area — and one of the best in all of the Bordeaux region — is Claude Darroze, in Langon, east of Sauternes. Claude Darroze is also an inn.

St.-Emilion

St.-Emilion *(sant eh mee l'yon)* is a historic town that was already famous for its wines in the fourth century. St.-Emilion is situated on a hillside overlooking the Dordogne Valley. The two châteaux in St.-Emilion definitely worth seeing are Château Ausone and Château Cheval Blanc — both of which also happen to make the finest wines in the region.

The best place to stay is right in St.-Emilion — the hotel-restaurant Hostellerie de Plaisance, in the Place du Clocher, on top of the hill. The Hostellerie has spectacular views of the town, and has an excellent restaurant, arguably the best in town, although there are several other fine restaurants in St.-Emilion. Another very good hotel-restaurant five minutes outside of St.-Emilion is Château du Grand Barrail.

Francis Goullée rivals the Hostellerie de Plaisance as the best restaurant in town. While in St.-Emilion, shop along the steep, cobblestone streets; many fine wine shops are in town.

Chapter 5

Red Bordeaux on a Budget

*A*fter browsing through the previous chapter, you might be thinking, "These classified red Bordeaux wines sound wonderful for special occasions, but I need affordable wines for drinking everyday." Don't we all! Fortunately, Bordeaux is a huge wine region, and lots of good Bordeaux wines — especially red wines — are available at all price ranges. We give you loads of suggestions for these wines in this chapter.

Where the Bargains Are

The elite wines of Bordeaux do have a way of grabbing the spotlight — and rightfully so, because they're among the very finest wines in the entire world. But they don't begin to tell the whole story of the Bordeaux region, where regular people make regular wine for drinking on a regular basis. Literally thousands of Bordeaux wines will cost you less than $20 a bottle, and many cost less than $10.

Besides costing less, these inexpensive red Bordeaux wines have the added advantage of being ready to drink sooner than the classified growths. Instead of waiting ten years or more to appreciate them, you can drink these relatively light-bodied, less tannic, inexpensive wines within a few years of the vintage.

For purposes of discussion, we divide all these inexpensive red Bordeaux wines into three categories:

✔ Cru Bourgeois wines from the Médoc peninsula

✔ Generic red Bordeaux

✔ Red Bordeaux from lesser-known appellations

Cru Bourgeois wines of the Médoc and Haut-Médoc

The Haut-Médoc is the southern section of the Médoc peninsula, which is in the northwest part of the Bordeaux region. The northern section, occupying about one-third of the peninsula, was formerly called the Bas-Médoc *(bah meh dock),* and now is known simply as the Médoc, just like the peninsula itself. Together, the Médoc and Haut-Médoc are particularly rich sources of good, inexpensive red Bordeaux wines — despite the fact that the Médoc peninsula is also the home of all but one of the elite red wines classified in 1855. (See "Classified Information" in Chapter 4 for more on the 1855 Classification and the Haut-Médoc district.)

As you can imagine, all of the properties in this area that weren't classified in 1855 felt left out, to say the least. Quite a few of these estates were, and are, making very good wines, in some cases on a par with — or even better than — a few of the classified growths. To remedy the injustice, in 1932, the Bordeaux Chamber of Commerce designated a group of wines in the Médoc peninsula as *Cru Bourgeois (crew boor j'wah).* The Chamber of Commerce let it be known that these châteaux ranked just below the *crus classés* (classified growths) of the 1855 Classification.

The 1932 list featured the wines of about 240 *Crus Bourgeois* properties; these wines make up about 40 percent of the production of the Médoc peninsula. The list was revised in 1966, and again in 1978, by the Syndicat des Crus Bourgeois, a self-regulatory association of châteaux. The syndicate organized the properties into the three following categories of wines: *Cru Bourgeois Exceptionnel, Cru Grand Bourgeois,* and *Cru Bourgeois.*

Of these terms, only *Cru Bourgeois* appears on a label, regardless of a property's rank — and sometimes even that term doesn't appear. Figure 5-1 shows the label of a *Cru Bourgeois* that does indicate the wine's status.

CRU BOURGEOIS

RED BORDEAUX WINE   PRODUCE OF FRANCE

Château d'Arsac

HAUT-MÉDOC

APPELLATION HAUT-MÉDOC CONTRÔLÉE

1996

ALCOHOL 12.5% BY VOL.   NET CONTENTS 750 ML

Mis en Bouteille au Château

12.5% vol.   750 ml

CHATEAU D'ARSAC PROPRIÉTAIRE A 33460 ARSAC FRANCE
PRODUCE OF FRANCE

LA 96

Figure 5-1: The labels of some *Cru Bourgeois* wines, such as this wine from the Margaux area of the Haut-Médoc, include the term *Cru Bourgeois*.

The *Cru Bourgeois* classification has its weaknesses. For example, a number of good estates never joined the syndicate, and therefore are not ranked; a few others joined after 1978, after the last revision was published, and they are therefore not ranked. But to some extent, the classification is valid.

Today, nearly 300 *Cru Bourgeois* properties exist — way too many to list here. To simplify matters, we name our favorite wines of the Médoc and Haut-Médoc that were not classified in 1855 — whether they are official *Crus Bourgeois* or not (a mere 81 wines!); let's call them "Crus Bourgeois wines and their friends." Many bear the appellation, "Médoc" or "Haut-Médoc"; some have specific village appellations. Most retail for $15 to $30; a few cost $30 to $40. We list them in alphabetical order:

Château d'Angludet
(Margaux)

Château d'Arsac (Margaux)

Château d'Agassac
(Haut-Médoc)

Château Arnauld
(Haut-Médoc)

Château Beau-Site
(St.-Estèphe)

Château Beaumont
(Haut-Médoc)

Château Bel Air
(Haut-Médoc)

Château Bellegrave (Listrac)

Château Le Boscq (Médoc)*

Château Le Boscq
(St.-Estèphe)*

Château Branas-Grand
Poujeaux (Moulis)

Château Brillette (Moulis)

Château Capbern-Gasqueton
(St.-Estèphe)

Château La Cardonne
(Médoc)

Château Chasse-Spleen
(Moulis)

Château Cissac (Haut-Médoc)

Château Citran (Haut-Médoc)

Château Clarke (Listrac)

Château Clément-Pichon
(Haut-Médoc)

Château La Commanderie
(St.-Estèphe)

Château Coufran
(Haut-Médoc)

Château Le Crock
(St.-Estèphe)

Château Duplessis-
Hauchecorne (Moulis)

Château Dutrarch-Grand-
Poujeaux (Moulis)

Château Fonbadet (Pauillac)

Château Fonréaud (Listrac)

Château Fourcas-Dupré
(Listrac)

Château Fourcas-Hosten
(Listrac)

Château Fourcas-Loubaney
(Listrac)

Château La France (Médoc)

Château du Glana (St.-Julien)

Château Gloria (St.-Julien)

Château Gressier Grand-
Poujeaux (Moulis)

Château Greysac (Médoc)

Château La Gurgue (Margaux)

Château Hanteillan
(Haut-Médoc)

Château Haut-Beauséjour
(St.-Estèphe)

Château Haut-Marbuzet
(St.-Estèphe)

Château Hortevie (St.-Julien)

Château Labégorce
(Margaux)

Château Labégorce-Zédé
(Margaux)

Château Lamarque
(Haut-Médoc)

Château Lanessan
(Haut-Médoc)

Château Larose-Trintaudon
(Haut-Médoc)

Château Larruau (Margaux)

Château Lestage (Listrac)

Château Liversan
(Haut-Médoc)

Château Loudenne (Médoc)

Château Malecasse
(Haut-Médoc)

Château Malmaison (Moulis)

Château Marbuzet
(St.-Estèphe)

Château Maucaillou (Moulis)

Château Mayné-Lalande
(Listrac)

Château Meyney
(St.-Estèphe)

Château Monbrison
(Margaux)

Château Moulin-Rouge
(Haut-Médoc)
Château Moulin à Vent
(Moulis)
Château Les-Ormes-de-Pez
(St.-Estèphe)
Château Patache d'Aux
(Médoc)
Château Peyrabon
(Haut-Médoc)
Château de Pez (St.-Estèphe)
Château Phélan-Ségur
(St.-Estèphe)
Château Pibran (Pauillac)
Château Plagnac (Médoc)
Château Potensac (Médoc)
Château Poujeaux (Moulis)
Château Ramage la Batisse
(Haut-Médoc)
Château Ségur (Haut-Médoc)
Château Sénéjac
(Haut-Médoc)

Château Siran (Margaux)
Château Sociando-Mallet
(Haut-Médoc)
Château Tayac (Margaux)
Château Terrey-Gros-Cailloux
(St.-Julien)
Château La Tour de By
(Médoc)
Château La Tour-de-Mons
(Margaux)
Château Tour Haut-Caussan
(Médoc)
Château Tour du Haut-Moulin
(Haut-Médoc)
Château La Tour St.-Bonnet
(Médoc)
Château Verdigan
(Haut-Médoc)
Château Vieux Robin
(Médoc)
Château Villegeorge
(Haut-Médoc)

* Two different châteaux; same names

Petits châteaux and generics

Perhaps that dot-com stock you invested in didn't pan out. Or you just wouldn't dream of spending $20 or more on a bottle of wine — at least not on a regular basis. Does that mean that Bordeaux is out of your price range? *Au contraire!* Many inexpensive Bordeaux wines are produced within every appellation in the region.

Many red Bordeaux wines are available in the $8 to $18 price range. They've never been classified, nor will they ever be; they go by the general name of *petits châteaux* (implying that the proprietors live in a small house, rather than a large château). These are the wines that the typical French man or woman picks up in his or her supermarket, along with some cheese, on the way home from work. The great advantage of the *petits châteaux* Bordeaux wines (besides their price) is that you can drink them as soon as you buy them; they do not require aging.

The advantages of inexpensive Bordeaux

Frankly, if you're just getting into red Bordeaux, it's kind of crazy to start at the top. Trying some inexpensive wines first, and then working your way up the price ladder, provides a context for evaluating and appreciating the finer wines. Even if you're lucky enough to be able to afford a great red Bordeaux every night, you probably won't appreciate it fully without the contrast of drinking lesser wines now and then.

Besides, every dinner doesn't call for a great wine. When you're having hamburgers, meat loaf, or a hearty soup on a Tuesday night, set your Château Lafite-Rothschild aside and open an inexpensive, ready-to-drink red Bordeaux.

In this price category, red Bordeaux is definitely better quality than white, in our opinion.

The term *petit château* is somewhat misleading, because it implies that a wine is an estate *(château)* wine; in fact, as the term is used today, it refers to all the least expensive Bordeaux wines, even those that do not come from a single property. Many of these wines are *generic* Bordeaux, meaning that their grapes come from all over the region, and they therefore carry the general "Bordeaux" appellation. But some carry more specific appellations, such as "Médoc," "Premières Côtes de Blaye," or "St.-Emilion." In other words, not every *petit château* is a generic Bordeaux, but neither is every *petit château* a château wine.

And don't look for the term *petit château* on the label; it isn't there. The price tells you the category. (Figure 5-2 shows the label of a *petit château* Bordeaux.)

Just like all other Bordeaux, these wines are made mainly from a blend of Merlot, Cabernet Sauvignon, and/or Cabernet Franc grape varieties. Literally thousands of such wines exist, and so we won't attempt any definitive listing. To give you an idea of the category of wine we're talking about, though, here's a list of a few of the more popular inexpensive red Bordeaux:

- ✔ Baron Philippe de Rothschild wines, including Mouton-Cadet, Mouton-Cadet Réserve, and Médoc

- ✔ Michel Lynch wines (from the owners of Château Lynch-Bages)

- ✔ Château Bonnet (available, and reliable, in both red and white)

- ✔ Château Cap de Faugères

- ✔ Château de Cruzeau (both red and white)

GRAND VIN DE BORDEAUX
1997

CHÂTEAU
LA TONNELLE
PREMIÈRES CÔTES DE BLAYE
APPELATION PREMIÈRES CÔTES DE BLAYE CONTRÔLÉE

Guy ROUCHI
Propriétaire - Viticulteur à Blaye - Gironde

MISE EN BOUTEILLE AU CHÂTEAU
PRODUCE OF FRANCE

CONTENTS 750 MILLILITERS
NATH' JOHNSTON & FILS
ESTABLISHED 1734
BORDEAUX
CONTAINS SULFITES

ALCOHOL 12% BY VOL.
IMPORTED BY
WILLIAM GRANT & SONS. Inc.
NEW YORK N.Y.
RED BORDEAUX WINE

Figure 5-2: Château La Tonnelle, from the Premières Côtes de Blaye, is a *petit château* wine, and one of Bordeaux's bargains.

All *petits chateaux* Bordeaux, plus the Bordeaux wines from the "other Bordeaux Appellations" in the next section, are at their best when they're consumed within five or six years of their vintage date; they are not made for aging.

Other Bordeaux Districts

In Chapter 4, we stress primarily the "Big Four" red Bordeaux districts: Haut-Médoc, Pessac-Léognan, Pomerol, and St.-Emilion. But a number of other Bordeaux districts exist on the Right Bank of the Gironde. These other districts make average to good Bordeaux wines at reasonable prices, for the most part. These other Bordeaux districts (and appellations) are the following:

- Fronsac
- Canon-Fronsac
- Côtes de Bourg
- Premières Côtes de Blaye
- Premières Côtes de Bordeaux
- Côtes de Castillon
- Côtes de Francs
- Lalande de Pomerol
- Puisseguin-St.-Emilion
- Lussac-St.-Emilion
- Montagne-St.-Emilion
- St.-Georges-St.-Emilion
- St.-Foy Bordeaux
- Bordeaux Supérieur (a general, regionwide appellation, mainly used for Right Bank Bordeaux)
- Bordeaux (a general, regionwide appellation, primarily used for Right Bank Bordeaux)

The wines from these districts are made from the same grape varieties as elsewhere in Bordeaux — with Merlot usually being the dominant variety. With the exception of the relatively more expensive Fronsac/Canon-Fronsac wines, all of the other Bordreaux wines in the following sections qualify, price-wise, as *petits chateaux* wines.

Although you can buy decent red Bordeaux wines from any of these districts or appellations, we believe that four of these areas are more important than the others for red wines. These four areas fall neatly into two pairs, because of how they're situated.

Fronsac and Canon-Fronsac

When you leave the city of Bordeaux heading east, and cross the Dordogne River into the Right Bank region, the very first wine districts you come across on your left are the adjacent areas of Fronsac and Canon-Fronsac. They lie just northwest of Libourne, the town that's the commercial center of the Right Bank Bordeaux districts (see Figure 4-1). Fronsac is three times larger than Canon-Fronsac and surrounds that district.

The word *canon (cah nohn)* means "hill" in French. The Canon-Fronsac appellation takes its name from two steep hills that dominate the district. But while this area is hillier than Fronsac, most of the vineyards of both appellations are situated on steep hillsides. Canon-Fronsac does have a higher percentage of finer wines, though.

In general, Canon-Fronsac and Fronsac have the highest reputation for quality of the lesser Bordeaux appellations, and their prices reflect their reputation. Whereas wines from the other appellations are mainly less than $18 a bottle — with many as low as $10 — the better wines from Fronsac and Canon-Fronsac are in the $18 to $25 range. Another factor affecting price is the size of the wineries: Many wineries in both districts are quite small, making as little as 2,000 to 6,000 cases a year.

Like Pomerol and St.-Emilion, Fronsac and Canon-Fronsac produce only red wines. Merlot is the dominant grape variety in both districts, although Cabernet Franc and Cabernet Sauvignon play a more important role in these two districts than in the other Right Bank appellations. Some properties in the Fronsacs produce a *prestige cuvée* as well as their regular wine, a practice that's quite unusual for the Bordeaux region.

Some of the better Fronsac and Canon-Fronsac wines include the following (listed in our rough order of preference):

Château La Croix-Canon
(Canon-Fronsac)

Château Canon de Brem
(Canon-Fronsac)

Château Canon-Moueix
(Canon-Fronsac)

Château La Dauphine
(Fronsac)

Château Haut-Carles
(Fronsac)

Château Fontenil (Fronsac)

Château Mazeris
(Canon-Fronsac)

Château Moulin-Pey-Labrie
(Canon-Fronsac)

Château La Vieille-Cure
(Fronsac)

Château Moulin-Haut-
Laroque (Fronsac)

Château Dalem (Fronsac)

Château Barrabaque
(Canon-Fronsac)

Château La Rivière (Fronsac)

Côtes de Bourg and Premières Côtes de Blaye

Côtes de Bourg and Côtes de Blaye are the two most northerly Right Bank districts. The regions are named after port towns on the Gironde (see Figure 4-1):

 ✔ Blaye *(bly)* is opposite St.-Julien on the Left Bank.

 ✔ Bourg, opposite Margaux and south of Blaye, is situated at the confluence of the Gironde into the Dordogne River.

The area called Côtes de Blaye is much larger than the Bourg district, and, confusingly, it actually comprises several separate AOC appellations. The appellation "Côtes de Blaye" itself applies to white wines, which historically were more important than the reds; the "Premières Côtes de Blaye" appellation applies to red wines and some of the area's better whites. White wines from this area can also carry the appellations "Blaye" or "Blayais."

Historically, both the Côtes de Bourg and Côtes de Blaye wine districts, especially Bourg, played an important role in the Bordeaux wine trade. With the emergence of St.-Emilion, Pomerol, and the Left Bank wine districts in the last century, Bourg and Blaye faded into the background, quietly making wines for consumption within France.

Today, both the Côtes de Bourg and the Premières Côtes de Blaye wines (particularly the Côtes de Bourg) are experiencing a resurgence in interest, not only in France, but in other European countries, as well as in the U.S. The reason is apparent: As prices continue rising at a rapid pace for red Bordeaux wines in the more prestigious districts, consumers are turning to the Bourg and Blaye districts for truly "great value" wines. Some wines from these districts are in the $8 to $10 retail price range!

Red wines predominate in both districts; about 99 percent of Côtes de Bourg wines are red, whereas in the Blaye district, about 90 percent are red. Merlot is the leading grape variety in both Bourg and Blaye red wines, with Cabernet Sauvignon, Cabernet Franc, and sometimes Malbec in the blend.

Both districts make about the same amount of wine annually, around 2.2 million cases. The wines from both these regions vary in quality, and include

✔ Simple, rustic, fruity, but powerful country wines (basically, the $8 to $15 wines)

✔ Sophisticated, elegant, complex, age-worthy red wines ($20 and up) that can compare in quality to fine wines from St.-Emilion or the Haut-Médoc, but at half the price

Some of the better Bourg and Blaye wines include the following (listed in our rough order of preference):

Château Roc de Cambes
   (Côtes de Bourg)
Château Tayac
   (Côtes de Bourg)*
Château La Tonnelle
   (Premières Côtes de Blaye)
Château de Barbe
   (Côtes de Bourg)
Château Gigault Cuvée Viva
   (Premières Côtes de Blaye)
Château Fougas-Maldoror
   (Côtes de Bourg)

Château Roland La Garde
   (Premières Côtes de Blaye)
Château Ségonzac (Premières
   Côtes de Blaye)
Château Les Grands-
   Maréchaux (Premières
   Côtes de Blaye)
Château Haut-Sociando
   (Premières Côtes de Blaye)

*Note that "Château Tayac" is also the name of a Cru Bourgeois red wine from the Margaux district, but the Château Tayac from the Côtes de Bourg district is probably the better wine of the two.

Chapter 6

White Bordeaux — Dry or Sweet, and Delectable

*T*he red wines of Bordeaux cast such a large shadow that it's easy to overlook the fact that this region also produces some of the world's finest white wines. And, not satisfied with making great red and white wines, Bordeaux also produces arguably the world's best dessert wine — Sauternes *(saw tairn)*. Both Sauternes and the finest dry white wines of Bordeaux are unique to the Bordeaux region; nowhere else in the world can you find such wines. As with many fine wines, however, their production is small. We point out some of the best examples of both in this chapter.

Dry White Bordeaux Today

The dry white wines of Bordeaux have experienced a metamorphosis. A generation ago, the Graves district — which then encompassed what is now Pessac-Léognan — produced far more white wine than it does now. In fact, its production was about ⅔ white to ⅓ red wine. But most of the white wine was not very good: It was not cleanly made, had too much added sulfur dioxide as a preservative, but it oxidized quickly, nonetheless. When red wines became popular, many wine-growers sacrificed their white grape varieties in order to plant red varieties. Today, the entire region has reversed itself: It now produces ⅔ red wines, ⅓ white. In fact, the northern third of Graves — the separate district of Pessac-Léognan — makes three times as much red wine as white wine.

And a funny thing happened: The white wines got a lot better! Today, all of Bordeaux's whites are much fresher and more flavorful than previously. (And now the Pessac-Léognan Leognan/Graves area can boast that it is the only part of Bordeaux that produces both world-class red wine and world-class white wine — as well as world-class dessert wines!)

Where the dry whites are born

The Bordelais make dry white wine in many districts of the region, including a few wines from the predominantly red-wine Haut-Médoc area. But most of Bordeaux's dry and semi-dry white wines come from the following three districts:

- ✔ Pessac-Léognan *(peh sack leh oh n'yahn)*
- ✔ Graves *(grahv)*
- ✔ Entre-Deux-Mers *(ahn treh douh mare)*

The Pessac-Léognan district is the home of Bordeaux's finest white wines. Most of these wines come from estates that also happen to make fine red wines. The Graves district makes good, dry white wines that are less expensive than those of Pessac-Léognan. This area also produces great dessert wines (covered later in this chapter).

Entre-Deux-Mers is a large area that lies east of the Pessac-Léognan/Graves districts, and between the Garonne and Dordogne Rivers; its name means "between two seas," a reference to these two rivers. (See Figure 4-1 for a map.) This district is known for its inexpensive dry, semi-dry, and sweet white wines, although it also grows reds.

Other white Bordeaux wines, mainly inexpensive versions, come from grapes grown throughout the Bordeaux region rather than in a specific district; these wines simply carry the region-wide appellation, *Bordeaux Blanc*.

The birthplace of Bordeaux

The busy city of Bordeaux, the fourth-largest in France, at the northernmost end of the Pessac-Léognan district, is the crossroad between the Médoc to the north, Pessac-Léognan/Graves to the south, and St.-Emilion to the east. (Figure 4-1 shows you all these locales.) The commune of Pessac begins in the southern suburbs of the city. Pessac-Léognan's two most important châteaux, Haut-Brion *(oh bree ohn)* and La Mission-Haut-Brion *(lah mee s' yohn oh bree ohn)*, are situated across the road from each other, in the midst of new suburban housing. A few miles south lies Château Pape-Clément *(pahp cleh mahn)*.

Here, on the outskirts of the city, Bordeaux wines, as we know them today, were born. Château Haut-Brion was already a noted winery in the 1500s, when the Médoc was just marshland; at that time La Mission-Haut-Brion was part of the Haut-Brion estate. Château Pape-Clément — once owned by the Bishop of Bordeaux, who later became Pope Clément V — had already planted its first vineyard in the early 1300s.

Ironically, the few white wines from the Haut-Médoc and Médoc, which are fairly expensive, must use the same *"Bordeaux"* or *"Bordeaux Blanc"* appellation as these inexpensive generic white Bordeaux, because no such thing as Médoc Blanc or Haut-Médoc Blanc (nor Margaux Blanc, and so forth) exists under AOC law.

Two white grapes — and neither is Chardonnay

The Chardonnay grape might rule the world of white wines, but it's not a permitted variety in Bordeaux. It's not needed, because Sauvignon Blanc and Sémillon, typically blended together here, have adapted extremely well to the *terroir* of Bordeaux. (A third permitted white grape variety, Muscadelle, plays a minor role in a few wines.)

Sauvignon Blanc is the dominant grape variety (60 to 100 percent) in most of Bordeaux's dry white wines, whereas Sémillon dominates the sweeter white wines. The very best dry white wines of Pessac-Léognan contain around 50 percent Sémillon (*seh mee yohn*).

Sauvignon Blanc and Sémillon have a fine symbiotic relationship, for the following reasons:

- ✔ The Sauvignon Blanc part of the wine offers immediate charm; it's crisp, lively, herbaceous, light-bodied, and develops early.

- ✔ The Sémillon part is slower to open; it's fuller-bodied, viscous, and honeyed, with lower acidity than the high-acid Sauvignon; it enriches the wine, but needs several years to unfold.

Most of the better dry white Bordeaux, which are blends of both varieties, are crisp and lively when they're young, but develop a honeyed, fuller-bodied richness with age. In good vintages, they can age a surprisingly long time — often for 30 or 40 years or more.

Drinking white Bordeaux

Dry white Bordeaux is a versatile wine, but we especially like it with chicken, turkey, veal, and delicate fish entrées. We also find that it goes well with soft, mild cheeses; goat cheese is particularly fine with white Bordeaux.

Like most fine white wines, dry white Bordeaux is best when you serve it slightly cool, but not cold! The ideal serving temperature is in the 58°F to 62°F (14°C to 16°C) range.

The 1998 vintage is the best white-wine vintage in Pessac-Léognan/Graves in the '90s decade. Two other very good vintages for dry white wines in these districts were 1994 and 1993. Older vintages to look for — if you can find the wines at this point — are the 1983, 1985, 1987, 1989, and 1990. (The least expensive wines are best young, up to five years of age.) For a complete listing of vintages, see Appendix C.

Good Producers of White Bordeaux

Unlike red Bordeaux, the best white Bordeaux wines form a small club. Nor have white Bordeaux wines experienced the same flurry of classifications as red Bordeaux wines. In 1959, the INAO, the regulatory body for French wines (see Chapter 3), classified the white Bordeaux of the Graves (Pessac-Léognan was then a part of Graves). They named only ten wines, all in Pessac-Léognan. (Refer to Appendix B for the complete listing.)

The star performers

Our personal tasting notes distinguish 20 top white Bordeaux: 13 from Pessac-Léognan (including eight of the ten classified wines), two from Graves, and five from the Haut-Médoc. These wines range in price from $250 for the incredible, rare Château Haut-Brion Blanc to about $20 or less for Château Olivier Blanc and Blanc du Château Prieuré-Lichine. We place the wines into three classes, according to our opinion of their quality. The approximate prices for the wines in each group are as follows:

- ✔ The wines in Class One retail from $95 to $250.
- ✔ The wines in Class Two retail for $30 to $75.
- ✔ The wines in Class Three go for $17.50 to $38.

In naming these wines, we use the word "Blanc" as part of the wines' names to distinguish them from the estates' red wines, even though "Blanc" often doesn't appear on the label; when we don't use "Blanc," only white wine is made under that name.

Here's our list of the top wines, arranged in our general order of preference, with the provenance of the wine indicated in parentheses:

Class One
Château Haut Brion Blanc
 (Pessac-Léognan)
Château Laville-Haut Brion
 (Pessac-Léognan)
Domaine de Chevalier Blanc
 (Pessac-Léognan)

Class Two
Pavillon Blanc du Château
 Margaux Bordeaux Blanc
 (Haut-Médoc)
Château Pape Clément Blanc
 (Pessac-Léognan)

Class Two (continued)
Château Smith Haut-Lafitte
Blanc (Pessac-Léognan)
Château Couhins-Lurton
(Pessac-Léognan)
Château de Fieuzal Blanc
(Pessac-Léognan)
Clos Floridène Blanc (Graves)
Château La Louvière Blanc
(Pessac-Léognan)
Château Latour-Martillac
Blanc (Pessac-Léognan)

Class Three
Aile d'Argent (Ch. Mouton-
Rothschild) Bordeaux
Blanc (Haut-Médoc)
Château Larrivet-Haut-Brion
(Pessac-Léognan)

Château Malartic-Lagravière
(Pessac-Léognan)
Château Carbonnieux
(Pessac-Léognan)
Blanc de Lynch-Bages
Bordeaux Blanc
(Haut-Médoc)
Caillou Blanc de Château
Talbot Bordeaux Blanc
(Haut-Médoc)
Château Rahoul (Graves)
Château Olivier Blanc
(Pessac-Léognan)
Blanc du Château Prieuré-
Lichine Bordeaux Blanc
(Haut-Médoc)

Where quality and value meet

With the prices of good wines, whether red or white, so high nowadays, it's refreshing to come across quality wines that are also excellent values. Our list of top white Bordeaux, in the previous section, contains nine wines that we believe offer great value. We list them here, along with their approximate retail prices per bottle. The first four wines are in our "Class Two" rating, and the other five are in our "Class Three" rating:

Class Two
Château Couhins-Lurton
($37 to $38)
Clos Floridène Blanc
($25 to $30)
Château La Louvière Blanc
($29 to $30)
Château La Tour-Martillac
Blanc ($27 to $30)

Class Three
Château Malartic-Lagravière
($25 to $30)
Château Carbonnieux
($26 to $28)
Caillou Blanc de Château
Talbot ($22 to $24)
Château Olivier Blanc
($19 to $20)
Blanc du Château Prieuré-
Lichine ($17 to $18)

Other notable dry whites

In our experience, 11 lesser-known, but very decent, white Bordeaux wines are worth considering for everyday consumption, because their prices are very reasonable. These are mainly the *petits châteaux* wines of Pessac-Léognan/Graves; most of them retail from $12 to $14. We list them, with their appellations, in alphabetical order:

Château d'Archambeau Blanc (Graves)

Château Baret Blanc (Pessac-Léognan)

Château Bonnet Blanc (Entre-Deux-Mers)

Château Chantegrive Blanc (Graves)

Château Chantegrive Cuvée Caroline (Graves)

Château de Cruzeau Blanc (Pessac-Léognan)

Château Ferrande Blanc (Graves)

Château de France Blanc (Pessac-Léognan)

Château Haut-Gardère Blanc (Pessac-Léognan)

Château Pontac-Monplaisir Blanc (Pessac-Léognan)

Château Rochemorin Blanc (Pessac-Léognan)

Sauternes and Barsac

Sauternes *(saw tairn)* and Barsac *(bar sack)* come from the southern part of the Graves district, about 25 miles southeast of the city of Bordeaux. These naturally sweet wines are products of one of nature's great, happy accidents, a fungus called *noble rot.*

In the autumn, mists rise from the Garonne River and its perfectly situated tributary, the Ciron, which runs through the heart of the Sauternes district. When the autumns are warm, dry, and prolonged, these mists enable a fungus called *botrytis cinerea (boh TRY tis sin eh RAY ah)* to grow on the grapes. This fungus makes the grapes ugly and wizened, sort of like raisins with a disease. But it also concentrates the sugars in their juice, and contributes certain unusual flavors. These intensely concentrated, sweet grapes retain plenty of acidity — giving the wine made from them a remarkable balance. The acidity in Sauternes and Barsac adds a zest to the wines, and prevents them from being cloyingly sweet.

Of course, the greatness of these wines comes at a price:

- ✓ **Production is small:** Each grapevine produces only a little (very concentrated) juice.

- ✓ **Production is very labor-intensive:** Workers must go through the vineyards several times to hand-pick only those individual grapes that are sufficiently infected with *botrytis*.

- ✓ **Weather conditions must be perfect:** Warm or hot summers must be followed by warm, dry, sunny, long autumns for the noble rot to attack the grapes. Rain (especially frequent rains), hail, or frost — all not uncommon in Bordeaux in the fall — can ruin the vintage for these wines.

Historically, the Sauternes/Barsac district has averaged only three good vintages of sweet wine per decade. But nature was very good to the sweet wine districts in the 1980s and in the second half of the 1990s. Six vintages in the 1980s and five in the 1990s have produced fine sweet wines.

This good fortune didn't come a minute too soon. Economically, the sweet wines of the Bordeaux region had been in dire straits until the 1980s. Numerous issues conspired against the châteaux that produced dessert wines, including a market trend favoring dry wines, the high costs of making these labor-intensive wines, and the infrequency of good vintages. But now things are looking up again, and the sweet wine regions are experiencing a renaissance.

The Sauternes wine district

Five communes, or villages, make up the Sauternes district: Barsac, Bommes, Fargues, Preignac, and Sauternes.

The sweet wines from all five of these communes are entitled to the "Sauternes" appellation. Barsac, the northernmost commune, makes wines that are so distinctive — in general, slightly dryer and lighter-bodied than those of the other communes — that its wines are entitled to a separate "Barsac" appellation. Each proprietor in Barsac can call his wine either "Barsac" or "Sauternes"; most of the better wines proudly use the Barsac appellation.

Isn't there a California Sauterne, also?

The "Sauterne" produced in California (note the difference in spelling; the original French wine has a final "s") bears absolutely no resemblance to true Sauternes from Bordeaux. California Sauterne is a semi-sweet, rather ordinary, inexpensive wine made from nondescript grapes; a few of the state's largest producers sell most of it in large 4- or 5-liter bottles.

Sauternes' grape varieties

Sauternes and Barsac use the same grape varieties as dry white Bordeaux, but in inverse proportions. Whereas Sauvignon Blanc is the most prominent variety in the dry whites, Sémillon is king of Sauternes. As much as 75 to 80 percent of Sémillon makes up the typical Sauternes or Barsac, with the rest usually Sauvignon Blanc, although a few wineries use a little Muscadelle — just as with the dry wines. Because each vintage brings different weather patterns, different proportions of each grape variety end up in the wine each year, depending on how each variety fared that season.

The golden, thin-skinned Sémillon grape plays the dominant role in these dessert wines because it's the perfect host for *botrytis cinerea*. Sauvignon Blanc adds freshness and acidity to the blend. After ten years or so, the characteristics of the two varieties blend together completely and make an outstanding, harmonious dessert wine.

Enjoying sweet Bordeaux

Sauternes, Barsac, and other sweet Bordeaux wines, because they are so rich, actually go well with *foie gras*. Personally, we prefer Sauternes after dinner, with ripe fruits (such as pears), lemon cake, or pound cake. It's also excellent as dessert.

Sauternes, Barsac, and other sweet Bordeaux wines taste best when they are served cold, at about 52 to 53°F (11°C). If a Sauternes or Barsac has some age (15 years or more), it can be served a bit warmer.

Producers of Sweet White Bordeaux

The greatest Sauternes is one of the world's most famous wines: Château d'Yquem *(dee kem)*. Château d'Yquem was the only Sauternes granted the status of First Great Growth in the 1855 Classification of Bordeaux wines. Wine collectors all over the world seek it out.

Château d'Yquem is almost ageless. Recently we tasted a half-bottle of 1893 d'Yquem, and it was glorious: all apricots, peaches, and honey, but with good acidity that gave it backbone. Château d'Yquem — and all the best Sauternes — needs 20 to 30 years to reach its plateau of greatness. When the wine turns the color of an old copper coin, that's the time when it has shed its baby fat, and begun to develop complex, exotic flavors. Its aftertaste is one of the lengthiest of all wines, lingering for several minutes on the palate.

As we write this, the currently available Château d'Yquem is 1993, compared to 1996 for most other Sauternes; the winery's owners age their wine longer than other Sauternes proprietors. That wine costs a mere $225, because 1993 is far from a great vintage for Sauternes. The really outstanding 1989 and 1988 Château d'Yquem retail for about $375, while the equally great 1990 goes for about $325. (Half bottles, 375 ml, cost about half as much; see the sidebar "Sauternes/Barsacs in half-bottles" later in this chapter.)

Sauternes/Barsacs in half-bottles

Frankly, we drink most of our Sauternes or Barsacs from half-bottles (375 ml). It's the perfect size for two to four people, because a rich wine such as Sauternes or Barsac goes a long way after dinner. Half-bottles are also a thrifty way to buy these dessert wines; decent half-bottles of Sauternes and Barsacs start at about $24 to $25. And Sauternes/Barsacs will keep for a few days after being opened, if you refrigerate them.

Château d'Yquem produces only about 6,000 to 7,000 cases each year. This amount is comparable to most major Sauternes/Barsac estates, which average 1,000 to 7,000 cases annually. But Château d'Yquem will always be the rarest and most expensive Sauternes because of its quality and because it is in high demand world-wide.

Beyond Château d'Yquem: great Sauternes/Barsacs

As great as Château d'Yquem is, at least six other superb Sauternes and Barsacs are almost in the same class. The little-known Château de Fargues, for example, which is owned by Yquem, is almost as good as Château d'Yquem, and at one-third the price. Here are six of our favorite Sauternes/Barsacs, listed in our order of preference, with their approximate prices. Vintages listed are the current ones available at the time of our writing:

1995 Château de Fargues
(Sauternes); $100
1996 Château Climens
(Barsac); $80
1996 Château Coutet
(Barsac); $60

1996 Château Suduiraut
(Sauternes); $55
1996 Château Rieussec
(Sauternes); $60
1995 Château Raymond-Lafon
(Sauternes); $80

Considering how labor-intensive great Sauternes and Barsacs are, these six wines are all excellent values, *and* both 1995 and 1996 are good vintages. In fact, the Sauternes/Barsac regions have been blessed with a rarity — four good vintages in a row — because 1997 and 1998 are also fine vintages, and 1999 looks promising. (See our vintage chart in Appendix C for a complete listing of recent vintages.)

More good Sauternes/Barsacs

We list here several other good Sauternes and Barsacs, almost all of which were ranked as "Premier Crus" in the 1855 Classification. (See Chapter 4 and Appendix B for more info on this famous ranking.) Most of these wines sell from $40 to $50. We list them in our unofficial "Class One" and "Class Two" rankings, in our rough order of preference. (This list does not include Château d'Yquem and the six Sauternes/Barsacs in the preceding section.)

Class One

Château Lafaurie-Peyraguey (Sauternes)

Château La Tour-Blanche (Sauternes)

Château Guiraud (Sauternes)

Château Rabaud-Promis (Sauternes)

Château Sigalas-Rabaud (Sauternes)

Château Nairac (Barsac)

Château Doisy-Védrines (Barsac)

Château Doisy-Daëne (Barsac)

Château Clos-Haut-Peyraguey (Sauternes)

Class Two

Château Bastor-Lamontagne (Sauternes)

Château de Rayne-Vigneau (Sauternes)

Château d'Arche (Sauternes)

Château de Malle (Sauternes)

Château Suau (Barsac)

Château Lamothe-Guignard (Sauternes)

Château Romieu-Lacoste (Barsac)

Château Liot (Barsac)

Bargain dessert wines

As good as Sauternes and Barsacs are, they will always be expensive. Other districts in Bordeaux make dessert wines from Sémillon and Sauvignon Blanc as well, and because they're all near the Garonne River, these wines also develop *botrytis*. None of these wines are as intensely concentrated or as complexly flavored as Sauternes/Barsac, but they are considerably less expensive — retailing for $15 to $25.

We recommend the wines of four areas in particular:

- ✔ **Cérons** is a commune within the Graves district, just north of Barsac.

- ✔ East of the Garonne River, in the Entre-Deux-Mares district, are the sweet wine areas of **Cadillac, Loupiac,** and **Sainte-Croix-du-Mont.**

These wines are perfect if you find Sauternes and Barsacs too intense, if you prefer a lighter-bodied dessert wine, or if you'd rather spend less money on your dessert wines.

Chapter 7

Burgundy — Queen of France

. . . .

In This Chapter

▶ Red Burgundy — Pinot Noir at its best

▶ Chablis — one of the world's great white wines

▶ *Grand cru, premier cru,* village wine, and regional wine

▶ Montrachet, a wine worth kneeling for

▶ Buying and enjoying Burgundy

. . . .

S ome of our wineloving friends swear that Burgundy is the greatest red wine in the world, while others insist that Bordeaux holds that claim. A legend about French red wine is that Burgundy seduces you when you're young, with all her voluptuous charms, but you grow into the safer, surer wines of Bordeaux with age. If our friends are any measure, however, some people remain devoted to Burgundy for life.

The châteaux wines of Bordeaux's major districts are more reliable, generally speaking, than Burgundies; you often have to try a few red Burgundies before you find a great one. But the search is part of the lure of great Burgundy, and the great wines, when you find them, are nothing short of magical. Nothing quite compares in aroma and flavor to a great red Burgundy. And among white wines, white Burgundies are some of the finest dry white wines in the world — when you select them carefully.

There's a bit of risk involved in loving Burgundy. But the reward is so worth it. In this chapter, we lead you past the pitfalls and help you uncover the secrets to enjoying the world's most seductive wine.

The Where and Why of Burgundy

Burgundy is a long, narrow wine region in eastern France, southeast of Paris (see Figure 7-1). The French call the region *Bourgogne,* pronounced *bor guh nyeh.*

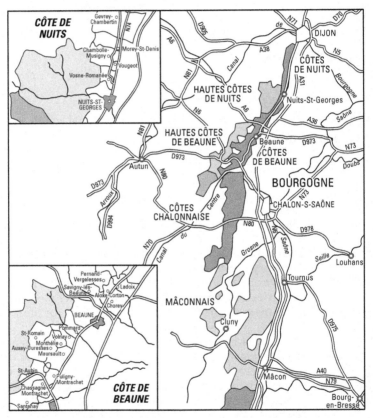

Figure 7-1: The Burgundy wine region encompasses several districts, including Chablis to the northwest. The Beaujolais region is south of Burgundy.

Burgundy is a slightly fragmented region, consisting of four somewhat contiguous districts and one district that's about 70 miles northwest of the rest of the region. The main part of

Burgundy begins just south of the city of Dijon, and continues south to the city of Mâcon. Some of the best food and wine in France (and in the world) come from this superb gastronomic region.

Because of its unique *terroir* — the special growing conditions in the vineyards — the Burgundy region excels in both white and red wines.

Soil and climate

The soils of Burgundy are extremely varied, in their richness, depth, and mineral content. The soils vary not only from one end of the region to the other, but also within a single area — for example, from the top of a hill to the bottom, or from one vineyard plot to the next, even if the two are separated only by the breadth of a dirt road. The variation of soils is the most feasible explanation for the enormous range of wines made in Burgundy.

Most vineyards have a base soil of limestone overlaid with limestone and marl (a mixture of clay and limestone), some-times mixed with sand or gravel. Where limestone is domi-nant, white wines grow; where more marl exists, grapes for red wine grow.

The climate in Burgundy is continental for the most part: fairly warm summers, with the constant threat of hail, and cold winters. The region is northerly enough and cool enough that the grapes just about ripen in most years. Not every year is a good vintage; some years bring too much rain, or are too cool. Fortunately, the grapes grown in Burgundy are suited to cool climates.

The two great Burgundy grapes

Nearly all the red wines of the Burgundy region derive from a single red grape variety, Pinot Noir.

Pinot Noir is notorious throughout the wine world for being difficult to cultivate, because it requires very specific soil and climate parameters to produce its best fruit. Burgundy has that climate and soil. (What's more, the variation in soil throughout the Burgundy region capitalizes on one of Pinot Noir's interesting attributes: that its wines reflect *terroir* differences clearly.) Few would argue the fact that the Burgundy region has more success with this grape than any other wine region, and that red Burgundy wines are the world's finest examples of this challenging, but delicious, variety.

Chardonnay is the other important variety in the Burgundy region, and the basis for the region's most important white wines. (Another white variety, Aligoté, grows here and there in Burgundy; its wines are clearly labelled "Bourgogne-Aligoté.") Although Chardonnay is a nearly universal variety today, it reaches its height in Burgundy, where it makes complex, masterful wines that can age for decades.

Both Pinot Noir and Chardonnay are thought to be native to the Burgundy region.

The scale of Burgundy

Burgundy's climate, soil and grape varieties make the wines what they are — but they don't tell the whole story of the region. To understand Burgundy, you have to comprehend the intricate scale of the vineyards and the wine production.

Whose Clos de Vougeot are you drinking?

As an example of vineyard fragmentation in Burgundy, consider one famous vineyard, Clos de Vougeot: Its 124 acres have about 82 owners. Each grower can make his own Clos de Vougeot *(cloh deh voo jhoh),* and many do; *négociants (neh go see ahn't)* also make Clos de Vougeot wines from grapes they purchase. As a result, many different Clos de Vougeots exist on the market. They all share the same pedigree, but they vary in quality according to the skill of their growers and winemakers, and the location of the vines within the vineyard. Knowing the best producers is essential in buying this, or any other, Burgundy wine.

Burgundy is a region of small vineyards, mixed ownership of vineyards, and relatively small production. Excluding the Beaujolais district, Burgundy produces a total of about 22 million cases of wine annually. (Beaujolais is technically part of Burgundy, but really a separate type of wine.) This quantity is only a small part of Bordeaux's production.

Burgundy's vineyards are also much smaller than Bordeaux's, meaning that less wine is available from any one vineyard. Where large vineyards do exist in Burgundy, they have multiple owners, so that many different wines exist from that one vineyard.

Some families own only two or three rows of vines in a particular vineyard, but they own small parcels of land in several vineyards. If they make their own wine, and they own vines in five or six vineyards, they make five or six different wines, each in very small quantities. The typical Burgundy winemaker's annual production varies from 50 to 1,000 cases of wine per type — far from enough to satisfy wine lovers all over the world who would like to buy that wine. (In Bordeaux, in contrast, the typical château makes about 20,000 cases of its principal wine annually.)

Not every grower in Burgundy makes, bottles, and sells the wines from his vineyard holdings, however. (The business of a Burgundy grower who does is known as a *domaine*.) Some families sell their grapes to companies called *négociants,* who consolidate the production of many growers into a single wine from that vineyard, or that village; others sell their grapes to cooperative wineries. *Négociants* and co-ops often have larger production of any one wine than domaines do, but their production of each wine is still generally quite small.

The limited scale of production in Burgundy has three repercussions:

- ✔ The wines are expensive because production is small.

- ✔ Multiple brands of any one wine are available.

- ✔ The name of a vineyard is not a reliable indication of a wine's quality, because every vineyard has several owners and winemakers, who vary in dedication and ability.

The hand of history

The small size of the vineyard holdings in Burgundy is due primarily to the French Revolution in 1789. Before the Revolution, French nobility and the Catholic Church were the major vineyard owners in Burgundy. After the fall of the monarchy, the government divided these large vineyards among the people, so that many families shared ownership of a vineyard.

France's Napoleonic Code added to the fragmentation; it requires that, at death, a person's land be equally divided among his or her heirs — making the small holdings even smaller. These laws of inheritance also explain why so many different Burgundian wineries have owners with the same surnames.

The best Burgundies start at about $40 retail, and their prices can be as high as $1,000 a bottle, or more. As an example of the heights red Burgundy prices can attain, consider Christie's auctions during the year 2000: Seven (!) of the ten most expensive wine lots were red Burgundies (six involved Romanée-Conti, normally the wine world's highest-priced wine when it's released). The other three lots were classified-growth red Bordeaux wines.

Inconsistent quality from one producer to the next, coupled with high prices, makes buying Burgundies very tricky. Knowing the best Burgundy producers for a type of wine is essential to anyone who plans to buy Burgundy wines on a regular basis. But — Catch 22! — the region has hundreds of producers who make thousands of wines.

If Burgundy is beginning to sound like a labyrinth to you — well, you've grasped the true complexity of the region. But like anything worth having, the reward of a fabulous Burgundy is worth the effort.

Burgundy's AOC System

Because Burgundy is one of France's classic wine regions, the vast majority of wines produced there are AOC wines. (For more information on France's AOC system of naming and defining wines, turn to Chapter 3.)

In some ways, Burgundy's AOC structure is straightforward, and follows the national norm for France:

- ✔ The appellation, or name, of a Burgundy wine is the place where the grapes for that wine grow.

- ✔ Some names refer to relatively broad areas, and some refer to small areas.

- ✔ The smaller and more precise the area referred to by the wine's name, the more elite the appellation, and, presumably, the wine.

But in some ways, Burgundy's AOC's are confusing. For one thing, the number of official appellations is staggering: More than 650 individual AOC wines exist, each from a different slice of territory within the Burgundy region. For another thing, the territory of many appellations overlap. And different wines carry similar, but slightly different appellations.

Burgundy's AOCs fall into four categories, according to the nature of their territory. From the most general to the most specific (and prestigious), these categories are the following:

- ✔ **Region-wide appellations:** The grapes for these wines can grow throughout the Burgundy region.

- ✔ **District-specific appellations:** These wines come from grapes grown in a single district of Burgundy, or part of a district. We name the various districts of Burgundy in the next section.

- ✔ **Village-specific appellations:** The grapes for these wines can grow only in the territory of certain villages (also called *communes,* or communities) that are named in the AOC regulations.

- ✔ **Vineyard-specific appellations:** The grapes for each of these wines must come from a single vineyard that is recognized in the AOC regulations.

The last category, vineyard-specific appellations, actually is a dual category, encompassing two levels of vineyards:

- ✔ *Premier cru* **vineyards:** 562 of these exist throughout Burgundy.

✔ *Grand cru* **vineyards:** AOC law recognizes 31 *grand cru* vineyards; these are the most prestigious of all the appellations of Burgundy. (This number does not include Chablis *grand cru;* the section,"Grand cru Chablis," later in this chapter, explains those wines.)

One difference between the two levels of vineyard-specific appellations is that *premier cru* vineyard names are subsidiary to the village where the vineyard is located — for example, the *premier cru* vineyard, Les Suchots, in the village of Vosne-Romanée, carries the appellation "Vosne-Romanée Les Suchots." *Grand cru* vineyards, in contrast, are freestanding appellations that carry no village name.

Table 7-1 gives examples of Burgundy wine names that correspond to each category.

Table 7-1	The Burgundy AOC System	
Type of Appellation	*Red Wine Example*	*White Wine Example*
Region-wide	Bourgogne Rouge	Bourgogne Blanc
District	Côte de Nuits-Villages	Mâcon
Commune (village)	Vosne-Romanée	Puligny-Montrachet
Premier Cru	Vosne-Romanée Les Suchots*	Puligny-Montrachet Les Combettes*
Grand Cru	Romanée-Conti*	Montrachet*

* Single vineyard sites

Region-wide and district appellations account for about 55 percent of all Burgundy wines; these wines range from about $8 to $40 a bottle at retail, depending mainly on the prestige of the producer. The most common appellation is Bourgogne, a region-wide appellation that translates as, simply, "Burgundy"; some producers name the grape variety, Pinot Noir, on the labels of their Bourgogne Rouge (red Burgundy) wines, and mention Chardonnay on the labels of their Bourgogne Blanc (white Burgundy) wines — but for any appellation higher than region-wide, you won't find the grape variety on the label. The region-wide category includes Burgundy's sparkling wine, Crémant de Bourgogne.

Wines with village-specific appellations usually come from several vineyards within the named village, such as Nuits-St.-Georges or Meursault. Village-level Burgundies represent about 34 percent of all Burgundy wines; 53 villages fall into this category. The retail price range for these wines varies widely ($20 to $60), according to the prestige of the village and the producer.

A village-level Burgundy sometimes comes from a single vineyard, instead of from the grapes of several vineyards. In such cases, the name of the single vineyard often appears on the label — and it's easy to confuse this name with a *premier cru* vineyard name. One key is that the single-vineyard village Burgundy label usually has smaller lettering for the vineyard name than for the village name, and the vineyard name appears on a separate line from the village name, such as in Figure 7-2. On labels of *premier cru* Burgundy, the village and vineyard usually appear in the same size print, and on the same line. Figure 7-3 shows a typical *premier cru* Burgundy label.

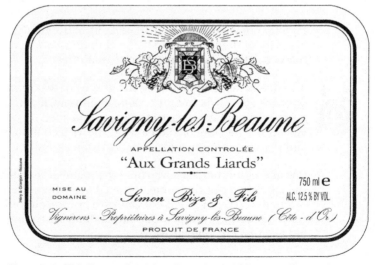

Figure 7-2: This Burgundy with a village-level AOC comes from a single vineyard.

FONDÉE EN 1859

MEURSAULT-GENEVRIÈRES

Appellation Meursault 1ᵉʳ Cru Contrôlée

MISE EN BOUTEILLES PAR

LOUIS JADOT

LOUIS JADOT, NÉGOCIANT-ÉLEVEUR A BEAUNE - CÔTE-D'OR - FRANCE

PRODUCE
OF FRANCE
ALC. BY VOL. 13,5%

KOBRAND Wines Spirits

750 ML
WHITE BURGUNDY
TABLE WINE

IMPORTED BY KOBRAND CORPORATION, NEW YORK, N. Y., SOLE U. S. IMPORTERS

Figure 7-3: The positioning of the vineyard name, Genevrières, next to the village name, Meursault, and the words *"premier cru"* ("1er") indicate that this is a *premier cru* Burgundy.

Premier cru wines make up 10 percent of Burgundy wines. The majority of them carry the name of their *premier cru* vineyard, but occasionally you can find one that doesn't.

If a wine is made by blending the grapes of two or more *premier cru* vineyards from the same commune, it can be called a *premier cru* but can't carry the name of a specific *premier cru* vineyard. The label of such a wine shows a commune name and the words *Premier Cru,* often written as *1er cru.*

Grand cru Burgundies carry only the name of the vineyard on the label, and not the name of the village where the vineyard is situated. The 31 *grand cru* vineyards represent only *1.5 percent* of Burgundy's wines. See Appendix B for a complete listing of *grand cru* vineyards.

Burgundy's Districts

Burgundy is a complex (and, some might say, complicated) region that encompasses four distinct wine districts. From north to south, they are Chablis, Côte d'Or, Côte Chalonnaise, and Mâconnais. The Côte d'Or is actually a compound district: It is made up of the Côte de Nuits and the Côte de Beaune, which are both districts in their own right.

Technically speaking, Burgundy includes another district, Beaujolais, south of the Mâconnais. Practically speaking, however, Beaujolais is not Burgundy; it has its own red grape variety (Gamay) and its own wines that are very different from those produced in the rest of Burgundy. We discuss Beaujolais in the next chapter, rather than here.

Although the four districts of Burgundy-proper all grow essentially the two same grape varieties, the wines of each district are unique in how they taste, and, in some cases, their nomenclature.

True Burgundy and Chablis — only from France

In your neighborhood wine shop, you can find inexpensive wines called "Burgundy" and "Chablis" in huge, four- or five-liter bottles or boxes. The producers' names include some of California's most well-known wineries: E & J Gallo, Almaden, Inglenook, Paul Masson, and so forth. These wines are not the authentic Burgundy or Chablis wines we talk about in this book.

In the early days of winemaking in the U.S., wineries borrowed the names of famous European wines — mainly French — for their own (American) wines. These "borrowed" wine names aren't as common as they once were, but they still exist. Novice wine drinkers can understandably confuse these wines with the real thing — or vice versa. But the domestic wines bear no resemblance to the wines whose names they borrow. For example, true red Burgundy is entirely Pinot Noir, grown only in the Burgundy region. It's highly unlikely that even a drop of expensive Pinot Noir juice is present in any of the mass-market California wines called "Burgundy." Real Burgundy and Chablis always have the words "Produce of France" or "France" on their labels — and, of course, the words "Appellation Controlée."

In the following sections, we describe the wines of the four main Burgundy districts.

Chablis, from Chablis, France

Yes, Virginia, there is a town called Chablis *(shah blee)*. It's a tiny town of less than 3,000 inhabitants, in the center of the Chablis wine district, about a two-hour drive southeast of Paris.

The Chablis district is far from the rest of the Burgundy region, over 70 miles, and yet it's a part of Burgundy — thanks to the Duke of Burgundy, who annexed the area in the 15th century. Chablis has a climate and soil distinct from the rest of Burgundy, but it does have a grape variety in common with the other districts: Chardonnay. This northernmost outpost of Burgundy produces white wines only, 100 percent Chardonnay.

Chablis's climate is generally cool, similar to that of the Champagne region to its north. The weather has a particularly strong effect on the wines of Chablis:

- ✔ The vineyards are prone to spring frosts; when a frost is severe, it can wipe out half of the crop.

- ✔ Too cool or rainy a year yields lean, ungiving wines that are too high in acidity.

- ✔ Years that are too warm produce uncharacteristically full-bodied, rich, ripe wines that are too low in acidity.

Chablis is one district for which you must pay particularly close attention to vintages; see the section, "Recent Chablis vintages" later in this chapter.

In a good vintage, however, Chablis can be magical: pale straw in color with hints of green, turning light gold with age; bone dry and medium-bodied, with lively acidity that makes the wine great with seafood; concentrated in delicate, minerally aromas and an appley flavor that lingers long after you swallow.

The soil in the Chablis area, which undoubtedly contributes to the wine's minerally qualities, has lots of limestone and chalky clay, of a type called Kimmeridgian clay; this soil contains fragments of billions of fossilized oyster shells, deposited by the sea which once covered Chablis. Is this the reason that Chablis goes so well with oysters? Probably so.

Chablis appellations

Chablis has a distinctly different appellation system from the rest of Burgundy. The wines of the Chablis district fall into four separate appellations. From least prestigious to most prestigious, they are:

- Petit Chablis
- Chablis
- Chablis Premier Cru
- Chablis Grand Cru

The Petit Chablis zone, which produces less than 10 percent of Chablis wine, is farthest from the town of Chablis, in the least interesting part of the district, soil-wise. The wine from this zone is quite forgettable, and very little is exported to the U.S.

Most Chablis wines fall into the "Chablis" appellation; sometimes wine people refer to these wines as "Chablis AC" (for *Appellation Controlée*), to distinguish them from Chablis Grand Cru or Chablis Premier Cru. These basic Chablis wines can be quite decent in good vintages, and they retail in the $16 to $24 price range. Drink Chablis AC wines within five or six years of the vintage.

Chablis is one wine where it pays to upgrade, however. *Grand cru* and *premier cru* Chablis are distinctly better wines than the basic Chablis AC wines, and are worth the extra money.

Grand Cru Chablis

On one slope just north of the town of Chablis lie seven vineyards that have been designated *grand cru*. These vineyards contain the highest percentage of Kimmeridgean clay, the limestone-clay soil unique to the area. The wines made from these *grand cru* vineyards are the most intensely flavored, concentrated, and longest-lived of all Chablis wines. They make up a mere 3 percent of all Chablis wines. The seven *grand cru* vineyards, listed according to their renown, are the following:

✔ Les Clos (*lay cloe*)

✔ Vaudésir (*voh deh zeer*)

✔ Valmur (*vahl moor*)

✔ Grenouilles (*greh n'wee*)

✔ Blanchots (*blahn shoh*)

✔ Les Preuses (*lay proo'z*)

✔ Bougros (*boo groh*)

Another small vineyard, La Moutonne, is part of Vaudésir and Les Preuses, but does not hold *grand cru* status in its own right. When you see "La Moutonne" on a Chablis label, you can consider the wine to be *grand cru* quality, however.

Although all seven *grand cru* Chablis vineyards are capable of producing excellent wines (depending upon the producer and the vintage), three vineyards have the finest reputations: Les Clos and Vaudésir, followed by Valmur.

Most *grand cru* Chablis wines retail in the $45 to $90 price range — not inexpensive, but still a bargain, considering their quality and the prices of comparable, good white Burgundies from the Côte d'Or (see "Burgundy Royalty: Côte d'Or" later in this chapter). In good vintages, *grand cru* Chablis can age and improve for 15 years or more.

Premier Cru Chablis

The best compromise between the great, but fairly expensive, *grand cru* Chablis and the simple Chablis AC wines are the *premier cru* Chablis. They're a big step up from Chablis AC, and yet they are reasonably priced in the $25 to $45 range. And in the hands of a good producer, a *premier cru* (sometimes written as *"1er Cru"* on the label) Chablis compares in quality to many *grand crus*. It's usually not quite so intensely flavored and a bit lighter-bodied than a *grand cru,* but a *premier cru* in a good vintage can age and improve for ten years or more.

About 40 *premier cru* vineyards exist, scattered in all directions around the town of Chablis. Some of the best are located right next to *grand cru* vineyards. Throughout the years, a few of the *premier cru* vineyards became the best-known (probably because they were the best, quality-wise). Now, lesser-known *premier cru* vineyards in the proximity of the well-known *premier crus* are allowed to use the more famous vineyards' names for their wines. Although on the surface this system seems deceptive, we've never found that it compromised the quality of the wines, assuming that the producer was good.

The six *premier cru* names that appear most frequently on Chablis labels are the following (the first three are the most favorably located):

- ✔ Montée de Tonnere *(mohn tay deh tonh nair)*
- ✔ Mont de Milieu *(mohn deh meh l'yew)*
- ✔ Fourchaume *(for shohm)*
- ✔ Vaillons *(vye yohn)*
- ✔ Montmains *(mohn man)*
- ✔ Les Forêts *(lay for ay),* also sold as "La Forest"

Good Chablis producers

Nowadays, producers make Chablis in three different styles:

- ✔ Many use just stainless steel tanks, with absolutely no oak barrels at all — either in fermenting or aging the wine — in order to preserve the purest expression of Chablis's flavors; the producer Louis Michel is the greatest proponent of this style; other "no oak" producers include Jean-Marc Brocard, Long-Depaquit, A. Régnard, and Jean Durup.

- ✔ A few producers ferment or briefly age their wines in oak barrels, mainly used barrels that give less oaky flavor than new barrels; this style of Chablis is typically more full-bodied, and can have some oaky aroma and flavor; Raveneau and René & Vincent Dauvissat are the leading producers of this style of Chablis.

- ✔ Quite a few producers take the middle ground, using no oak for their less-expensive Chablis, and some oak aging for their more serious wines; these producers include Collet, Jean-Paul Droin, Jean Dauvissat, William Fèvre, and Domaine Laroche.

Your Burgundy buying strategy

Regardless of the district, the strategy for choosing a Burgundy wine is to choose a good producer first; then choose a good vintage; then consider the level of the appellation: *grand cru,* *premier cru,* village wine, and so forth.

At any rate, you can find good Chablis producers in all three style categories. Our favorite Chablis producers, in our rough order of preference, are the following (the first three are virtually tied for first):

Class One
François & Jean-Marie
    Raveneau
René & Vincent Dauvissat
Louis Michel & Fils
Jean Collet
Jean-Paul Droin
Jean Dauvissat
Verget

Class Two
Gérard Duplessis
Christian Moreau Père et Fils
Jean-Claude Bessin
William Fèvre
Domaine Laroche

Long-Depaquit
Billaud-Simon

Class Three
Jean-Marc Brocard
Jean & Daniel Defaix
Domaine A. & F. Boudin
Jean Durup
Jean-Pierre Grossot
Domaine Pinson
Robert Vocoret et Fils
Simonnet-Febvre
A.Regnard & Fils (also known
    as Albert Pic)
La Chablisienne
    (Coopérative)

Recent Chablis vintages

The most recent classic vintage for Chablis has been 1996. Another very good vintage is 1995 (but the wines are a bit harder and more austere than in '96). If you like a more forward, rich, plush style of wine, then you'll probably enjoy the 1997s. Older vintages worth buying, if you can find well-stored bottles of *premier* or *grand cru* wines, are 1992, 1990, 1989, 1986, and 1985. Just about all the Chablis from these vintages are ready to drink; some may be past their best drinking stage.

TIP

Near the Chablis district

The small town of Chablis has only one decent hotel-restaurant, the Hostellerie des Clos (the restaurant, in fact, is excellent). About ten miles west of Chablis, however, is the much larger town of Auxerre, with many good hotels and restaurants, plus some old, historic churches.

Two very interesting wine villages near Chablis that are definitely worth a visit are St.-Bris-le-Vineux and Irancy. About 11 miles southwest of Chablis, the St.-Bris-le-Vineux vineyards are the only ones in the area to produce a Sauvignon Blanc (instead of Chardonnay). The wine is called Sauvignon-de-St.-Bris *(san bree)*, and it's quite good! The charming village of Irancy *(ee rahn see)*, a bit farther south of St.-Bris, makes one of the best dry rosé wines in Burgundy (simply called Irancy) — a truly delightful wine for warm weather lunches; Irancy also produces a decent, light-bodied red Burgundy, also called "Irancy." Neither village's wines are common in the U.S.

Burgundy Royalty: Côte d'Or

Most wine lovers associate the word "Burgundy" specifically with the wines from the Côte d'Or, the heart of the Burgundy region. The Côte d'Or is the name of a *département,* or county, in the Burgundy region. In wine terms, it's a narrow strip of villages and vineyards that starts just south of the city of Dijon and runs south-southwest about 30 miles to its southernmost major village, Santenay. The Côte d'Or is the northernmost area in the world producing world-class red wines.

All the vineyards of the Côte d'Or are situated on a sunny, east- and southeast-facing slope that's only about a mile and a half wide at its widest point, and less than a quarter mile wide at its narrowest. The word "côte" refers to this slope; some say that the phrase "d'or" means the slope is golden, because of the quality of wines grown there, but it actually refers to the slope's eastern (Orient) exposure.

Although we list the Côte d'Or as a single district of Burgundy, it's actually two districts in one, because it encompasses two individual areas: the Côte de Nuits and the Côte de Beaune:

✔ The more northerly Côte de Nuits, named after its
most important commercial town, Nuits-St.-Georges, is
renowned for its great red Burgundies. (White
Burgundies are a rarity here.)

✔ The Côte de Beaune is named after Beaune, the major
commercial town of the Côte d'Or, and the most centrally-
located place to stay when visiting Burgundy. It is equally
renowned for its white and red Burgundies. Many wine
lovers consider Côte de Beaune white Burgundies the
world's finest dry white wines.

The Côte d'Or produces all levels of Burgundy wine. District-
level appellations that you might occasionally see on wine
labels include Côte de Nuits-Villages, Côte de Beaune-Villages,
Hautes-Côtes-de-Nuits, and Hautes-Côtes-de-Beaune.

The Côte d'Or wine villages

If you think real estate is expensive in New York, Beverly Hills,
or San Francisco, try buying a vineyard in the Côte d'Or, let's
say, in the village of Vosne-Romanée. Vineyard property in a
few Côte d'Or villages might be the most expensive real estate
in the world.

Although all the wines of the Côte d'Or come from the same
grape varieties — Chardonnay (if they're white) or Pinot Noir
(if they're red) — the wines are subtly different according to
the village near which the grapes grow. And some villages
have *premier cru* or *grand cru* vineyards which produce wines
that are again different from the basic village-level wine. These
differences occur primarily because of soil variations along
the slope.

We list here, from north to south, the main wine villages in the
Côte d'Or — first the northern Côte de Nuits, and then the
more southerly Côte de Beaune — and mention each village's
typical style of wine, as well as any wines for which the village
is renowned.

The main wine villages in the Côte de Nuits are the following:

✔ **Marsannay** *(mahr sah nay):* Delicate rosés (from Pinot
Noir) are its specialty

- ✓ **Fixin** *(fee san):* Earthy red wines; best vineyard, Clos du Chapitre *(1er cru)*

- ✓ **Gevrey-Chambertin** *(jehv ray sham ber tan):* Full-bodied, rich, red wines; nine *grands crus,* such as Chambertin and Chambertin-Clos de Bèze

- ✓ **Morey-St.-Denis** *(maw ree san d'nee):* Full, sturdy red wines; *grands crus* include Clos de la Roche, Clos St.-Denis, Clos de Tart, Clos des Lambrays, and Bonnes Mares (a small part)

- ✓ **Chambolle-Musigny** *(shom bowl moo sih nyee):* Finesseful, elegant red wines; *grands crus* include Musigny and Bonnes Mares (the larger part); superb *1er crus*

- ✓ **Vougeot** *(voo joe):* Full-bodied red wines; the one *grand cru* is Clos de Vougeot

- ✓ **Vosne-Romanée** *(vone roh mah nay):* Elegant, rich, velvety red wines; *grands crus* include the famous Romanée-Conti, La Tâche, Richebourg, Romanée-St.-Vivant, La Romanée, and La Grande Rue; also very fine *1er crus*

- ✓ **Flagey-Échézeaux** *(flah jhay eh sheh zoe):* Hamlet of Vosne-Romanée; *grands crus* are Grands-Échézeaux and Échézeaux

- ✓ **Nuits-St.-Georges** *(nwee san johr'j):* Sturdy, earthy, red wines; no *grand cru,* but a few excellent *premier crus* (such as Les Saints-Georges, Les Vaucrains)

The main wine villages in the Côte de Beaune are the following:

- ✓ **Ladoix** *(lah dwah):* Inexpensive, medium-bodied red and white wines; encompasses part of two *grand crus,* Corton (red) and Corton-Charlemagne (white)

- ✓ **Pernand-Vergelesses** *(per nahn ver jeh less):* Good-value red and white wines; encompasses about a quarter of *grand cru* Corton-Charlemagne (white)

- ✓ **Aloxe-Corton** *(ah luss cor ton):* Full, sturdy wines; several red *grand crus* vineyards — all include the name "Corton"; one great white *grand cru* (Corton-Charlemagne)

- ✓ **Chorey-lès-Beaune** *(shor ay lay bone):* Good-value red wines; a few white wines

- ✓ **Savigny-lès-Beaune** *(sah vee nyee lay bone):* Mostly red wines; fine values

- **Beaune** *(bone):* Elegant, medium-bodied reds; some whites; fine *1er crus* in both colors

- **Pommard** *(pohm mahr):* Sturdy, full red wines; some good *1er crus* (such as Rugiens and Épenots)

- **Volnay** *(vohl nay):* Finesseful, elegant red wines; good *1er crus* (such as Caillerets and Clos des Ducs)

- **Auxey-Duresses** *(awe see duh ress),* **Monthélie** *(mon tel lee),* **St.-Romain** *(san roh man),* **St.-Aubin** *(sant oh ban):* Four little-known villages producing mainly red, but some white, wines; excellent values, because they are less known

- **Meursault** *(muhr so):* First important white Burgundy commune; full-bodied, nutty wines; some excellent *1er crus* (such as Les Perrières, Les Genevrières, and Les Charmes)

- **Puligny-Montrachet** *(poo lee nyee mon rah shay):* Elegant white Burgundies; *grands crus* include Montrachet (a part), Chevalier-Montrachet, Bâtard-Montrachet (a part), and Bienvenues-Bâtard-Montrachet, plus very fine *1er crus*

- **Chassagne-Montrachet** *(shah sahn nyah mon rah shay):* A bit sturdier than Puligny; encompasses the rest of the Montrachet and Bâtard-Montrachet, plus Criots-Bâtard-Montrachet, *grands crus;* also, some earthy, rustic reds

- **Santenay** *(sant nay):* Light-bodied, inexpensive red wines

- **Maranges** *(ma rahnj):* Little-known, mainly red, inexpensive wines

Reading through this list of villages, you might be struck with the desire to try a Volnay, let's say, or a Chambolle-Musigny. (And we hope that you are!) Before you run out to buy one, however, remember the situation we describe in the section, "The scale of Burgundy": fragmented ownership of the vineyards, many different brands of each wine, and some wines that don't live up to the reputation of their village or vineyard. Rather than choosing a Burgundy according to its appellation, we recommend that you choose a wine according to the producer. We can't emphasize enough the importance of *knowing the producer* when you choose Burgundy wines.

No shortcuts allowed

The names of Burgundy wines can be cumbersome, and shortening them can be tempting. But when you shorten the names of a village-level wine from the Côte d'Or, you end up referring to a very different wine. In a wine shop, for example, we heard someone ask for a "Montrachet," as a quick (and easy) way of saying Puligny-Montrachet or Chassagne-Montrachet; the retailer took the customer into the special, chilled room where he keeps all his $100-plus botttles, because Montrachet is a *grand cru* white Burgundy, the priciest of all white Burgundies — as opposed to the village-level Puligny-Montrachet that sells for about $35 to $40. Likewise, "Chambertin" and "Gevrey-Chambertin" — and several other villages. Use the wine's full name. The pronunciations we provide will help you.

Côte d'Or wines in the market

The reds and whites of the Côte d'Or are the best that Burgundy has to offer — and they are priced accordingly. If you want to spend about $20 or less, seek out the reds and whites from the Côte Chalonnaise district or the whites from the Mâcon district (information on these wines follows later in this chapter). Or look for a Bourgogne Blanc or a Bourgogne Rouge — wines that can be grown anywhere in Burgundy — from a serious producer who has vineyards in the Côte d'Or; chances are, that wine will have plenty of Côte d'Or grapes in it.

Lesser-known Côte d'Or village-level wines are the least expensive Côte d'Or wines; their retail price for both red and white wines can be as low as $20 to $30 per bottle. Village-level wines from the better-known villages are in the $40 to $55 price range.

Premier cru and *grand cru* Burgundies from the Côte d'Or have vast price ranges — depending upon the producer and the appellation. The less prestigious *premier cru* wines, both red and white, can range from $25 to $40 per bottle, but the better-known *premier cru* Burgundies go from $40 to $150 a bottle.

Prices for *grand cru* Burgundies, both red and white, start around $70 a bottle, but can go up as high as $900 a bottle for a Montrachet (white) from a great producer — or as high as $1400 (a bottle!) for Romanée-Conti. The *grand cru* wine Romanée-Conti is normally Burgundy's — if not the world's — most expensive wine, based on the initial price of the wine when it is first released.

So that you can spend your Burgundy dollars wisely, we recommend that you follow the following criteria, listed in order of importance, when choosing your red or white Burgundy wines:

- ✓ **The producer's reputation:** Consult recent newsletters, review the list in the next section of this book, or ask a knowledgeable wine merchant.

- ✓ **The vintage:** The Burgundy region experiences considerable variation in quality and style from year to year (see our Vintage Chart, Appendix C).

- ✓ **The appellation:** The name of the commune and/or the vineyard, although significant, is invariably less important than the producer or the vintage.

Côte d'Or producers to buy

Burgundy producers, especially in the Côte d'Or, have undergone a number of changes during the last decade or so. Some are better than ever, some are new, others have not kept up with the times, and some have retired — such as the legendary Henri Jayer, the winemaking genius from Vosne-Romanée.

Producers named "Domaine" own the vineyards from which they make their wines; those named "Maison" are *négociants* who buy grapes and wine, as well as growing grapes themselves, and sell wine made from their various sources of supply. *Négociants* usually are larger than grower-producers, and their wines are more readily available.

We list here our favorite producers of Burgundy in the Côte d'Or, first red Burgundy, then white Burgundy. Some producers make wines from two or more communes, and make both white and red wine; we list those producers under the type for which they are most known.

Our top 30 Côte d'Or Red Burgundy producers (in our rough order of preference) are the following:

Domaine (and Maison) Leroy (also makes white Burgundy)
Domaine de la Romanée-Conti (also makes Montrachet)
Domaine du Comte de Vogüé
Domaine Anne Gros
Domaine Hubert Lignier
Domaine Claude Dugat
Domaine Robert Groffier
Clos de Tart
Domaine Joseph Roty
Domaine Jean Grivot
Domaine Denis Mortet
Domaine Armand Rousseau
Domaine Georges et Christophe Roumier
Domaine Jean et Jean-Louis Trapet
Domaine Bertrand Ambroise (also, white Burgundy)
Domaine Dujac
Maison Dominique Laurent
Domaine Jacques-Frédéric Mugnier
Maison (and Domaine) Faiveley
Domaine Bruno Clair (also, white Burgundy)
Domaine Jayer-Gilles
Domaine Robert Chevillon
Domaine Méo-Camuzet
Domaine Robert Arnoux
Domaine du Marquis d'Angerville
Domaine Georges Mugneret / Mugneret-Gibourg
Maison Louis Jadot (also, white Burgundy)
Maison Bouchard Père et Fils (also, white Burgundy)
Domaine Henri Gouges
Domaine Michel Lafarge

Other fine Red Burgundy producers (listed in alphabetical order) include the following:

Domaine Amiot-Servelle
Domaine de l'Arlot
Domaine du Comte Armand
Domaine Ghislaine Barthod (also called Barthod-Noëllat)
Domaine Simon Bize (also, white Burgundy)
Domaine Jean-Yves Bizot
Domaine Chandon de Briailles (also, white Burgundy)
Domaine Chauvenet-Chopin
Domaine du Clos des Lambrays
Domaine Jean-Jacques Confuron
Domaine Edmond et Pierre Cornu
Domaine de Courcel
Domaine Drouhin-Laroze
Maison Joseph Drouhin (also, white Burgundy)
Domaine René Engel
Domaine Forey
Domaine Fourrier
Domaine Jean Garaudet
Domaine Antonin Guyon (also, white Burgundy)
Domaine Fernand Lécheneaut et Fils
Domaine René Leclerc
Domaine Bernard Maume
Domaine Mongeard-Mugneret

Domaine Albert Morot
Domaine des Perdrix (owned by Maison Antonin Rodet)
Domaine Henri Perrot-Minot
Maison Nicolas Potel
Domaine Jacques Prieur (also, white Burgundy; owned by A. Rodet)

Domaine Daniel Rion
Domaine Rossignol
Domaine Emmanuel Rouget
Domaine Christian Sérafin
Domaine Tollot-Beaut (also, white Burgundy)

Our recommended Côte d'Or White Burgundy producers (listed in alphabetical order) include the following:

Domaine Guy Amiot et Fils
Domaine Bachelet-Ramonet
Domaine Bitouzet-Prieur
Domaine Blain-Gagnard (also, red Burgundy)
Domaine Jean Boillot (also, red Burgundy; plus Maison Henri Boillot)
Domaine Jean-Marc Boillot (also, red Burgundy)
Domaine Bonneau du Martray (also, red Burgundy)
Domaine Boyer-Martenot
Domaine Louis Carillon & Fils*
Domaine Jean-François Coche-Dury*
Domaine Marc Colin et Fils
Domaine Michel Colin-Déléger
Domaine Arnaud Ente
Domaine Jean-Philippe Fichet
Domaine Fontaine-Gagnard
Domaine Jean-Noël Gagnard
Domaine Génot-Boulanger
Maison Vincent Girardin (also, red Burgundy)
Domaine Patrick Javillier

Domaine François Jobard
Domaine Rémi Jobard
Domaine des Comtes Lafon* (also, red Burgundy)
Maison Louis Latour (also, red Burgundy)
Domaine Latour-Giraud
Domaine Leflaive*
Maison Olivier Leflaive Frères
Château de la Maltroye
Domaine Joseph/Pierre Matrot
Domaine (and Maison) Bernard Morey et Fils
Domaine Jean-Marc Morey
Domaine Marc Morey
Domaine Pierre Morey
Maison Morey-Blanc
Domaine Michel Niellon
Domaine Paul Pernot
Domaine Ramonet*
Domaine Roland Rapet (also, red Burgundy)
Maison Antonin Rodet (also, red Burgundy)
Domaine Guy Roulet
Domaine Étienne Sauzet*
Maison Verget

* Particularly outstanding producer

The allure of Côte d'Or Burgundies

A red Burgundy from the Côte d'Or can be like no other wine in the world. It lacks the black-red, inky color of Cabernet Sauvignon or Syrah, because Pinot Noir just doesn't deliver much color — but it can have a lovely, light cherry-red to deep-ruby hue. Most red Burgundies are medium-bodied and low in tannin, with an utterly captivating, silky texture — unless they have an uttterly captivating velvety texture. But, ah, the aromas and flavors are even more irresistible — red fruits such as cherries and/ or raspberries, or black fruits such as blackberries or blueberries, combined with a note of damp earth or woodsiness. The memory of a good red Burgundy from the Côte d'Or stays with you for a long time.

Of all the dry white wines that we have consumed, great white Burgundies — such as Montrachet, Bâtard-Montrachet, Chevalier-Montrachet, *premier cru* Meursaults, and Corton-Charlemagne — have been the most memorable. The *grand cru* Montrachets combine rich structure and texture with a delicate floral character, and/or a touch of butterscotch. (The great French author Alexander Dumas once said that Montrachet should be drunk only when one is on one's knees!) Meursaults deliver unique aromas and flavors of hazelnuts and honey, often combined with ripe peaches. Austere, magisterial Corton-Charlemagne combines power with rich texture, always needing at least eight to ten years to fully develop. White Burgundies support the thesis that the Chardonnay variety — in the right location — is the finest white wine grape in the world.

The Côte Chalonnaise: Affordable Burgundies

Shortly after you leave the village of Santenay in the southern end of the Côte d'Or, you enter another Burgundy district called the Côte Chalonnaise. The first town you come across is Chagny, the home of a fine Michelin three-star restaurant and inn, Lameloise. After Chagny, the vineyards begin, and you're in Burgundy wine country once more.

The Côte Chalonnaise district boasts five wine villages that are good sources of very decent, affordable red and white Burgundies — about $15 to $30 a bottle, retail. Côte Chalonnaise Burgundies aren't quite so fine as most Côte d'Or

Burgundies; they tend to be a bit earthier and have less complex aromas and flavors. But they are good values, and they are excellent choices in restaurants or for everyday drinking.

Like Côte d'Or whites — and unlike many whites from Chablis or the Mâconnais district (discussed in the next section) — the white wines of the Côte Chalonnaise tend to have smoky, toasty flavors from being fermented or aged in oak barrels. As in the rest of Burgundy, Pinot Noir is the red grape of the Côte Chalonnaise, and Chardonnay is the white grape — but the white Aligoté *(ah lee go tay)* variety happens to be a speciality of the village of Bouzeron.

Côte Chalonnaise appellations

A new district-level appellation, Bourgogne Côte Chalonnaise, applies to the vineyards in this area. But many grapes grown in this district end up as wines with region-wide appellations, such as Bourgogne Rouge/Blanc or Crémant de Bourgogne.

Five Côte Chalonnaise villages boast village-level appellations, and some of them have *premier cru* vineyards. From north to south, these villages are the following:

- ✔ Bouzeron *(boo zuh rohn)*
- ✔ Rully *(roo lee)*
- ✔ Mercurey *(mair coo ray)*
- ✔ Givry *(jee vree)*
- ✔ Montagny *(mohn tah n'yee)*

The specialty of Bouzeron is Bourgogne Aligoté de Bouzeron, a lively, light-bodied wine with refreshing acidity. Aubert de Villaine (an owner of the great Domaine de la Romanée-Conti in the Côte d'Or) is the best producer; his Bouzeron property is called A & P de Villaine. The A & P de Villaine Bourgogne Rouge and Bourgogne Blanc come mainly from grapes of this area, and are good wines.

Rully's production is about half red and half white, but the whites are considerably more interesting. Some Rully vineyards have *premier cru* status. Antonin Rodet is a leading producer of Rully (and Mercurey) Burgundies.

The best red Burgundies of the Côte Chalonnaise come from Mercurey; in fact the Chalonnaise district is sometimes even called the "Région de Mercurey." Mercurey Rouge is equivalent in quality to some of the lesser Burgundies of the Côte d'Or, but at lower prices; the more-difficult to find Mercurey whites are also quite good. A whopping 95 percent of Mercurey's production is red, and 5 percent is white; several *premier cru* vineyards exist in Mercurey.

Givry's red wines are higher in quality than its whites — and reds dominate the village's production, accounting for about 90 percent of Givry wine. They tend to be earthy and rather rustic in style.

The entire production of Montagny, the southernmost Chalonnaise wine village, is white, and some of it is *premier cru*. The wines offer good value, but generally they aren't quite so good as the more expensive Rully and Mercurey whites.

Chalonnaise producers to buy

We recommend the following producers of Côte Chalonnaise wines (listed in alphabetical order):

Domaine Bertrand
 (Montagny)
René Bourgeon (Givry Blanc)
Domaine Jean-Claude Brelière
 (Rully)
Domaine Michel Briday
 (Rully)
Château de Chamirey
 (Antonin Rodet —
 Mercurey Rouge and Blanc)
Château de Rully (Antonin
 Rodet — both Rully Blanc
 and Rouge)
J. Faiveley (Mercurey Rouge
 and Blanc; Rully Blanc;
 Montagny)
Domaine de la Folie (Rully
 Blanc; Rouge, especially
 Clos St. Jacques)
Château Genot-Boulanger
 (Mercurey)

Domaine Joblot (Givry)
Domaine Michel Juillot
 (Mercurey Rouge and
 Blanc)
Louis Latour (Mercurey
 Rouge; Rully Blanc; Givry
 Blanc; Montagny)
Olivier Leflaive Frères (Rully
 Blanc; Mercurey Blanc)
Domaine Thierry Lespinasse
 (Givry)
Domaine de la Rénarde
 (Rully)
Domaine Thénard (Givry)
Domaine A & P de Villaine
 (Bouzeron Aligoté;
 Mercurey Rouge; Rully
 Blanc)

The lingo of Burgundy

Although "Burgundy" technically refers to all the region's wines, most of the time people use the term for red or white Burgundies from the Côte d'Or, or for the region-wide wines Bourgogne Rouge or Bourgogne Blanc. When people talk about a wine from the Côte Chalonnaise, they usually specify the village — such as "Mercurey" — or refer to the wine as a Burgundy from the Côte Chalonnaise. For the other districts, common usage is to call the wine by its district or village name — such as "Chablis," "Mâcon-Villages," or "Pouilly-Fuissé," rather than to call it "Burgundy."

Everyday Whites: Mâcon

The city of Mâcon *(mah cawn)* is an important crossroads in France: a passageway to Provence, Switzerland, and Italy. It's located at the southern end of the Mâconnais — a wine district directly south of the Côte Chalonnaise, and north of Beaujolais. As you travel into the Mâconnais, you notice the slight change in climate. The weather becomes warmer and sunnier, more and more Mediterranean; palm trees actually grow in Mâcon!

Some of the greatest white wine values in the world come from the Mâconnais *(mah cawn nay)*. Where else can you buy a very decent white wine — 100 percent Chardonnay — for $8 to $10?

Mâcon's appellations and wines

Almost all of the Mâcon wine that's exported is white. About ⅓ of the wine from the Mâconnais is red, however; it's called Mâcon Rouge, and it comes mainly from the Gamay grape variety, of Beaujolais fame. (After all, Mâcon is adjacent to Beaujolais.) Because Beaujolais is a more successful wine commercially, the production of Mâcon red wine has been declining steadily; it was once more common than white Mâcon. Bourgogne Rouge, which legally can be made only from Pinot Noir, is also produced in the Mâconnais, as well as an interesting red wine called Bourgogne Passetoutgrains *(pass too gran)*. The colorful name translates roughly as "Burgundy Let all the Grapes In"; the wine is usually ⅔ Gamay and ⅓ Pinot Noir, and is always attractively priced. But white wine is the main game in the Mâconnais today.

Mâcon and Mâcon-Villages

Most Mâcon white wines carry the appellations Mâcon, Mâcon Supérieur (which contains 1 percent more alcohol), or Mâcon-Villages *(mac cawn vee lahj)*. Mâcon-Villages wines come from 43 specific villages, and they are slightly better than simple "Mâcon" wines. Also fairly common are wines with one specific village name attached to the word "Mâcon," such as "Mâcon-Viré" or "Mâcon-Lugny." These last two appellations are common because large cooperative wineries (wineries that pool the grapes of private growers) are located in Viré and Lugny. About 90 percent of Mâcon wine is made by cooperatives, in fact; the economy of scale enjoyed by co-ops is one of the main reasons that Mâcon is so reasonably priced.

All of these Mâcon white wines range in price from $8 to $14. They are medium-bodied, fresh, crisp, lively, and almost always made without the use of oak. Drink them when they are young — within three years of the vintage.

Pouilly-Fuissé and St.-Véran

The best Mâcon wines have more specific appellations. They're all white wines, and they all come from the southernmost part of the Mâconnais, just north of Beaujolais.

The most famous Mâcon wine is undoubtedly Pouilly-Fuissé *(poo yee fwee say)*, the most full-bodied and, at $18 to $45, clearly the most expensive wine of the Mâconnais. Pouilly-Fuissé wines come from a vineyard area around the villages of Pouilly and Fuissé, and, unlike simpler Mâcon white wines, are usually aged in small oak barrels.

Two similar but somewhat lighter-bodied and less expensive Mâcon whites are Pouilly-Vinzelles *(van zell)* and Pouilly-Loché *(lo shay)*. Pouilly-Loché is seldom seen because it can be legally sold as the better-known Pouilly-Vinzelles; actually, the combined production of both these wines is less than ⅒ that of Pouilly-Fuissé, and so they are fairly rare.

A Chardonnay story

Thought Chardonnay was just a grape name? There is actually a village in the northern part of the Mâconnais called Chardonnay. This village most probably gave its name to the world's most popular white wine variety.

St.-Véran *(san veh rahn)* wines have about half the production (250,000 cases annually) of Pouilly-Fuissé, and, at $11 to $17, are far better values. The St.-Véran sub-district, at the very southern end of the Mâconnais, includes the village of St.-Vérand. These wines are similar to Pouilly-Fuissé, but are less full-bodied. A new AOC, Viré-Clessé, just established in 1998, now includes some of the better Mâcon white wines from the vicinity of Viré and Clessé.

Mâcon producers to buy

The following are our recommended producers of Mâcon, Mâcon-Villages, Viré-Clessé, and St.-Véran wines, listed in our rough order of preference:

Verget	Louis Jadot
Domaine Jean Thévenet	Joseph Drouhin
Domaine Valette	Manciat-Poncet
Jean-Claude Thévenet	André Bonhomme
Roger Lasserat	Emilian Gillet
Louis Latour	Olivier Merlin

The following are our recommended producers of Pouilly-Fuissé wines, listed in our rough order of preference:

M. Vincent/Château Fuisse	Manciat-Poncet
Daniel Barraud	Thierry Guérin
Domaine J.A. Ferrat	Château de Beauregard
Domaine Robert Denogent	Roger Lasserat
Verget	Louis Latour
Domaine Valette	Louis Jadot

Serving Burgundy

Unlike red Bordeaux, red Burgundy from the Côte d'Or can be consumed when it's relatively young, after five or six years. The reason is that the Pinot Noir grape contains far less tannin than Cabernet Sauvignon or Merlot — Bordeaux's grape varieties — and this makes red Burgundy approachable in its youth.

On the other hand, red Côte d'Or Burgundies from good producers in good vintages (see the Vintage Chart in Appendix C) are easily capable of aging for 20 years or more, when stored in a cool place. (Red Burgundy is especially vulnerable to heat.) Red Burgundies from the Côte Chalonnaise should generally be consumed within 10 to 12 years, however.

Serve your red Burgundies slightly cool — about 60° to 62°F (17°C) in a fine, wide-bowled glass. Do *not* decant red Burgundies; pour them straight from the bottle. Too much aeration causes you to lose some of your wine's wonderful aromas — one of its greatest qualities.

Recent good red Burgundy vintages include the 1997, 1996 (especially), 1995, and 1990.

Enjoying white Burgundy

White Côte d'Or Burgundies are among the most long-lived white wines in the world. In good vintages, the best white Burgundies, such as Corton-Charlemagne or a *grand cru* Montrachet, can age for 20 years or more. Unlike red Burgundies, the better whites need time, often ten years or more, to really develop and open up. We recommend that you *do decant your serious white Burgundies;* they truly benefit from the extra aeration.

Here are our recommendations for best drinkability periods for other white Burgundies:

  ✔ *Grand Cru* Chablis is at its best after about eight to ten years of aging, and can live for at least another five years or more after that.

✓ *Premier Cru* Chablis needs at least five or six years of aging to develop, and will still be fine for drinking for another seven or eight years.

✓ Côte Chalonnaise white Burgundies, such as Rully Blanc, can be consumed in their youth, but should last for up to ten years.

✓ All Mâconnais wines are best in their youth; the better Pouilly-Fuissés, however, can age for eight to ten years — although they don't necessarily improve with age.

Serve fine white Burgundies slightly cooler than red — about 55° to 58°F (13 to 15°C). You can't appreciate their wonderful, complex flavors when they are too cold. We enjoy our good white Burgundies in a wide-bowled glass, just slightly smaller than the glass we use for red Burgundies.

Recent good white Burgundy vintages include the 1999, 1997, 1996 (especially), 1995, 1992, 1989, and 1986. The wines of the last three, 1992, 1989 and 1986, are completely developed and ready to drink. (Because the Chablis climate marches to a different drum, we discuss Chablis vintages separately, earlier in this chapter.)

Pairing Burgundy with food

Red Burgundy is the ideal red wine in restaurants, not only because it's enjoyable when it's young, but also because it's so food-friendly. The fairly low tannin level of most red Burgundies makes them fine companions for poultry and fish, such as white meat turkey or salmon, whose flavors would grate with a tannic red. In general, red Burgundy accompanies meat as well as fish — as long as the fish is not too delicately flavored.

With chicken, turkey, or ham, try a lighter-bodied red Burgundy. With beef, game, or game birds (including duck), a full-bodied red Burgundy is ideal.

White Burgundies go well with fish, seafood, or poultry; just avoid any fruity sauces, because the wines themselves are not fruity, and they taste austere against the sauce. Lobster accompanied by a full-bodied white Burgundy is a particularly fine pairing.

Chapter 8
Beaujolais, The Fun Red

● ●

In This Chapter
▶ Wine without attitude
▶ One region, one grape
▶ France's youngest and freshest
▶ Delicious *cru* wines that aren't *grand*
▶ Twelve variations on the Beaujolais theme

● ●

*E*very now and then, we get wined out. Sometimes this condition affects us for weeks at a time, such as the whole month of July. Sometimes it hits us on a Friday evening after a heavy week of tasting serious wines. Whenever it comes, we're ready with the antidote: a bottle of grapey, unpretentious Beaujolais.

The Beaujolais region is unique among French wine regions because it makes wines that are happy to please without trying to impress. Some Beaujolais wines are better than others, sure — but even the best wines, such as a good Moulin-à-Vent, don't require contemplative attention. Beaujolais is for drinking. How refreshing!

What Makes Beaujolais

Beaujolais wine is the product of the Beaujolais region and the red Gamay grape variety. (White Beaujolais, or "Beaujolais Blanc," — mostly from the Chardonnay grape, but Aligoté is permitted — does exist, but it's a relative rarity.) A particular type of winemaking used in the region also shapes the character of Beaujolais wines.

The Beaujolais region lies south of the Mâcon district of Burgundy, extending from the Mâconnais border southward to within a few miles of the city of Lyons. Administratively, Beaujolais is a district of the Burgundy region, but the red wine of Beaujolais is so different from those in the rest of Burgundy — made from a different grape variety grown in different soil and a warmer climate — that we consider Beaujolais to be a wine region in its own right, distinct from Burgundy.

The Beaujolais terroir

Beaujolais is a large wine region by Burgundy's standards: It's about twice the size of Rhode Island and larger than any Burgundy district. The Monts du Beaujolais (Beaujolais Mountains) form the western border of the region; the terrain descends from these mountains eastward, toward the Saône River Valley. The region encompasses nearly 50,000 acres of vineyards, which extend 34 miles in length and seven to nine miles in width. The vineyards are situated in the eastern part of the region, on undulating hills.

Beaujolais is near enough to the Mediterranean Sea to experience Mediterranean-like summer weather, which is warm and dry; but the region is also interior enough to experience cold, dry weather from the northeast, including spring frosts. Overall, the climate is temperate.

Soil variations are the most significant factor in defining the character of the region's various wines:

- In the southern part of the region, south of the town of Villefranche, the soils are sandstone or clay and limestone.

- In the north, the soils are granite or schist (crystalline rock) on the upper slopes, with stone and clay soils on the lower slopes.

Just as the soils are different in the north, so are the wines. The sturdiest, firmest Beaujolais wines come from the northern vineyards, while the lightest, most supple wines come from southern vineyards.

The Gamay grape

Except for a small amount of Chardonnay, 99 percent of the Beaujolais vineyards are covered by a single grape variety, Gamay; all red Beaujolais wine derives entirely from Gamay.

Gamay exists in a few other places — France's Loire Valley, for example, and Switzerland — but the Beaujolais region is truly the stronghold for this variety, and the finest Gamay wines come from this area. (Neither the grape called Gamay Beaujolais in California nor the grape called Napa Gamay is true Gamay.)

The Gamay variety makes wines that are fairly deep in color, with a bluish tinge. They tend to have light to medium body, relatively low acidity, moderate tannin, and aromas and flavors of red berries.

Beaujolais winemaking

We don't discuss technical issues such as winemaking very much in this book, but for Beaujolais, the topic is unavoidable. A particular winemaking technique that's widely practiced in the region contributes significantly to the style of Beaujolais wines. (If you want more information on winemaking in general, we suggest that you read Chapters 1 and 3 of *Wine For Dummies,* 2nd Edition.)

That particular technique is called *carbonic maceration* (because the grapes *macerate,* or soak, in a carbon dioxide–rich environment). It's a fairly simple process in terms of what the winemaker does, but it's more complicated chemically. The effect of the process is a reduction in the wine's tannin and an enhancement of particular fruity aromas and flavors in the wine.

The principal behind carbonic maceration is that when whole grapes are deprived of oxygen, they begin to ferment (their sugars convert to alcohol) from the inside; certain other changes occur within the grape berries, such as the formation of particular aroma and flavor compounds. This internal fermentation happens without the help of yeasts; normal fermentation, in contrast, occurs because yeasts come in contact with the juice of crushed grapes.

For the lightest Beaujolais wines — specifically, the style called Beaujolais Nouveau — the fermentation can be as short as three days. Other styles ferment for about ten days, during which time they gain more color and tannin from the grape skins than the lighter styles do.

From Frivolous to Firm

Not all Beaujolais wine is the same. Soil differences through-out the region and subtle variations in winemaking technique cause the wines to vary considerably in style — from light-bodied, precocious wines at one end of the spectrum to denser, fuller-bodied wines at the other end. All these wines are dry.

Beaujolais and Beaujolais-Villages

The lightest wines, from the southern part of the region, usu-ally carry the region's most basic appellation, "Beaujolais." In theory, a wine with a simple "Beaujolais" appellation can come from anywhere in the region, but in practice, these wines originate almost entirely from the southern one-third of the region, where the soil is sandy or clayey. They account for about 75 million bottles a year, half of the region's total production.

Wines with the simple Beaujolais appellation are generally light-bodied with low tannin and pronounced, youthful fruity aromas and flavors; they are wines to drink young, in the first year after the harvest. Wines with the appellation Beaujolais Supérieur are basic Beaujolais wines that have a higher minimum alco-hol content.

A separate type of Beaujolais comes from grapes grown in the territory of 39 villages in the northern part of the region: "Beaujolais-Villages" (*bo jho lay vee lahj*). These wines are fuller and more substantial than simple Beaujolais wines, thanks to the schist and granite soils of the north — but they are still fruity, fresh, youthful wines for consuming young, until they are about two years old. Beaujolais-Villages wines account for 25 percent of all Beaujolais production.

Beaujolais Nouveau

Beaujolais Nouveau, *new Beaujolais,* is the lightest, fruitiest, most exuberant style of Beaujolais. It differs from other Beaujolais wines not according to where it comes from, but according to how it's made: with minimum aging and maximum personality. Beaujolais Nouveau is designed to be delicious when it is barely two months old.

Beaujolais Nouveau is the first French wine to be released from each year's new crop of grapes. The grapes are harvested in the Beaujolais and Beaujolais-Villages vineyards in late August or September, depending on the weather. (About two-thirds of the wine from these two areas is made into Beaujolais Nouveau.) By mid-November, the wine is already bottled and on its way to market. On the third Thursday of November the wine becomes legal: Wine drinkers all over the world open bottles to celebrate the harvest.

Some wine lovers like to deride Beaujolais Nouveau, criticizing it for not being a serious wine. Actually, they're right: It's not a serious wine. But it *is* delicious and it is definitely fun; we can't imagine letting November end without our drinking a bottle or two of the wine. Since when do all wines have to be serious, anyway?

Cru Beaujolais

The best Beaujolais wines come from ten specific zones in the north. They carry the name of the area where the grapes grow; their official appellations don't use the word "Beaujolais" at all. (Many labels for the U.S. market do carry the words "Red Beaujolais Wine" in small print, however.) Figure 8-1 shows a label of a *cru* Beaujolais wine.

The wines from these ten areas are known as *cru Beaujolais.* (Unlike in Burgundy and Alsace, these top wines are simply *crus,* not *grands crus.*) Cru Beaujolais wines are firmer, richer and more refined than other Beaujolais wines. But generalizations about these wines are problematic, because the *cru* wines vary in style from one *cru* to another. Some are perfumed and charming in personality, while others are dense and relatively powerful in style.

Vin du Beaujolais

Juliénas

Appellation Juliénas Contrôlée

RED BEAUJOLAIS WINE

DOMAINE DU CLOS DU FIEF

Michel TETE

Propriétaire-Récoltant à JULIÉNAS 69840 France

Mis en Bouteille au Domaine

ALC.13% BY VOL.   PRODUCE OF FRANCE   750 ML

Figure 8.1: Labels of *cru* Beaujolais wines carry the word "Beaujolais" only in fine print — if at all.

The ten *cru* Beaujolais, from south to north, are:

- ✔ **Brouilly** *(broo yee)*
- ✔ **Côte de Brouilly**
- ✔ **Régnié** *(ray nyay)*
- ✔ **Morgon** *(mor gohn)*
- ✔ **Chiroubles** *(sheh roob leh)*
- ✔ **Fleurie** *(flehr ee)*
- ✔ **Moulin-à-Vent** *(moo lahn ah vahn)*
- ✔ **Chénas** *(shay nahs)*
- ✔ **Juliénas** *(jool yay nahs)*
- ✔ **St.-Amour** *(sant ah more)*

The names of all of these wines are the names of specific villages, with the exception of Brouilly and Côte de Brouilly (named for the volcanic Mont Brouilly) and Moulin-à-Vent (named for a windmill).

Brouilly, Régnié, and Chiroubles tend to be the lightest of the *cru* wines (although they have more substance than many Beaujolais-Villages wines). Brouilly, in fact, is the largest of the *cru* territories. Régnié happens to be the newest *cru,* recognized in 1988. One of our favorites — not only of the lighter *crus,* but of all ten — is Chiroubles, a wine with lovely aromatic delicacy, and a perfumed, pretty style; to us, it embodies the very personality of Beaujolais.

In the middle group, stylistically, are Côte de Brouilly, Fleurie, and St.-Amour. Of these, St.-Amour is generally the lightest, a soft and charming wine with delicious berry flavors. Côte de Brouilly, from a very small area of vineyards on the higher slopes of Mont Brouilly, is considerably more concentrated than Brouilly itself. Fleurie is a popular *cru* that's quite reliable but relatively pricey for a Beaujolais (about $15) because it is popular.

Morgon, Juliénas, Chénas, and Moulin-à-Vent are the fullest of the *cru* Beaujolais. Chénas is harder to find than the other *crus,* because many of the wines of Chénas are (quite legally) labelled as Moulin-à-Vent — a recognizable name that's an asset to sales; stylistically, it's fairly substantial, similar to Moulin-à-Vent. Morgon (a favorite of ours) is a full, earthy, wild cherry-scented wine that ages as well as any Beaujolais wine, developing a Burgundian silkiness after about five years. Juliénas is always a wise choice, because the wines are consistently high in quality.

Moulin-à-Vent wines can differ from other Beaujolais wines because some producers age them in small oak casks that give oaky aromas and flavors to the wine, along with extra tannins. These oak-aged Moulin-à-Vents can probably age longer than other *cru* wines — how long is uncertain, because the practice is fairly new — but at the sacrifice of some of the wine's traditional character. You can sometimes identify these wines by the words *"fûts de chêne"* (oak casks) on the label.

Producers and prices

Large *négociant* companies produce most Beaujolais wines; they buy grapes and wine from private growers and then blend, bottle, and sell the wine under their own labels. Many of these companies are Burgundy *négociants,* who also sell a full range of Burgundies; some of them own vineyards in Beaujolais, as well as purchasing grapes from growers. A single *négociant,* Georges Duboeuf, produces about 15 percent of the region's entire production.

Individual estate Beaujolais wines exist as well. Some are wines of private growers, such as Jacky Janodet, Michel Tête, Domaine Dalicieux, and Jean-Paul Brun. Other estate wines come from *négociants* who segregate certain wines from private estates. Duboeuf, for example, bottles and sells the wines of his best growers separately, as estate wines, when he believes they are distinctive. And the Louis Jadot firm owns the fine Château des Jacques estate in Moulin-à-Vent, and sells that wine separately.

Wines from single estates are generally higher in quality and more distinctive than the normal *négociant* wines, but they're also less widely available and usually cost more.

The price of Beaujolais depends on the type:

✔ Beaujolais Nouveau costs about $6 to $8 a bottle after Thanksgiving; the bottles available the week before Thanksgiving are more expensive because they're shipped by air.

✔ Simple Beaujolais wines sell for $8 to $11.

✔ Beaujolais-Villages wines cost a dollar or two more than simple Beaujolais.

✔ Cru Beaujolais range in price from about $10 to $15, but single estate wines from the best *crus* can cost more.

Enjoying Beaujolais

Here's our advice for enjoying Beaujolais wines:

1. **Chill wine.**

2. **Open bottle.**

3. **Pour wine into glass.**

4. **Drink wine.**

Of all the wines of France, Beaujolais is the one that requires the least preparation and the least expertise to enjoy. Just do it!

Nevertheless, certain situations and certain foods can help you appreciate Beaujolais all the more. When we daydream of being in Paris, eating roast chicken and *pommes frites* at a neighborhood bistro, it's a bottle of Beaujolais-Villages that's on the table, because Beaujolais strikes just the right tone in informal settings. Likewise a summer picnic, with cold cuts, potato salad, and crusty bread — or a neighborhood potluck dinner.

Beaujolais goes well with a wide range of foods, from poultry to game birds, red meats, stews, game, and cheeses from light to strong. Choose the type of Beaujolais according to the richness of the dish (or vice versa!): For example, Beaujolais-Villages or a light *cru* such as Chiroubles with poultry, and a fuller *cru* such as Morgon with stews or game. But don't obsess about the pairings — that would definitely go against the Beaujolais spirit.

The lighter the Beaujolais wine, the more it accommodates chilling. We like to drink Beaujolais Nouveau almost as cool as white wine (about 52°F), Beaujolais and Beaujolais-Villages at cellar temperature (56° to 57°F), and *cru* Beaujolais at about the same temperature as red Burgundy, 60°F to 62°F.

Beaujolais Nouveau with age

This really happened. We walked out to the curb one evening in late 2000 to deposit a can into our recycle bin before the next morning's pick-up. Atop the bin we found a plastic bag with three bottles of wine in it: a half-bottle of inexpensive bubbly, a raspberry wine, and a 1997 Beaujolais Nouveau from Prosper Maufoux. We didn't know where they came from, but we did know that we couldn't leave full bottles sitting at the curb — so we brought them inside to empty them down the sink. When we opened the Beaujolais Nouveau, we poured a glass (in the interest of research) and, to our surprise, the wine was quite drinkable. At three years of age, it had lost its zip, but it was in no way spoiled. Thanks to that experience, we've revised our usual advice to drink Beaujolais Nouveau by March of the following year.

Beaujolais is best when it's young, because with age it loses its distinctiveness. The lighter the style, the younger the wine should be. Here are some general guidelines:

- **Beaujolais Nouveau:** Drink as young as possible; it will still be drinkable at one or even two years old, but you sacrifice personality along the way.

- **Simple Beaujolais wines:** Ready from their release, about one month after the nouveau style, to about one year later.

- **Beaujolais-Villages:** Drinkable from about March of the year after the harvest until they're about two years old.

- **Lighter *cru* wines:** Drink within three years of the vintage.

- **Medium-bodied *cru* Beaujolais:** Best from one to four years after the vintage.

- **The fullest *crus*:** Drink four to seven years after the vintage, up to ten years for Moulin-à-Vent.

Chapter 9

Robust Rhône Reds and Unique Whites

....

In This Chapter

▶ The Syrah grape shines at home

▶ Generous blends born of southern sun

▶ Viognier at the source

▶ Characterful reds, from affordable to rare

....

*A*lmost as soon as we began drinking French wines, we became passionate about Bordeaux, Burgundy, and Champagne. Rhône wines didn't do it for us, at first. The newsletters we subscribe to extolled the virtues of the Rhône, our friends shared their favorite bottles with us, and we even invested in some top Rhône reds for our cellar, but the wines just didn't ignite the same spark with us as other French wines.

Now, we love them. What changed? For one thing, a trip to the Rhône Valley (and then another, and another) brought the wines alive for us. And we suddenly "got" Syrah, the Rhône's truly great red variety. We also became more accepting of untamed wines that puncture the veil of refinement to offer an animalistic sort of pleasure. You could say that Rhône wines have put us in touch with our primitive selves. Are you ready to explore the dark pleasures of the Rhône?

Two Regions in One

The rich wine region known as the Rhône Valley lies in south-eastern France, south of Beaujolais (see Figure 1-1). The region takes its name from the Rhône River, which rises in the Swiss Alps and courses westward, then southward through France, emptying into the Mediterranean Sea. The Rhône River runs right through the Rhône Valley wine region for about 120 miles.

In terms of both the terrain and the wines, the Rhône Valley has two distinct parts: the Northern Rhône and the Southern Rhône. The two parts have different grape varieties, different winemaking philosophies, different soils, and, to some extent, different climates. What unites the two into a single wine region is the river itself, a mighty, continuous presence, and the sultry spirit of the wines.

The Rhône Valley produces red, white, rosé, sparkling, and sweet dessert wines — but red wines dominate, representing 91 percent of the region's production. Among its red and white wines, the Rhône Valley makes both inexpensive wines for drinking young, and more expensive wines that require aging to reach their prime drinkability. The Rhône Valley makes so much wine — more than 40 million cases a year — that the region is the number two producer of AOC wine, after Bordeaux. This huge quantity does encompass plenty of quality, too.

The nature of the North

The Northern Rhône is a long, narrow wine region that begins 16 miles south of the city of Lyons (in French, Lyon, pronounced *lee ohn*) and continues 40 miles southward to just below the town of Valence. It's an area of steep, terraced hills sloping down toward the river from the west, and slightly more open hills facing the river on the east. Vineyards cover these hills in a nearly continuous stretch on the western side of the Valley; vineyards also occupy the river's eastern shore, but don't continue as far northward as on the western side of the river. Figure 9-1 shows the vineyards of the Rhône Valley.

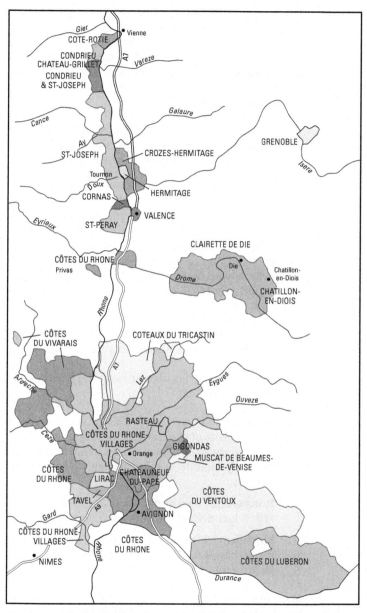

Figure 9-1: The Northern Rhône and the Southern Rhône are two distinct vineyard areas.

The Northern Rhône has a continental climate; summers are warm, with lots of sun; the winters are cold. A cold, hurricane-force wind from the north, called the *mistral,* funnels down the narrow river valley, jeopardizing flowering of the vines in the spring and ripening of the grapes in the fall. The slope of the hills, and a south-facing orientation for some vineyards, help to hasten ripening.

The soils of the Northern Rhône are mainly porous granite and schist — generally light, infertile soils. The best vineyard areas, usually on steep hills, have these soils; where the soil is heavier, in the plain along the river, grapes for lesser wines grow.

The single red grape variety of the Northern Rhône is Syrah *(see rah),* one of the highest-quality red varieties in the world. It is a dark, fairly tannic grape with enormous complexity of flavor. Depending on where it grows, Syrah can make a wine with aromas and flavors that are fruity, floral, spicy, smoky, meaty, and vegetal — quite a range for a single variety! Although Syrah grows in many parts of the world — including Australia, South Africa, California, Washington State, and Italy — the Northern Rhône is the one area where Syrah consistently expresses its widest aromatic range.

Several white varieties also grow in the Northern Rhône. They include the following:

- **Viognier** *(vee oh n'yay):* The most important white variety in terms of the unique character of its wines. Viognier has pronounced, but delicate, aromas and flavors that typically include floral notes, as well as peach and apricot.

- **Roussanne** *(roos sahn):* Another high quality white variety; it has delicate aromas and crisp acidity.

- **Marsanne** *(mar sahn):* A variety that's much easier to grow than Roussanne, giving more body to its wines but lacking finesse.

Marsanne and Roussanne typically co-star in some of the white wines of the Northern Rhône, but Viognier stands alone in the white wines that feature it.

The nature of the South

The main vineyard area of the Southern Rhône begins about 30 miles south of the vineyards of the North, and continues to just south of the city of Avignon *(ah vee n'yon)*. The region is much larger than the Northern Rhône, and it produces much more wine; about 95 percent of all Rhône Valley wine comes from the South.

The shape and the topography of the Southern Rhône are completely different from that of the Northern Rhône: It's a wide, open area with lots of flat land and some gentle hills. The climate is Mediterranean rather than continental, because the region is quite close to the sea, and far less interior than the Northern Rhône. This means that it's a milder area, with plenty of summer heat to ripen the grapes, but sometimes insufficient rain. The *mistral* wind from the north blows forcefully through the area, requiring grape-growers to take special precautions to protect their vines from damage.

Like the terrain, the assortment of grape varieties in the Southern Rhône is wide open. Numerous red and white varieties grow there, and most wines are blends of several varieties. Grenache *(gren ahsh)*, a red variety, is the main grape; in fact, on the strength of its acreage in the Southern Rhône, Grenache is also the main grape variety of the Rhône Valley overall. At low crop levels, it makes fairly dense, dark wines with meaty and black pepper flavors; when the crop is large, however, Grenache's color tends to fade, and its flavors become dilute. In order to beef up Grenache's color and tannins, winemakers of the Southern Rhône usually blend it with other varieties grown there.

The other red varieties important in the Southern Rhône are the following:

- ✔ **Syrah:** This variety is growing in use among many producers intent on improving the quality of their wines.

- ✔ **Mourvèdre** *(more ved'r):* A deep-colored variety with fruity aromas that's also increasing in use.

- ✔ **Cinsault, or Cinsaut** *(san soh):* A variety that makes relatively light wines that are soft and perfumed.

Other red varieties of the Southern Rhône include Carignan (a dark, tannic variety of Spanish origin), Picpoul, Terret Noir, Counoise, Muscardin, and Vaccarèse.

White grape varieties hardly figure in the Southern Rhône, because the region's wine production is mainly red. The following white varieties are largely responsible for the few white wines that do exist in the region:

- **Grenache Blanc:** A white version of the red Grenache variety; it's soft and full-bodied but short in aroma and flavor.
- **Clairette:** A variety that makes soft, full-bodied whites. It's also used in local sparkling wines.

Other white varieties used in Southern Rhône blends include Roussanne, Bourboulenc *(bore boo lahnk)*, Ugni Blanc *(oo n'yee blahn'k)*, Muscat, Marsanne, Picardan *(pee car dan)*, white Picpoul, and Viognier.

The Northern Rhône, Up Close

If the film *True Grit* were set in wine country, the Northern Rhône would be the ideal location. Most Northern Rhône vineyards occupy dry, scraggy, terraced hillsides rising steeply above small towns perched along the Rhône River. Old, gnarled vines grow in burnt-looking earth. The vineyards look rustic and somewhat primitive.

In a sense, the vineyards reflect the taste of the wines: dry, concentrated, a bit tough, gritty of spirit. The red wines of the Northern Rhône are survivors, born of challenging conditions and enduring for years in the bottle. They vary by degree — some of them being lighter and smoother, others being fuller and more intense — but they're all of the same mold. This is in part due to the fact that a single red grape variety, Syrah, is the basis for all of them.

White wines grow in this region, too, and like the landscape, they're dramatic wines. As generalizations go, they're full-bodied, dry whites, with intriguing and unusual aromas; some of them need many years of bottle age to express themselves best.

Like most French wines, the wines of the Northern Rhône carry the names of the places where their grapes grow. Eight *terroirs* give their names to wines: two for red wine only; three for red or white wine; and three for white wine or sparkling wine. Roughly from north to south, these AOC wines are the following:

- **Côte-Rôtie** *(coat ro tee):* Red

- **Condrieu** *(con drew):* White

- **Château Grillet** *(sha tow gree yay):* White

- **Hermitage** *(er mee tahj):* Mainly red, some white

- **Crozes-Hermitage** *(crows er mee tahj):* Mainly red, some white

- **St.-Joseph** *(san jhoe sef):* Mainly red, some white

- **Cornas** *(core nahs):* Red

- **St.-Péray** *(san peh ray):* Mainly sparkling, some white

The reds rule

Most of the wine made in the Northern Rhône is red. These red wines fall into two groups:

- **The most prestigious, expensive, and age-worthy wines:** Hermitage, Côte-Rôtie, and Cornas fall into this category; of these, Hermitage and Côte-Rôtie are the real stars.

- **The less prestigious, less expensive wines for earlier drinking:** St.-Joseph and Crozes-Hermitage are examples.

Côte Rôtie

The Côte Rôtie ("roasted slope") vineyards are the northern-most of the Rhône, covering nearly 500 acres on the western bank of the Rhône around the village of Ampuis. Because the river runs southwest for six miles at this point, the hills above the river face south or southeast rather than east, giving the vines a bonus of sunshine and ripening potential.

The Côte Rôtie vineyards vary in altitude, incline, and soil. The most famous distinction within Côte Rôtie is between the northern vineyards, called the Côte Brune, and the southern vineyards, called the Côte Blonde. The Côte Brune ("brown slope") has an iron-rich, relatively dark schistous soil, while the Côte Blonde has a schist and granite soil that's paler in color. The names of these two areas were born of a legend involving the blonde and brunette daughters of a local lord.

Traditionally, Côte Rôtie wines derived from grapes of both areas blended together, but today a number of producers also make single-vineyard Côte Rôties, which contain the grapes of one area only. These single-vineyard wines command higher prices than most other Côte Rôties, and reflect the particular character of their zone. (Côte Blonde wines are elegant, more finesseful, more balanced, and readier to drink sooner; Côte Brune wines are more tannic and austere, and need more time to develop in the bottle.)

Côte Rôtie wine may be made entirely from Syrah, or it may contain up to 20 percent of white Viognier grapes; in practice, most producers use less than 5 percent Viognier, if any, in their wines.

One of the most beguiling characteristics of Côte Rôtie wines is their perfume, a fragrant mix of violets, raspberries, green olives, bacon, and underbrush. Although they're full-bodied, dense, tannic, and rustic in the general Rhône paradigm, these wines have finesse and smoothness. They're enjoyable beginning about five to six years after the vintage (depending on the vintage's quality), but the best wines require ten to 15 years to mature fully, and can age gracefully for 20 years or more.

Côte Rôtie wines sell for about $40 to $75 a bottle, but the most sought-after single-vineyard bottlings cost as much as $150 a bottle or more.

Marcel Guigal has done more to popularize Côte Rôtie than any other producer. We recommend his firm and other reliable firms that specialize in Côte Rôtie, listed alphabetically:

Domaine Gilles Barge
Domaine Bernard Burgaud
Domaine Champet
Domaine Clusel-Roch
Domaine Gentaz-Dervieux
Domaine Jean-Michel Gerin

E. Guigal
Domaine Jamet
Domaine Robert Jasmin
Domaine Michel Ogier
Domaine René Rostaing
Domaine Vidal-Fleury

Three other reliable producers make Côte Rôtie but don't specialize in it: M. Chapoutier, Delas Frères, and Paul Jaboulet Aîné.

Hermitage

The broad, dramatic Hermitage hill lies on the eastern bank of the Rhône River. The river takes a propitious turn eastward around the town of Tain L'Hermitage, causing the hill and its vineyards to face southward, and making Hermitage perhaps the single finest *terroir* of the entire Rhône Valley.

With about 318 planted acres, Hermitage is only two-thirds the size of Côte Rôtie. The soils vary across the Hermitage hill, and the altitude of the vineyards varies, too, creating subtly different wines according to where the vines grow. Unlike in Côte Rôtie, however, single-vineyard Hermitage wines are less common — although many producers do make a super-Hermitage as well as a standard version. La Chapelle, the legendary, nearly eternal Hermitage of the Paul Jaboulet Aîné winery, is perhaps the most famous premium Hermitage.

Quite a few wine critics (present company included) consider Hermitage to be the greatest Syrah wine on the planet. Technically, it can contain up to 15 percent of two white varieties, Marsanne and Roussanne, but it rarely contains any; instead of blending their white grapes into their red Hermitage, producers make a separate white wine, Hermitage Blanc (described in the next section).

Hermitage is a full-bodied, intense, tannic red wine with long aging potential. Its aromas and flavors reflect Syrah's full spectrum: spice, cedar, cassis, smoke, meat, leather, and, sometimes, tar. With age, Hermitage becomes soft and slightly sweet, and its aromas grow even more complex. It is truly one of the greatest wines of France.

Hermitage from a great, or even good, vintage (and a good producer) needs many years to develop — at least ten years from the vintage and as much as 20. If you drink an Hermitage when it's young, you'll probably be impressed by its power and weight, but you won't experience the true majesty of this wine.

Hermitage has six particularly outstanding producers. These firms each produce more than one red Hermitage, generally a standard wine and a premium version. These six producers, listed aphabetically, are Domaine Jean-Louis Chave, M. Chapoutier, Delas Frères, Paul Jaboulet Aîné, Domaine Marc Sorrel, and Domaine Bernard Faurie.

Red Hermitage costs from about $40 to $100 per bottle. A few elite, premium, or single-vineyard Hermitages can cost $150 or more.

Cornas

Cornas is a very small town on the western bank of the Rhône. The Cornas vineyards are planted entirely with Syrah.

Some Cornas producers believe that Cornas is comparable to Hermitage as a *terroir* for Syrah, and that it's superior to most of the vineyards of Côte Rôtie. (*They're* not biased.) We like Côte Rôtie too much to accept that premise — but we do believe that Cornas is a far better site, and wine, than it traditionally has gotten credit for. And stylistically, Cornas wines do resemble Hermitage more than Cote Rôtie: dense, powerful wines with aromatic finesse that can take long aging.

Cornas is a tiny area — only 250 acres shared by 38 growers — and is the smallest and southernmost appellation for red wine in the Northern Rhône. Despite its small size, some growers, such as Jean-Luc Colombo, perceive the area to have several distinct *terroirs,* according to the vineyards' altitude. Because of these perceived differences, some of these growers bottle single-vineyard Cornas wines.

Traditionally, Cornas wines needed 20 years to reach their best drinking, but today's wines are less ferocious when they're young. We recommend that you drink them when they're at least eight years old, up to 20 years or even longer in the best vintages. Because Cornas is a relatively unsung wine, it's a good value; most Cornas wines sell for $30 to $60.

Eight producers make very good Cornas; alphabetically, they are Domaine Guy de Barjac, Domaine Auguste Clape, Jean-Luc Colombo, Domaine Marcel Juge, Paul Jaboulet Aîné, Domaine Robert Michel, Domaine Noël Verset, and Domaine Alain Voge.

St-Joseph

The St.-Joseph vineyards are on the western bank of the Rhône, north of Cornas and across the river from Hermitage. They occupy a fairly large area of hills as well as flatter land above and below the slopes, stretching along almost the whole length of the Northern Rhône region. Since the formation of the St.-Joseph appellation in 1956, the territory has expanded considerably, encompassing land that is not ideal for growing Syrah. Local growers and the AOC committee have now redrawn St.-Joseph's boundaries, but vineyards in the less suitable areas may continue to grow the wine until 2022. As a result of the large area, the quality of St.-Joseph wine is variable according to where the vineyards for a particular wine are situated.

About 90 percent of St.-Joseph wine is red; it may contain up to 10 percent of the white varieties Marsanne and Roussanne. Red St.-Joseph wines are generally the lightest, fruitiest, and most approachable Northern Rhône reds. They're usually medium-bodied and only moderately tannic, with black cherry aromas and flavors.

Most red St.-Joseph wines can be enjoyed within three to five years from the vintage; a few sturdier (and more expensive) ones can age for up to ten years. Most St.-Joseph red wines range from $14 to $25.

Good producers who specialize in St.-Joseph include Bernard Gripa, Domaine Louis Chèze, Domaine Courbis, Domaine Pierre Coursodon, Jean-Louis Grippat, and Raymond Trollat.

Crozes-Hermitage

The vineyards of Crozes-Hermitage lie on the eastern bank of the Rhône, surrounding the Hermitage hill and stretching far north, south, and east of it. Compared to other Northern Rhône vineyards, the territory is fairly flat and quite large: With about 2500 acres of vines, it's the largest AOC territory in the North. Naturally for such a large area, the terrain is not uniform; soils, slope, and altitude vary, and consequently the wines vary in quality and intensity.

The producers also vary. In addition to established growers and established *négociant* companies, the area includes several fairly new growers who have brought fresh energy to

Crozes-Hermitage and make some of the area's best wines. Altogether, Crozes-Hermitage producers make almost 12 times as much wine as Hermitage.

Red Crozes-Hermitage wine may legally contain up to 15 percent white grapes, but, as for Hermitage itself, the wine is almost always entirely Syrah. Some producers make their wines for early consumption, using methods similar to the carbonic maceration practiced in Beaujolais (see the section "Beaujolais winemaking" in Chapter 8); these wines are soft and exude grapey Syrah flavor, and they are best within three to four years from the vintage. Other Crozes-Hermitage wines are more traditional: fairly robust and firm wines that evolve slowly over 15 years.

The more forward-styled Crozes-Hermitage wines are usually the least expensive, about $14 to $18, while the more traditional wines tend to run about $22 to $28. Good Crozes-Hermitage, in fact, can be one of the best values in French wine today — but choose carefully.

Four producers who specialize in Crozes-Hermitage include Domaine Albert Belle, Domaine Alain Graillot, Bernard Chave and Domaine du Pavillon. You can also find very good Crozes-Hermitage from M. Chapoutier, Delas Frères, Jean-Luc Colombo, and Paul Jaboulet Aîné. Jaboulet's Crozes-Hermitage from the family's "Domaine du Thalabert" estate is consistently fine, and a real value at $23.

Uncommon whites

White wines make up only a small percentage of the Northern Rhône's production, but they are not incidental wines that you can basically ignore. The white wines of the Northern Rhône are among the most unusual white wines of the world.

Condrieu and Château Grillet

The territory of Condrieu runs for 12 miles along the western bank of the Rhône, in the north of the region, just south of Côte Rôtie. The tiny territory of Château Grillet — another, separate AOC wine — lies within the borders of Condrieu.

Condrieu versus Viognier

We describe Condrieu as a wine that's rare and expensive because of the difficulty in growing Viognier — but you can find varietally-labelled Viognier wines from France in your wine shop for as little as $10. What gives?

In recent years, breeders have isolated clones of Viognier that are easier to grow and produce a decent-sized crop; the newer Viognier vineyards in the south of France and in minor Rhône areas such as the Ardèche (a *vin de pays* zone) have these more productive clones. Also, these new vineyards are in areas that are less expensive to farm than the limited hills of Condrieu (240 acres!). The inexpensive Viogniers can give you a good idea of the grape's exotic aromas, but they are less intriguing than Condrieu.

Both Condrieu and Château Grillet wines derive entirely from the Viognier grape. Because this variety has very small berries that give low yields of juice, these two wines are small in production, and somewhat rare. Condrieu production is less than 30,000 cases annually, and that of Château Grillet is about 1,000 cases.

A good Condrieu is a fascinating wine — rich in exotic aromas and flavors that suggest peach, flowers, and dried fruits, but dry and quite full in body. The aroma makes one statement (delicacy, finesse), and the wine's body and richness say something else entirely (weight, substance). Château Grillet is similar to Condrieu but generally drier and a bit crisper, due to aging for 18 months in oak barrels; we find good Condrieu far more satisfying than the often over-rated Château Grillet, which excels only in very good vintages.

Condrieu costs about $45 to $50 a bottle or more, and Château Grillet costs about double. In our experience, these wines don't age well; we prefer to drink them no later than three years after the harvest. We also prefer to drink them with very delicately flavored foods, such as light fish or simple chicken dishes (or by themselves), so that the wines' delicate aromas are not overpowered.

Only one winery makes Château Grillet, and that's the Château Grillet estate. The leading producers of Condrieu include the following, in alphabetical order:

Château du Rozay

M. Chapoutier

Domaine Clusel-Roch

Domaine Yves Cuilleron

Delas Frères

Pierre Dumazet

E. Guigal

Paul Jaboulet-Aîné

Domaine Robert
 Niero-Pinchon

Domaine André Perre

Domaine Alain Paret

Domaine Georges Vernay

Hermitage Blanc

White Hermitage, or Hermitage Blanc, comes from the same area as red Hermitage, on the eastern bank of the Rhône. The wine is a blend of two varieties, Marsanne and Roussanne. Marsanne, the easier variety to grow, is the main constituent of most Hermitage Blanc wines, but Roussanne, the finer, more fragrant variety, has gained favor with winemakers in recent years, and it constitutes an increasing percentage of the blend.

Hermitage Blanc is a statuesque and exotic wine, dry and full-bodied with pronounced honey and floral (and earthy, citrusy, nutty, or marmalade-like) aromas and flavors. It's delicious when it's young, and it's compelling when it's old: richer in texture, its aromas flattened out but its character magnified. In the in-between years — when the wine is about four to fifteen years of age — disappointment lurks. Like some red wines, but unlike most whites, Hermitage Blanc goes "dumb" and has nothing to say for a period, but eventually rediscovers its tongue and can be wonderful for decades thereafter. If you have, say, an eight-year-old Hermitage, resist the urge to open the bottle now.

Hermitage Blanc costs about $35 to $55 per bottle, but some wines, such as Chapoutier's Cuvée de l'Orée, sell for more than $100.

Some producers who make red Hermitage also make white Hermitage. We particularly like the Hermitage Blanc from the following producers, listed alphabetically:

Domaine Jean-Louis Chave
M. Chapoutier
Jean-Luc Colombo
Delas Frères

Jean-Louis Grippat
Paul Jaboulet-Ainé
Domaine Marc Sorrel

Chave and Chapoutier have particularly fine reputations for their Hermitage Blanc, and we would personally add Jaboulet to that elite group.

Crozes-Hermitage Blanc and St.-Joseph Blanc

Both the Crozes-Hermitage and the St.-Joseph appellations apply to white wine as well as red. In both cases, the whites derive from a blend of Marsanne and Roussanne, but Roussanne (the finer of the two) is more common in Crozes-Hermitage than in St.-Joseph.

Crozes-Hermitage Blanc resembles Hermitage Blanc but is somewhat lighter in body and in aromatic intensity, and it can't live as long — nor does it withdraw during its adolescent years. We prefer white Crozes young, up to about four years of age. St.-Joseph Blanc is lighter yet charming and quite easy to enjoy during its first four years, which is its best period. Both types of wine generally cost from $14 to $25.

M. Chapoutier, Delas Frères, and Paul Jaboulet Ainé — three good wineries that market a wide range of Rhône wines — all make both Crozes-Hermitage Blanc and St.-Joseph Blanc. Specialists in Crozes-Hermitage Blanc include the four producers we name for red Crozes: Domaine Albert Belle, Domaine Alain Graillot, Bernard Chave, and Domaine du Pavillon.

Top producers of St.-Joseph Blanc include the following:

Domaine Louis Chèze
Domaine Pierre Coursodon
Domaine Yves Cuilleron

Jean-Louis Grippat
André Perret
Raymond Trollat

St.-Péray

St.-Péray is a town slightly larger than tiny Cornas, situated south of Cornas on the western bank of the Rhône; it is the southernmost AOC area of the Northern Rhône. St.-Péray is the lone appellation of the Northern Rhône that does not make red wine. In fact, it makes very little white wine, either: Its production is mainly sparkling.

The sparkling wine called St.-Péray is mainly Marsanne, with some Roussanne and a local variety called Roussette (which might or might not be Roussanne). It's made using the traditional method of second fermentation in the bottle. (Chapter 15 of *Wine For Dummies,* 2nd Edition, explains this process, as does Chapter 3 of *Champagne For Dummies,* both published by Hungry Minds.) It's rather full in body for a sparkling wine because its vineyards are so southerly. Very little of this wine is available in the U.S.

Jean Lionnet produces a very good St.-Péray. Incidentally, he also offers a good Cornas called "Domaine de Rochepertuis."

The Southern Rhône in the Spotlight

What a difference 30 miles make! When you drive from the Northern Rhône into the South, the steep, rugged landscape disappears behind you, and a windswept tableau of lavender, olive groves, and cypress trees opens ahead. By the time you reach the heart of the region, you are nearly in Provence. Clearly, such a terrain and such a warm, sunny climate cannot produce wines of the same personality as the North.

The wines of the Southern Rhône are more generous and approachable than the northern wines — and wine in the South is also more abundant. Largely on the strength of a single type of wine, Côtes du Rhône, the South produces about 19 times more wine than the North.

The wines of the South have place names, but some of the places are very large areas, while others are more limited and specific. A total of 18 AOC designations exist in the Southern Rhône or its vicinity. Seven of these are the most important, either for the quantity of wine they produce, the quality of the wine, or their historic standing. These seven AOC areas all produce non-sparkling, dry wines; they are the following:

- **Côtes du Rhône** *(coat dew rone):* Mainly red; also rosé or white

- **Côtes du Rhône-Villages** *(coat dew rone vee lahj):* A higher quality Côtes du Rhône

✔ **Châteauneuf-du-Pape** *(sha toe nuff dew pahp):* Mainly red, but also white

✔ **Gigondas** *(gee gohn dah's):* Mainly red but also rosé

✔ **Vacqueyras** *(vac keh rah's):* Red, rosé, and some white

✔ **Lirac** *(lee rak):* Red, rosé, and white wines

✔ **Tavel** *(tah vell):* Rosé wine only

Another seven AOC's for still, dry wines are less important. Some of these areas attained AOC status only in the past few years, and their wines are therefore practically unheard of outside France — while other areas do export their wines, which are mainly inexpensive. We discuss these wines in the sections, "Satellite wine zones of the Southern Rhône" later in this chapter.

Another four AOC areas produce either sweet wines or sparkling wines; these wines are the following:

✔ **Muscat de Beaumes-de-Venise** *(moos cah deh bohm deh veh nees):* Sweet white from Muscat grapes

✔ **Rasteau** *(raah stow):* Sweet, fortified red wine

✔ **Clairette de Die** *(clar et deh dee):* Sparkling wine

✔ **Crémant de Die** *(cray mahn't deh dee):* Sparkling wine

The major wines of the South

Although white grape varieties grow throughout the Southern Rhône, red wines are by far the dominant type. One wine — Châteauneuf-du-Pape — stands out both historically and for its quality. Two other wines, Côtes du Rhône and Côtes du Rhône-Villages, account for a huge volume with variable quality, but include some very good wines.

Châteauneuf-du-Pape

The rather large Châteauneuf-du-Pape territory (7,700 acres of vineyards) lies on the eastern bank of the Rhône River, south of the city of Orange. Its name means "new castle of the Pope," a reference to the fact that Pope John XXII constructed a summer residence there in 1318. In wine terms, the area is famous because a local grower, Baron de Roy, developed the idea for France's AOC system, in 1923. When France implemented the system in 1935, Châteauneuf-du-Pape was one of France's first AOC wines.

The Châteauneuf-du-Pape territory encompasses a variety of soil types, of which the *galets* — large, smooth round stones — is the most famous. To see vines growing in rocks — no dirt in sight! — is quite amazing. These stones reflect the stored heat of the day onto the vines at night, assisting the ripening of the grapes.

Red Châteauneuf-du-Pape can be made from as many as 13 different grape varieties, including four white varieties. These 13 varieties are Grenache (red and white); Syrah, Mourvèdre, Picpoul, Terret Noir, Counoise, Muscardin, Vaccarèse, and Cinsault (all red); also Picardan, Clairette, Roussanne, and Bourboulenc (white).

In modern practice, however, most Châteauneuf-du-Pape reds come from three or four varieties, all red:

- ✔ Grenache typically dominates the wine, making up 50 to 70 percent of the blend.

- ✔ Syrah constitutes from 10 to 30 percent of the blend.

- ✔ Mourvèdre makes up the balance, sometimes along with Cinsault, Counoise, or Vaccarèse.

The renowned Château Rayas has often produced Châteauneuf-du-Pape entirely from Grenache, grown so that it produces very small crops and delivers an intensity atypical of this variety. And some producers do use all 13 varieties — notably the fine Château de Beaucastel.

Châteauneuf-du-Pape wines can also vary from producer to producer according to how they're made. A few producers vinify the grapes traditionally, to make sturdy, full-bodied, tannic, high-alcohol wines that need several years to develop and can evolve for up to 20 years. Other producers are experimenting with vinification techniques — such as the carbonic maceration method used in Beaujolais (see Chapter 8) — to make wines that are less tannic, fruitier, and easier to drink young. Both styles generally have aromas and flavors that are earthy, herbal, and fruity — especially jammy black cherry or raspberry.

Long-lived Châteauneuf-du-Papes made in the traditional style cost about $40 to $50 a bottle or more; the more modern-styled wines are less expensive, about $25 to $30 a bottle.

More than 120 producers grow and bottle Châteauneuf-du-Pape — not counting the *négociant* brands. The 17 estates we list alphabetically here all make top-quality, traditional style red Châteauneuf-du-Pape:

Château de Beaucastel	Château de la Gardine
Domaine de Beaurenard	Domaine de la Janasse
Henri Bonneau	Domaine de Marcoux
Les Cailloux	Château de la Nerthe
Clos des Papes	Domaine du Pégau
Clos du Mont Olivet	Château Rayas
Domaine de Mont Redon	Le Vieux Donjon
Font de Michelle	Domaine du Vieux-
Château Fortia	Télégraphe

In addition to these estates, Paul Jaboulet Aîné, Jean-Luc Colombo, and M. Chapoutier also make good, reliable red Châteauneuf-du-Pape.

Châteauneuf-du-Pape Blanc

White Châteauneuf-du-Pape also exists. It may be made from six white varieties: Clairette, Grenache Blanc, Bourboulenc, Picpoul Blanc, Viognier, and Roussanne.

Although it represents only about 7 percent of the zone's production, the quantity of white Châteauneuf-du-Pape is increasing. The quality of the wine has increased as well, thanks to winemaking changes — such as less oak aging and earlier bottling — which help retain the freshness of the wine. At its best, Châteauneuf-du-Pape Blanc is a dry, full-bodied white with aromas and flavors that are earthy, minerally, fruity (pear, pineapple, and melon), and honey-like. Wines from the best producers can age for ten years, but most are at their best at no more than three or four years of age.

Because not every Châteauneuf-du-Pape producer makes a white wine, we list here, alphabetically, our favorite producers that do make it:

Château de Beaucastel	Domaine de Marcoux
Les Cailloux	Château de la Nerthe
Clos des Papes	Domaine de Nalys
Font de Michelle	Château Rayas
Château de la Gardine	Domaine du Vieux-
Domaine de la Janasse	Télégraphe

Côtes du Rhône

The Côtes du Rhône AOC is a region-wide appellation: The grapes can come from anywhere within the Rhône Valley region, including the vineyards of the North. Practically speaking, however, the vast majority of this wine comes from the Southern Rhône. Various vineyard areas in the center of the Southern Rhône region, on both sides of the river, are designated specifically for its production. Together with its sister appellation, Côtes du Rhône-Villages, this area makes a huge amount of wine — almost 28 million cases annually, twice as much as Beaujolais.

Côtes du Rhône is mostly a red wine; only 2 percent of the production is white, and another 2 percent is rosé. Red Côtes du Rhône is a blend of various grape varieties, which may be combined according to a complicated formula. Since the 2000 harvest, the regulations regarding varieties are as follows:

- ✔ Grenache must represent at least 40 percent of the wine (except in the Northern Rhône, where the wine can be entirely Syrah).

- ✔ Syrah and Mourvèdre are also principal varieties; along with Grenache, they must constitute at least 70 percent of the blend.

- ✔ Secondary red varieties — ten in all, including Carignan and Cinsault — may constitute no more than 30 percent of the wine; white varieties may constitute no more than 5 percent.

Most Côtes du Rhône wines are inexpensive (under $10 to $12), soft, fruity, low-tannin reds. They are the everyday wines of the region, tasty reds to enjoy with hamburgers or other casual meals, and the majority of them are for enjoying young. Some producers make a more serious style, however; these better Côtes du Rhônes, in our rough order of preference, are Château de Fonsalette, of Château Rayas; Coudoulet de

Beaucastel, of Château Beaucastel; Cuvée des Te...
Domaine Brusset; Domaine Gramenon Côtes du Rhône,
Château des Tours Côtes du Rhône.

Côtes du Rhône-Villages

Côtes du Rhône-Villages wines are a higher class of Côtes du
Rhônes, made from a more limited vineyard area and fewer
grape varieties. That said, the vineyard area is not all that lim-
ited: It encompasses the vineyards of about 70 communities in
Southern Rhône. But production is only 13 percent that of
Côtes du Rhônes.

Grenache may constitute a maximum of 65 percent of the
Côtes du Rhône-Villages blend; Syrah, Cinsault, or Mourvèdre
form a minimum of 25 percent, and other local red varieties
are no more than 10 percent.

Sixteen of the Côtes du Rhône-Villages communities enjoy
special status: They may append their name to the appellation, if the grapes for a wine come specifically from that village. The name of the wine then reads either "Côtes du
Rhône-Villages-Cairanne," for example, or "Cairanne-Côtes du
Rhône-Villages." Other villages of note are Vinsobres, Rasteau,
Chusclan, and Laudun.

Côtes du Rhône-Villages wines are slightly more expensive
than simple Côtes du Rhônes; expect to pay about $12 to $14
a bottle. Some wines worth seeking out include the following:

Domaine de l'Oratoire-St.-
  Martin Côtes du Rhône-
  Villages-Cairanne
Domaine Rabasse-Charavin
  Côtes du Rhône-Villages-
  Rasteau
Domaine Marcel Richaud
  Côtes du Rhône-Villages-
  Cairanne

Domaine de la Soumade
  Côtes du Rhône-Villages-
  Rasteau
Domaine de Ste.-Anne Côtes
  du Rhône-Villages
Domaine de Deurre Côtes du
  Rhône-Villages-Vinsobres

Gigondas

Until 1971, Gigondas was a village name appended to Côtes du
Rhône-Villages, but then the Gigondas area, on the eastern side
of the Rhône, became an AOC in its own right. Today Gigondas
is a thriving appellation, producing about 30 percent as much
wine as the larger Châteauneuf-du-Pape territory.

The winds of change

How does the new formulation for Côtes du Rhône differ from the old? Three varieties — Carignan, Terret Noir, and Cinsault — were demoted to secondary status, thus limiting their use. And increased emphasis now rests on Grenache, Syrah, and Mourvèdre, as the official backbone of the wine. Of course, many good producers relied on these three top varieties all along.

Gigondas wine is red or rosé only. Grenache constitutes up to 80 percent of the blend; Syrah and Mourvèdre must be at least 15 percent, and other local varieties (excluding Carignan) may represent up to 10 percent of the blend.

Of the Southern Rhône reds, Gigondas wines are considered second in quality only to Châteauneuf-du-Pape. Like that wine, they are made in two styles, a lighter, more approachable style (costing about $20 to $25), and a denser, fuller-bodied style ($30 or more). The lighter-style wines are best up to six years of age, while the fuller wines usually drink best from seven or eight years of age up to 15 years.

Good producers of Gigondas, listed alphabetically, include the following:

Domaine du Cayron
Domaine Roger Combe
Domaine de Font-Sane
Domaine Les Goubert

Domaine Raspail-Ay
Domaine Saint Gayan
Domaine de Santa Duc

Vacqueyras

Vacqueyras is a fairly small area directly south of Gigondas, east of the Rhône River. Like Gigondas, Vacqueyras was originally a Côtes du Rhône-Villages area; it was promoted to free-standing AOC status in 1990. Its grape varieties are similar to those of Gigondas, but the wines are not quite as good, at least not yet. Like Gigondas, most (96 percent) of Vacqueyras wine is red.

Because Vacqueyras is a fairly new appellation, and is therefore not well known, its wines tend to be relatively inexpensive. Good Vacqueyras can cost you as little as $15, although some of the best wines are $20 to $30. Good producers of Vacqueyras, listed alphabetically, include Domaine des Amouriers, Domaine Le Clos des Cazaux, Domaine La Fourmone (Roger Combe), Domaine des Garrigues, and Paul Jaboulet Aîné.

Lirac and Tavel

Lirac is a sizeable area encompassing four villages on the western banks of the Rhône. Although 80 percent of the wines made there are full-bodied, soft reds (and 4 percent are whites), the area is best known in the U.S. as a producer of dry rosé wines, along with the neighboring Tavel appellation. Lirac red and rosé derive from Grenache (maximum 40 percent), Cinsault, Mourvèdre, and Syrah, plus Carignan.

The neighbouring Tavel AOC covers rosé wines only. These wines derive mainly from Grenache and Cinsault. They're dry, with refreshing berry flavor, and they tend to be quite high in alcohol for rosés, up to 14 percent. Because it's better known, Tavel Rosé is more expensive than Lirac Rosé: about $20 to $25 compared to $15 or less for Lirac.

Château St.-Roch (produced by Cantegril-Verda), Domaine Pélaquié, and Château de Ségriès are reliable producers of Lirac Rosé. Château d'Aquéria and Domaine Méjan-Taulier are top Tavel producers; the latter also makes a small amount of Lirac Rosé.

Muscat de Beaumes-de-Venise and Rasteau

Rasteau and Beaumes-de-Venise are two of the 16 villages within the Côtes du Rhône-Villages area that are entitled to append their names to that appellation. But each of these villages also has separate AOC status for a special type of sweet wine, called _Vins Doux Natural,_ or VDN (pronounced _van doo nah too rahl,_ and translated as "naturally sweet wines"). These are wines made by adding alcohol to grape juice that has fermented only slightly; the alcohol stops the fermentation and fixes the natural grape sugar in the wine.

Rasteau AOC is a VDN from Grenache grapes grown in three villages: Rasteau, Cairanne, or Sablet. The wine can be red or even tawny, depending on the winemaking and aging techniques. It's not common in the U.S., but it can occasionally be found for about $18 to $20.

The VDN wine of Beaumes-de-Venise is called Muscat de Beaumes-de-Venise *(moos cah deh bohm deh veh nees)*. It comes entirely from the Muscat grape — the best type of Muscat, the Muscat Blanc à Petits Grains. It's a particularly delicious wine, redolent with floral Muscat perfume, yet full-bodied and substantial. It sells for about $18 to $30.

Satellite wine zones of the Southern Rhône

Several outlying areas of the Southern Rhône also produce wine. Most of them lie east and south of the Côtes du Rhône production area, but some are north of that wine zone (see Figure 9-1). Their production accounts for 23 percent of the Rhône Valley's total each year.

The wines of these areas are far less renowned than other Rhône wines. Although these areas all have AOC status, some of them were elevated from the VDQS to the AOC level only in the past decade. (Chapter 3 explains the relationship of VDQS to AOC.) In time, their wines will certainly become better known to wine lovers outside of France.

Côtes du Vivarais *(coat dew vee vah ray)* earned AOC status only in 1999. Situated to the west of the Côtes du Rhône territory, its vineyards are on both sides of the Ardèche River, a tributary of the Rhône. Grenache must constitute at least 40 percent of red Côtes du Vivarais, and Syrah, another 30 percent. The local whites are based on Grenache Blanc, and the rosés, on Grenache.

The **Coteaux du Tricastin** *(coh toh dew tree cas tan)* vineyards lie across the Rhône River from the Côtes du Vivarais zone, in a very windy area with stony soil. Red wines are the main type; they're made from Grenache, Cinsault, Syrah, Mourvèdre, and Carignan. Some rosé comes from the same varieties. The small amount of white is made from Grenache Blanc, Clairette, Picpoul, Ugni Blanc, and Bourboulenc.

Côtes du Ventoux *(coat dew vahn too)* is one area whose wines are somewhat familiar to wine lovers, thanks to the success of the brand, La Vieille Ferme, and to Paul Jaboulet Aîné's well-distributed Côtes du Ventoux. This large territory, named for Mount Ventoux, lies east and south of Châteauneuf du Pape, including some hillside vineyards. Red wines dominate, with 87 percent of the production; Grenache, Cinsault, Syrah, Mourvèdre, and Carignan are the varieties used.

Côtes du Lubéron *(coat dew loo bear on)* is south of Côtes du Ventoux. The red, rosé, and white wines are generally soft, easy to drink, and inexpensive. Red varieties are Syrah and Grenache, with Mourvèdre, Cinsault, and (up to 20 percent of the blend) Carignan. White varieties are Grenache Blanc, Clairette, and Bourboulenc, with Marsanne, Roussanne, and (maximum 50 percent) Ugni Blanc.

Coteaux de Pierrevert *(coh toh deh pee air vair't),* another area newly elevated to AOC status, lies east of the Côtes du Luberon. Local wines include light reds and rosés made from Grencahe, Syrah, Cinsault, and Mourvèdre, plus Carignan, Terret, and Oeillade, and white wines from Clairette, Marsanne, Picpoul Blanc, Roussanne, and Ugni Blanc.

Four other AOC wines come from a far-flung area around the town of Die *(dee),* which lies east of the Rhône River on the Drôme, a tributary of the Rhône; in terms of its latitude, it's about equidistant from the end of the Northern Rhône and the beginning of the main southern Rhône vineyards. This district is called the Diois *(dee wah),* and is historically important for the production of sparkling wines. It encompasses four AOC wines:

- ✔ **Clairette de Die** *(clar et deh dee):* A slightly sweet, youthful sparkling wine with gentle carbonation. It derives mainly from Muscat (the finer, Muscat à Petits Grains variety), with no more than 30 percent Clairette. The wine is made by a particular process called the *méthode dioise* (pronounced *meh tode dee wahze*) that involves bottle fermentation and only brief aging.

- ✔ **Crémant de Die** *(cray mahn deh dee):* A dry sparkling wine from Clairette grapes, formerly called Clairette de Die Brut, made in the traditional method used in Champagne. (Refer to Chapter 10 for more information on Champagne.)

- ✓ **Coteaux Diois** *(coh toh dee wah)* or **de Die:** Since 1993, a non-sparkling white wine from Clairette.

- ✓ **Châtillon-en-Diois** *(sha tee yon on dee wahs):* Youthful red and rosé wines from Gamay (75 percent), Pinot Noir, and Syrah.

Enjoying Rhône Wines

Recent good vintages for Northern Rhône red wines are 1999, 1998, 1997, 1995, 1991 (for Côte Rôtie especially), 1990, 1989 (especially for Hermitage), 1988, and 1985. Recent good vintages for Southern Rhône red wines are 1999, 1998 (especially), 1995, 1990, and 1989.

Serve Rhône red wines at cool room temperature, about 62°F to 64°F (17°C to 18°C). Simple Côtes du Rhône red wines can be served a few degrees cooler. Northern Rhône whites and Châteauneuf-du-Pape Blanc should be only slightly cool, about 58°F to 62°F (15°C to 17°C), so that you can appreciate their wonderful aromas. Rosé wines are best when served cold — about 50°F to 52°F (10°C to 11°C).

Serve your better Rhône wines — both red and white — in a tall glass with an oval-shaped bowl (similar to a Bordeaux or Cabernet Sauvignon glass) that has a minimum capacity of 10 to 12 ounces.

The sturdier red Rhône wines are good with roasts of beef or lamb, steaks, stews (especially hearty meat and/or bean stews, such as *cassoulet*), full-flavored game, such as venison, and game birds. The lighter red Rhône wines, such as Crozes-Hermitage, St.-Joseph, and Côtes du Rhône — are good accompaniments to roast chicken, grilled hamburgers, or pizza.

Enjoy Hermitage Blanc and Châteauneuf-du-Pape Blanc with veal or robust poultry dishes. The wines made from the Viognier variety — Condrieu and Château Grillet — are difficult to pair with food; they're really best as apéritifs. Delicate, white fish or simply-prepared chicken dishes can work, but any strongly-flavored entrée is inadvisable; it will mask the delicate aromas and flavors of the wines.

Part III
France's Other Wine Regions

In this part . . .

You could say that this part of the book speaks a *patois,* because it embraces a wide variety of French wine regions, from the celebrated, and celebratory (Champagne!), to the obscure. These regions make every type of wine imaginable: stylish whites from Alsace, lively Cahors reds, engaging Provençal rosés, untamed reds from the South of France, luscious sweet wines and delicate bubblies from pockets of history in the South, and, from the Loire Valley, *everything* — especially some of the best value, high-quality white wines anywhere.

If "adventure" and "discovery" are among your favorite words, don't wait another minute to begin your journey through the rest of French wine.

Chapter 10

Champagne: The World's Greatest Sparkling Wine

. . . .

In This Chapter

▶ Champagne from Champagne, France

▶ Vintage versus non-vintage

▶ The great Champagne houses

▶ The rise of the grower-producer

. . . .

*I*s there a better-known, more popular wine in the world than Champagne? When it comes to sparkling wines, the sparkling wine we call "Champagne" has no peer. We can seriously debate what the best red wine, white wine, or dessert wine is, but it's no contest for the best sparkling wine.

What makes Champagne the best of its kind? What are the differences in various types of Champagne? And what are the best Champagnes? We'll answer all of these questions and more in this chapter.

What Champagne Is

Champagne is a white or rosé sparkling wine that starts its life like any other wine — as the fermented juice of grapes. But a subsequent, vital step transforms Champagne, and all the other serious sparkling wines of the world. Bottle the wine with yeast and a little sugar-wine solution, and it undergoes a *second* fermentation; this time, the bottle traps the carbon dioxide (a by-product of fermentation), so that it takes the form of tiny bubbles in the wine. Voila! You have Champagne — at least you do if this process takes place in the Champagne region of France. And that's the catch. True Champagne comes only from this one wine region. All other bubbly wines are simply "sparkling wines" — no matter what they choose to call themselves on the label.

But Champagne is more than just the right place and the right process. In almost all cases, Champagne is an extremely complex blended wine — not only a blend of grape varieties, but also a blend of wines from various vineyards throughout the region (the blend, called the *cuvée,* combines the strengths of each vineyard), and in most cases, a blend of wines from different vintages. For a wine that's so easy to enjoy, Champagne is very difficult to create! (See *Champagne For Dummies* by Ed McCarthy, published by Hungry Minds, for details on how Champagne is made.)

When "Champagne" is not Champagne

If "Imitation is the sincerest form of flattery," Champagne producers should feel mighty flattered. If they were to walk into just about any wine store in the U.S. — and many other non-European countries — they would find bottles of inexpensive sparkling wines, *not* made in France, but called "Champagne." If they perchance opened one of these bottles — some priced as low as $3 — their reaction would probably be, "Sacrebleu, Monsieur! Dees ees not Champagne!"

The European Union does not permit any of its member countries except France to call its sparkling wines "Champagne." And of course, sparkling wines made in French wine regions other than Champagne cannot legally be called Champagne. But, beyond the borders of Europe, many countries continue to cash in on the popularity of the Champagne name — and confuse legions of novice wine drinkers — by calling their sparkling wines "Champagne." Usually these wines are the least expensive, mass-produced, poorest quality sparklers; most of the better sparkling wines do not use the word. Just remember: *True* Champagne always has the word "Champagne" *plus* "Product of France" or "France" on the label. Anything selling for less than $15 is *not* Champagne!

The Champagne Region

The cool, agricultural region called Champagne *(sham pah n'yah)* is about an hour and a half northeast of Paris by auto or train — roughly 90 miles. (Figure 1-1 shows the location of the region.) Besides hardy grains such as wheat, its main crop is grapes, because the soil is not very fertile and the climate too forbidding to grow much of anything else. It's not France's most beautiful region. Nor is its cuisine one of France's best. But it *does* produce one of the greatest wines in the world. And it *does* have some great restaurants, inns, and cafés where you can enjoy as much Champagne as you desire.

The Champagne vineyards occupy about 75,000 acres of the sparsely populated region; vineyards in 321 villages in the region, also known as *crus,* provide the grapes for Champagne.

Most of the large Champagne *houses* — the name used for producers who make and sell most of the Champagne — are located in the following three communities (see Figure 10-1):

- ✔ **Rheims** *(*French spelling, *Reims;* pronounced *rhaams): *Champagne's only city (190,000 inhabitants), and its capital; home of many of Champagne's most important houses (15, in all), the Cathedral of Reims (one of the world's most beautiful Gothic churches), and one of France's greatest restaurants, the three-star Michelin restaurant-inn, Boyer Les Crayères.

- ✔ **Épernay:** The town that's the geographical center of the Champagne region, and the home of the most Champagne houses, 25, including the largest, Moët & Chandon; about a 20-minute drive south of Rheims.

- ✔ **Aÿ** *(eye ee):* A small town about ten minutes to the east of Épernay; home of nine Champagne producers, and the source of one of Champagne's few good red wines (made from Pinot Noir).

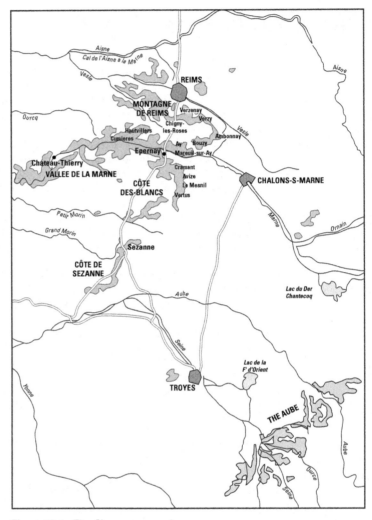

Figure 10-1: The Champagne region.

The proximity of these three communities and Champagne's closeness to Paris make a short tour of the region very feasible for wine lovers. (For a complete list of Champagne houses to visit, as well as hotels and restaurants in the region, see Chapter 15 of *Champagne For Dummies,* by Ed McCarthy.)

Appellation Champagne Contrôlée

Only one appellation applies to all of Champagne's sparkling wines: *"Appellation d'Origine Champagne Contrôlée."* Unusually for France, however, producers aren't actually required to use these words on their labels. A few producers do use the phrase, but many don't. The only statement of authenticity required on Champagne labels is "Champagne" and either "Product of France," or simply "France."

Champagne's climate and soil

The location of the Champagne region really pushes the envelope for grape-growing: It's practically at the northernmost latitudinal limit (a little below 50 degrees latitude) in which vines can be cultivated in the northern hemisphere. It's the most northerly wine region in the world, with the exception of two of Germany's minor regions and the vineyards of southern England. The annual mean temperature in Champagne is 50°F (10°C) — about one-half degree Centigrade above the annual temperature in which grapes can grow.

In most years, wine grapes just about ripen in this marginal growing climate, and (typical of less-ripe fruit) they retain lots of acidity. Even in warmer-than-average years, the grapes are quite acidic. Such high acidity is a real problem for *still* (non-sparkling) wines, but an asset to, and the *raison d'être* for, sparkling wines, which need acidity for their palate-cleansing liveliness.

It rains quite a bit in Champagne, even in the summer, but the better vintages have enough sun for the grapes to ripen. The big enemy is late spring frosts, which can wipe out much of the crop.

The chalky soil of Champagne is something special. As you drive through the region, you can actually see mounds of pure white chalk. This soil originated about 65 million years ago, when the region was covered by the sea; the sea left huge deposits of seashells behind as it receded. The type of soil is poor for many crops, but ideal for wine grapes, which thrive in infertile soils.

The influence of Dom Pérignon

No, Dom Pérignon didn't "invent" Champagne. Naturally occurring "sparkling" wines existed in Champagne and elsewhere long before the now-famous 29-year-old Benedictine monk arrived in 1668 at the Abbey of Hautvillers *(oh vee lay)* to take on the duties of cellarmaster.

During his 47 years at Hautvillers, Dom Pierre Pérignon did play a vital role in perfecting the bubbly wine that we know today as Champagne. Among his many talents, he was a "master blender" — balancing all the characteristics (body, acidity, elegance, intensity, and so forth) of wines made from grapes grown in villages throughout the region. He was also among the first winemakers to make white wine from red grapes; Pérignon recognized that white wine was better than red for sparkling wines. (Both of these practices are common today; in fact, the leading requirement of a modern Champagne cellarmaster is to be an outstanding blender.) He was the first to use cork as a stopper for Champagne bottles, and possibly the first winemaker to recognize the potential of aging wines in cold, dark cellars.

What Dom Pérignon did for the Champagne region was truly remarkable. Before his arrival at the abbey, winemaking wasn't an important occupation among the Champenois. But thanks to his work and the work of other monks, Champagne — the wine they perfected — has become synonymous with the region itself, and has become one of the most famous wines in the world. The Champagne named after him, Cuvée Dom Pérignon, has become so famous today that people just ask for "the Dom" or "DP" when ordering it.

The chalk is hundreds of feet deep in most of the best vineyard areas, and the vines' roots dig deep into the earth for nourishment. The chalky subsoil retains enough water for dry spells, but is porous enough to prevent the roots from becoming damaged by too much water during rainfalls — essential in this rather rainy region. The chalk also absorbs the heat of the sun during the day and radiates it to the vines during the cool nights.

As a result of the climate and soil, the grapes that grow in the Champagne region tend to be rather tiny, but have lots of concentrated nutrients. Champagne's cool climate and its chalky, limestone soil are undoubtedly the leading factors contributing to the excellence of its sparkling wine.

The grape varieties of Champagne

Champagne is made mainly from three grape varieties:

- ✔ **Pinot Noir** (a red wine variety)
- ✔ **Pinot Meunier** (a red variety related to Pinot Noir)
- ✔ **Chardonnay** (a white variety)

A few minor grapes — such as Petit Meslier, Arbanne, and Pinot Blanc — still survive in some of the region's vineyards and are still permitted, but they cannot be replanted and are of little consequence.

Most Champagnes — about 85 to 90 percent of them — are a blend of about ⅔ red grapes and ⅓ Chardonnay. A few Champagnes (less than 5 percent) are 100 percent Chardonnay (they are called *blanc de blancs*); fewer yet are 100 percent red grapes (and called *blanc de noirs*). Rosé Champagnes, a small category, are usually, but not always, made from a blend of white and red grapes.

Although Champagne is primarily a white wine, the two red varieties predominate; they make up about 72 percent of the Champagne vineyards. The current percentage of planting of the three grape varieties in Champagne is 38 percent Pinot Noir, 34 percent Pinot Meunier, and 28 percent Chardonnay.

The reason that most Champagnes are blends of Pinot Noir, Pinot Meunier, and Chardonnay is that each grape variety has strengths to contribute to the final blend:

- ✔ Pinot Noir adds body, structure, aroma, and a complexity of flavors. This difficult variety likes the cool climate of the region, and it grows well in the chalky limestone soil.

- ✔ Chardonnay, a star performer in the Champagne region, gives freshness, delicacy, elegance, and finesse. For this reason, many producers make a *blanc de blancs* (Chardonnay) Champagne.

- ✔ Pinot Meunier contributes fruitiness, floral aromas, and a precocious character (readiness-to-drink sooner).

Pinot Meunier is especially valuable because it buds later in the spring than Pinot Noir and Chardonnay. It is therefore less prone to damaging frosts and can thrive in areas like the Marne River Valley, where Pinot Noir and Chardonnay would not be successful. It also ripens earlier in the fall than the other two varieties, thus often avoiding autumn rains. But Pinot Meunier has a disadvantage: Its wines tend to age more quickly than those of the other two varieties. Also, many producers think it is not quite so fine as Pinot Noir and Chardonnay, and therefore do not use it in their most prestigious Champagnes. Its champions — such as the houses of Krug, Deutz, and Alfred Gratien — say that you just have to know where it grows best.

The four grape-growing districts

As it happens, each of the three grape varieties does best in different areas of the Champagne region. The region has four main grape-growing districts, each specializing in certain varieties (see Figure 10-1). These districts are the following:

- **Montagne de Reims** *(mohn tahn yeh deh rhaams):* These chalky hillsides are directly south of the city of Rheims, north of Épernay, and north of the Marne River. Pinot Noir is the dominant variety here, but some Chardonnay and a little Pinot Meunier are also grown.

- **Côte des Blancs** *(coat day blahnk):* This district, directly south of the town of Épernay, is by far *the* most important vineyard area for Chardonnay. Most of the best *blanc de blancs* Champagnes use grapes from the villages on the Côte des Blancs; huge deposits of chalk are in the soil here. The Côte de Sézanne prolongs the Côte des Blancs to the south.

- **Vallée de la Marne** *(val lay deh lah marn):* The largest district, located directly west of Épernay. It includes Épernay itself and stretches beyond the town of Château-Thierry. Pinot Meunier is the most-planted grape variety, by far, in this area, but some Pinot Noir and a little Chardonnay also grow here.

- **The Aube** *(oh'b):* Also known as the Côte des Bar, this district is well south of Épernay, near the city of Troyes *(twah).* Pinot Noir is clearly the predominant variety, although its wine is heavier and not so fine as the Pinot Noir in the Montagne de Reims.

The greatest Champagne villages

Over hundreds of years of grape growing in the Champagne region, certain villages (or *crus,* as they are called) emerged as the best vineyard areas. These *crus,* numbering 321, started to gain recognition in the second part of the 19th century. The Champagne trade organization called the CIVC (*Comité Interprofessionnel du Vin de Champagne*), which was formed during World War II and has become Champagne's regulatory body, now ranks 17 villages as *grands crus* and another 40 villages as *premiers crus.* Each *cru* has an official quality rating on a scale of 100: *Grand cru* vineyards all rate 100, and *premier cru* vineyards rank from 90 to 99 points.

The remaining 264 designated Champagne villages rate between 80 and 89. The rating is not static; the CIVC periodically revises the rankings (the last revision took place in 1985).

If a Champagne is made from all *grand cru* grapes, it is entitled to use the name *"Grand Cru"* on its label. Likewise, if it is made from all *premier cru* grapes, it can use the term *"Premier Cru"* (or *"1er Cru"*) on its label. A combination of *grand cru* and *premier cru* grapes entitles a Champagne to only a *premier cru* designation.

Usually only grower-producers — grape-growers who also make their own Champagne — are small enough to use only *grand cru* and/or *premier cru* grapes in their Champagnes. The large houses produce so much wine that they must use grapes from other villages in addition to *grand cru* or *premier cru* grapes. The exception for the large houses is their premium Champagnes, which are usually made from only, or mainly, *grand cru* and/or *premier cru* grapes. With several exceptions, the large houses usually refrain from using these designations on their Champagnes, so as to not denigrate their less expensive Champagnes in comparison.

The 40 *premier cru* villages provide about 22 percent of the grapes for Champagne. Most of the *premiers crus* are in the Montagne de Reims or the Côte des Blancs, but some very good *premier cru* villages are also in the part of the Vallée de la Marne that's located close to the town of Épernay.

The best of the best

About 8.6 percent of Champagne's grapes come from *grand cru* villages. Nine *grand crus* are in the Montagne de Reims, six in the Côte des Blancs, and two in the Vallée de la Marne. Of the 17 *grand cru* villages, Aÿ *(eye ee)* and Verzenay *(ver zeh nay)* are generally regarded as the two best for the Pinot Noir grape, with Bouzy *(boo zee)* close behind. Le Mesnil-sur-Oger *(leh meh neal seur oh jhae)*, Cramant *(crah mahn)*, and Avize *(ah veeze)*, all in the Côte des Blancs, are considered the finest *grand cru* villages for the Chardonnay grape. Look for these village names on some of the better Champagnes, especially from grower-producers.

Styles of Champagne

Enormous variation exists among Champagnes. Some of them are sweeter than others, for example, or lighter, or more complex. We refer to the different types and tastes of Champagnes as the various *styles* of Champagnes. The spectrum of Champagne styles encompasses the following categories:

- ✔ Non-vintage, vintage, and prestige cuvée (premium) Champagnes
- ✔ Standard, *blanc de blancs, blanc de noirs,* and rosé Champagnes
- ✔ Brut, extra dry, and demi-sec Champagnes
- ✔ Light-bodied, medium-bodied, and full-bodied Champagnes

We discuss the last category in the "The Great Champagne Houses" section, later in this chapter.

Non-vintage, vintage, and prestige cuvées

Once you understand these three styles, you can distinguish them from one another fairly easily. The challenge is that the labels don't tell you which type a Champagne is. Here is a thumb-nail description of each:

✔ **Non-vintage Champagnes:** The most common type by far, these wines are blends of wines from several years, and no vintage date appears on the label; they're called "non-vintage" because they don't derive from just *one* vintage; also known as "Classic"; the least-expensive type (with a few exceptions).

✔ **Vintage Champagnes:** These are made from grapes of a single year, which is usually, but not always, a better than average year; the vintage year is on the label.

✔ **Prestige *cuvées*:** These are the producers' best Champagnes, mainly vintage Champagnes, but possibly non-vintage; the most expensive type of Champagne; Cuvée Dom Pérignon and Roederer Cristal are examples.

Non-vintage Champagnes

Most of the time when you drink a Champagne, you probably drink a non-vintage. Non-vintage Champagnes make up 85 to 90 percent of all Champagnes produced today. (Wine lovers in the U.S. *do* buy a higher percentage of prestige *cuvées* than those in any other country, however.)

Non-vintage Champagnes are the foundation of the Champagne business by necessity. Because of the region's marginal climate, not every year can be a perfect "vintage" year. If producers didn't blend the wines of several years together, evening out the faults of one year with the virtues of another, they would have been out of business a long time ago.

Non-vintage Champagnes are also called "classic" Champagnes because they were the original type of Champagne. Some producers prefer the term "multi-vintage." Sometimes "Classic" appears on the label, but "non-vintage" never does, because Champagne producers believe that this term is disparaging.

Non-vintage Champagnes are the least expensive Champagnes, mainly $20 to $45 per bottle. Every Champagne producer makes a non-vintage Champagne, which is always his biggest-selling wine. (The one exception is a small house, Salon, which produces only a vintage *blanc de blancs*.)

Most non-vintage Champagnes are made from approximately ⅔ red grapes (Pinot Noir and Pinot Meunier) and ⅓ white (Chardonnay). A large part of each year's non-vintage blend is made up of wines from the current harvest. Then, older wines (known as *reserve* wines) are added to the blend. Most producers use between 5 and 25 percent reserve wines in their non-vintage blends. A few high-quality producers, such as Charles Heidsieck and Krug, use even higher percentages of reserve wines, up to 45 or 50 percent.

Although vintage Champagnes are generally superior to non-vintage Champagnes, there's absolutely nothing wrong with the quality of most non-vintage Champagnes. And they are generally $10 to $15 a bottle less expensive than standard vintage Champagnes.

When you consider the number of wines used in the blend, from different grape varieties, several different vintages, and different *crus,* you understand that the cellar master must be gifted with an exceptional palate and taste memory.

Vintage Champagnes

Vintage Champagne comes from the grapes of one year only: 100 percent of the grapes must be from the vintage stated on the label.

Standard vintage Champagnes (those that are not prestige cuvées) make up a small part of the Champagne market — less than 10 percent of production and sales. This is ironic because vintage Champagnes usually represent the best value in Champagne. Yes, they do average $10 to $15 a bottle more than non-vintage Champagnes (about $45 to $60 a bottle), but they are invariably higher in quality because:

- ✔ They're made from better grapes, usually from better vineyards. As a result, vintage Champagnes are richer and more concentrated than non-vintage Champagnes.

- ✔ They're aged for two to three years longer by the producer; the extra aging adds more complexity and maturity.

- ✔ Most producers use only the two finest grape varieties, Pinot Noir and Chardonnay, for vintage Champagnes; the quicker-maturing Pinot Meunier is used mainly in non-vintage Champagnes.

- ✔ They're made from the grapes of at least a good, and sometimes a superb, vintage.

Custodians of the house style

Champagne drinkers do become accustomed to their favorite Champagne's flavor and style —especially in non-vintage Champagnes — and they expect to find that same style every time they drink that brand.

The person responsible for the consistency of a house's style from one year to the next is the cellarmaster (the *chef de caves*). He (most cellarmasters are male) manages to recapture the house style each year by blending 30 to 50 wines — sometimes more — from various villages throughout the Champagne region. His goal is to make a harmonious, balanced blend that will tastes like the "style of the house" when the Champagne has finished aging and is released three or four years later.

Producers normally make vintage Champagnes only when the weather has been especially good — warm and dry — especially in the autumn, near harvest. On the average, about five or six years each decade are good enough for vintage Champagnes to be produced. But each producer decides whether he will make a vintage Champagne in any given year. Some vintages have been so good — such as 1982, 1985, 1988, 1989, 1990, 1995, and 1996 — that just about every producer made a vintage Champagne in these years.

Prestige cuvées

The best Champagne a producer makes is usually called his "prestige cuvée" — also known as "premium Champagnes" — although you will not find any of these words on the label. The way that you normally identify a Champagne as a prestige cuvée is by its price, which starts at about $70 a bottle and can go well over $100.

Most prestige cuvées are also vintage Champagnes, but a few are non-vintage. Almost every large Champagne house, and most of the smaller ones, makes at least one prestige cuvée; some houses make two prestige cuvées, a white and a rosé.

The most famous prestige cuvées are

 ✔ Moët & Chandon Cuvée Dom Pérignon (the largest-selling prestige cuvée in the world)

✔ Louis Roederer Cristal

✔ Perrier-Jouët (*pehr ree yay jhoo et*, not *jhoo ay!!*) Fleur de Champagne (the renowned "flower bottle")

Other well-known prestige cuvées include the following:

Krug Grande Cuvée
Laurent-Perrier Cuvée
 Grand Siècle
Pol Roger Cuvée Sir
 Winston Churchill
Pommery Louise

Dom Ruinart Blanc de Blancs
Salon Le Mesnil
Taittinger Comtes de
 Champagne
Veuve Clicquot La Grande
 Dame

When you're spending quite a bit of money on a bottle of Champagne, you probably want to know that you're getting your money's worth. In the case of prestige cuvée Champagne, you are, for two reasons. First, prestige cuvées are made from the finest grapes from the very best locations — usually from grand cru or a blend of grand cru and premier cru vineyards. Second, they're aged longer in the producer's cellars than any other Champagnes (typically from five to eight years). Both of these factors ensure high quality.

How are they different from other Champagnes? Let us count the ways:

✔ Their bubbles are finer — very tiny and delicate.

✔ Their aromas and flavors are more complex, more elegant, and more intense.

✔ They have greater length on the palate (their flavors persist longer) than other Champagnes.

✔ They have greater longevity than other Champagnes; they're usually at their best 15 or more years from the vintage date.

And of course there's the status value of a prestige cuvée. When you want to impress someone, nothing quite works like a prestige cuvée Champagne.

Blanc de blancs, blanc de noirs, and rosé Champagnes

Over 90 percent of all Champagnes are "traditional" or standard Champagnes — a blend of at least two grape varieties (Pinot Noir and Chardonnay), but usually all three, and white in color. But three other types of Champagne exist — all made in small quantities:

- ✔ **Blanc de blancs Champagne:** White; from Chardonnay only

- ✔ **Blanc de noirs Champagne:** White, actually more golden; from one or two black grapes

- ✔ **Rosé Champagne:** Pink; made from one or more grape varieties

Blanc de blancs Champagne

In the 1920's, Eugène-Aimé Salon started selling a Champagne made exclusively from Chardonnay; this was the first commercial *blanc de blancs* (literally, "white from white") Champagne. Today Salon (*sah loan*) Champagne still exists, but it is an expensive (over $100) prestige cuvée made in small quantities, and is difficult to find.

Blanc de blancs Champagnes didn't really catch on internationally until 1957, when Taittinger, a large, family-owned house, released its first blanc de blancs Champagne, the 1952 Comtes de Champagne prestige cuvée. Now, a good many houses and grower-producers make a blanc de blancs. They are always *brut* (very dry) Champagnes.

Blanc de blancs Champagnes come in all forms — as non-vintage, vintage, and prestige cuvée Champagnes. Because the Chardonnay grape is so suited to the cool climate and chalky soil of the Champagne region, the quality of these wines is quite high.

Most, but not all, blanc de blancs Champagnes are lighter-bodied, more acidic, and more elegant than other Champagnes. Many have vibrant, tart lemony flavors. They tend to be slightly more expensive than other Champagnes, but they also age extremely well.

Some of the most famous blanc de blancs Champagnes are the following (listed alphabetically):

Billecart-Salmon *(bee ay car sal mohn)* Blanc de Blancs

Deutz Blanc de Blancs

Mumm de Cramant *(crah mahn)*

Pol Roger *(pole ro jhay)* Blanc de Chardonnay

Dom Ruinart Blanc de Blancs

Taittinger *(tate tahn jhay)* Comtes de Champagne

Two blanc de blancs Champagnes, Krug Clos du Mesnil and Salon, are rather atypical of the genre in that they are very full-bodied and austere, and require *so* many years — at least 15 to 20 — to mature. Krug Clos du Mesnil is also that rare Champagne whose grapes come from a single vineyard (the "Clos du Mesnil"). And at $300 a bottle, it's also the most expensive Champagne when it's first released.

Blanc de noirs Champagnes

Blanc de noirs are the rarest type of Champagnes, especially among the larger Champagne houses; a few grower-producers do make one. Blanc de noirs, typically golden in color, are made from one or both of the black grapes — Pinot Noir and/or Pinot Meunier — but most are 100 percent Pinot Noir. This is the fullest-bodied type of Champagne, and can accompany main courses at dinner very nicely. Like blanc de blancs, blanc de noirs are always *brut* (very dry) Champagnes.

Rosé Champagnes

About 97 percent of all Champagne is white. That leaves only three percent for rosé Champagnes.

Rosé Champagnes come in all different hues of pink, from the palest salmon or onion-skin to the deepest rose. They are always *brut* Champagnes, and are, therefore, always dry. They get their color from a little Pinot Noir wine that's added for that purpose (or, in a few cases, the grape juice remains in contact with the dark skins of Pinot Noir and/or Pinot Meunier during the first fermentation).

Rosé Champagnes are usually blends of Pinot Noir and Chardonnay, but sometimes also Pinot Meunier. In a few cases, rosés are 100 percent Pinot Noir, but unlike blanc de noirs Champagnes, rosés always are some shade of pink.

Most houses make at least one rosé Champagne. Like blanc de blancs, rosés come in all forms — non-vintage, vintage, and prestige cuvées — and they're usually slightly higher in price than other Champagnes. Most of them have aromas and flavors of wild strawberries. Like blanc de noirs Champagnes, rosés are more full-bodied than most other Champagnes, and go well with main courses at the dinner table.

A few popular rosé Champagnes — all of which happen to be non-vintage — are the following:

- ✔ Billecart-Salmon *(sal mohn)* Brut Rosé
- ✔ Gosset *(go say)* Grand Rosé Brut
- ✔ Laurent-Perrier *(laur ahnt pehr ree yay)* Cuvée Rosé Brut
- ✔ Pommery Brut Rosé

From dry to sweet: Brut, Extra Dry, and Demi-Sec Champagne

Most Champagnes benefit from a *dosage (doh sahj),* a wine-sugar solution added as a final adjustment to the wine after its second fermentation and aging; the *dosage* balances the wine's high acidity and makes the wine more palatable. Depending on the amount of sugar added, and the amount of counter-balancing acidity in the wine, you might or might not perceive the sweetness.

The French nomenclature for categorizing Champagnes on a dryness-sweetness scale can be quite confusing. For instance, Extra Dry Champagne is not that dry at all! And *Demi-Sec* (medium-dry) Champagne is rather sweet. We're living in an age in which no one wants to admit that anything is sweet, including Champagne producers.

Technically, six different levels of dryness are permitted in Champagne but, practically speaking, we see only three types: *Brut,* Extra Dry, and *Demi-Sec.*

Table 10-1 shows the six categories of dryness/sweetness, the amount of residual sugar expressed in grams per liter, and the real meaning of the dryness categories.

Table 10-1   Dryness-Sweetness Levels in Champagne

Category	Residual Sugar (grams/liter)	Description
Extra Brut (bone dry)	0-6	From totally dry (0) to extremely dry
Brut (very dry)	0-15	From totally dry (0) to fairly dry
Extra Sec (extra dry)	12-20	From fairly dry to off-dry
Sec (dry)	17-35	Medium dry
Demi-Sec (medium dry)	35-50	Quite sweet
Doux (sweet)	50+	Very sweet

Actually, more than 95 percent of all Champagne produced today — regardless of whether it's non-vintage, vintage, rosé, and so forth — is labelled as *Brut*. But the term *"Brut"* is somewhat of a misnomer, because many so-called *Brut* Champagnes, those whose residual sugar is close to the maximum 15 grams per liter, are not really all that dry.

Virtually no producer makes *"doux"* Champagne any more; it was popular in the 19th century, but it's too sweet for today's tastes. No *"Sec"* Champagne is presently sold in the U.S. — and very little is made. The first category, "Extra *Brut*," is quite rare, also. Extra *Brut* Champagnes are *very* dry (some contain absolutely no sugar at all). Only one large Champagne house, Laurent-Perrier, produces an Extra *Brut* Champagne today (which they call *"Ultra Brut"*), and a few small grower-producers also make an Extra *Brut* (sometimes called *"Brut* Zero"), but these Champagnes are difficult to find.

Brut Champagnes

Brut Champagnes constitute the largest category of Champagnes, but it's not a uniform category: The only way to determine how dry or sweet a *Brut* Champagne actually is, within the range allowed by law, is to know the producer's style.

Most *Brut* Champagnes are in the 10- to 15-gram category. The following six major Champagne houses make *Brut* Champagnes that have *less than* 10 grams of sugar. If you crave truly dry Champagnes, check out these houses (listed alphabetically):

Bollinger   Krug
Gosset *(go say)*   Bruno Paillard
Jacquesson   Salon *(sah loan)*

Extra Dry and Demi-Sec Champagnes

Extra Dry Champagnes are "on the dry side," but somewhat sweeter than *Brut* Champagnes. This category is really marketed only in the U.S. (our national sweet tooth?). In fact, one brand, Moët & Chandon's White Star (an Extra Dry Champagne) is the best-selling Champagne in the U.S.

Although Extra Dry Champagnes are sweeter than *Bruts*, they aren't sweet enough for dessert. The only Champagne that has enough sweetness for after dinner and/or dessert is *Demi-Sec* Champagne. *Demi-Sec* Champagnes are not very common, but at least four houses (Moët & Chandon, Veuve Clicquot, Laurent-Perrier, and Louis Roederer) still make this style.

The Great Champagne Houses

When we talk about the "great Champagne houses," we are referring to the Champagne *négociants*. In the Champagne region, a "*négociant* house" is a firm that buys grapes from growers, makes and blends the wines, ages and bottles them, and sells them under the company's own label; most *négociant* houses also own some vineyards as well. The French term for these *négociant* houses is *négociant-manipulant* (Look for the initials "NM" on the labels of *négociant* Champagnes.).

Many of the *négociant* houses are huge, such as Moët & Chandon, Mumm, and Veuve Clicquot. The Champagne region's 261 *négociant-manipulants* dominate Champagne sales with a 71 percent share of the total market. (Outside Europe, they are responsible for a whopping 97 percent of all Champagne sales!)

About 2,000 of the region's 15,000 grapegrowers actually make Champagne themselves. Another 3,000 have it made for them, from their own grapes, at their local cooperative, where the wine is bottled with their own label. These 5,000 grower-producers account for 22 percent of all Champagne sales (mostly within France itself). The prices of their wines are comparable to those of the big *négociant* brands, except at the prestige cuvée level, where the grower Champagnes represent better value.

Cooperatives account for the remaining 7 percent of all Champagne sales. Champagnes from grower-producers and cooperatives combined account for only 3 percent of Champagne sales outside of Europe; this fact proves that, with a few exceptions, almost all of the Champagne sold in the U.S. is made by *négociant* houses. But sales by growers and cooperatives have been rising during the past decade.

"House styles"

We classify 25 major producers into three categories (listed alphabetically within the category) according to their house styles: light and elegant, medium-bodied, or full-bodied. The house styles of the producers is most evident in their non-vintage *Brut* (and Extra Dry) Champagnes, which they produce every year, and which make up the largest part of their production. Although producers do try to express their house styles in their vintage Champagnes, the influence of the climate in a particular vintage year can sometimes mask the house style.

Light, Elegant Style
Billecart-Salmon
Henriot
Jacquesson
Lanson
Laurent-Perrier
G.H. Mumm
Bruno Paillard
Perrier-Jouët
Piper-Heidsieck
Pommery
Ruinart
Taittinger

Medium-Bodied Style
Cattier
Deutz
Charles Heidsieck
Moët & Chandon
Philipponnat
Pol Roger

Full-Bodied Style
Bollinger
Gosset
Alfred Gratien
Krug
Louis Roederer
Salon
Veuve Clicquot Ponsardin

All 25 of these houses make excellent Champagne. Which style you prefer really boils down to personal taste. (For a complete description of all the Champagnes that these houses produce, see Chapters 8 and 9 in *Champagne For Dummies,* by Ed McCarthy, published by Hungry Minds.)

Grower-producer Champagnes

In the early 1990s, you might have been able to find only six or seven grower-producer Champagnes in the U.S., if you really searched. But by the year 2000, we found about 30 such Champagnes in the U.S. The increasing prosperity of the larger grower-producers (those who make their own Champagnes; the initials "RM" are on the bottom of the front labels of their wines) has given them the means to start exporting their Champagnes. This development is excellent for wine lovers, who now not only have a larger group of Champagnes from which to choose, but who also have the opportunity to buy prestige cuvée Champagnes at reasonable prices.

Grower-producer Champagnes generally offer more individualistic flavors than Champagnes of the large *négociants*. The reason is simple: The grapes of grower-producers usually come from the vineyards of just one village, whereas most of the *négociant* Champagnes (excepting their prestige cuvées) typically are made from a blend of grapes from many villages throughout the region. Also, most of the better grower-producers — those who export their Champagnes — own vineyards in *grand cru* and/or *premier cru* villages, and so they have access to superior raw material, even for their least expensive Champagnes.

In future years, you can look forward to many other grower-producer Champagnes coming to the U.S. and other countries. Just about all the grower-producer Champagnes now available in the U.S. are of very fine quality, but we name 11 of our favorites. We divide these growers according to the style of their Champagnes, and list the village and district where each grower is situated. The growers are listed alphabetically within each group:

Powerful, Pinot Noir-Dominated

Paul Bara (Bouzy, Montagne de Reims)

Henri Billiot (Ambonnay, Montagne de Reims)

Egly-Ouriet (Ambonnay, Montagne de Reims)

Tarlant (Oeuilly, Vallée de la Marne; a balance of all three grape varieties)

Rich, Chardonnay-Dominated

J. Lassalle (Chigny-les-Roses, Montagne de Reims)

Vilmart & Cie (Rilly-la-Montagne, Montagne de Reims)

Full, Rich Blanc de Blancs

Guy Charlemagne (Le Mesnil-sur-Oger, Côte des Blancs)

Diebolt-Vallois (Cramant, Côte des Blancs)

Larmandier-Bernier (Vertus, Côte des Blancs)

Pierre Peters (Le Mesnil-sur-Oger, Côte des Blancs)

Alain Robert (Le Mesnil-sur-Oger, Côte des Blancs)

Aging Champagne

Champagne producers don't encourage you to age Champagne, probably because they suspect that many people don't have proper storage conditions. They insist it's ready to drink when you buy it.

Well, that's not necessarily true, especially for vintage Champagnes and prestige cuvées — which are *seldom* ready to drink when you buy them. Champagne does age well, when stored in a cool place. Even non-vintage Champagnes improve with two or three years of aging. The extra aging allows the blended wines more time to "marry," and adds complexity and maturity to the Champagne. You know how homemade soups always taste better a day or two after they're made? The same principle applies here. Properly stored non-vintage Champagnes should last at least four or five years without any signs of deterioration.

Vintage Champagnes and prestige cuvées often don't really start developing until about ten years from the vintage date, and can age for 15 to 20 years or more in good vintages. *Blanc de blancs* Champagnes age particularly well (15 to 20 years or more), while rosés and *blanc de noirs* Champagnes are usually best consumed within ten years.

Champagne with Food

Champagne is a natural as an apéritif. A *blanc de blancs* Champagne or light-to medium-bodied non-vintage *Brut* — such as Bruno Paillard's, Deutz's, or Ruinart's — works well. Accompany the Champagne with seafood hors d'oeuvre, such as shrimp, scallops, or crab dip. Stuffed mushrooms; smoked oysters, clams, or mussels; and an assortment of nuts, especially almonds and hazelnuts, are all great with Champagne.

Even though Champagne is great for celebrations of all kinds, it's also an excellent accompaniment to dinners. Or try it for brunch with an egg-mushroom dish. If you're having Mimosas, fill your glass two-thirds with a decent Champagne and one-third with orange juice.

Champagnes go well with pasta or risotto, but not pasta with tomato sauce; tomato dishes clash with Champagne. Champagne is also fine with most vegetables, and is truly superb with fish and seafood dishes. If you're having that special treat — caviar and Champagne — choose a light-bodied Champagne, such as Billecart-Salmon Blanc de Blancs or Pommery Louise; a full-bodied, heavy Champagne overwhelms the delicate caviar.

Champagne for weddings

If you can afford it, a reasonably priced non-vintage Champagne would be a fine choice to serve at your wedding, or, if you're in our age bracket, your daughter's or son's wedding. Whatever you do, don't leave the choice of the wine in the hands of the caterer! Too many caterers serve the poorest-quality, least-expensive sparkling wine they can find — and then add insult to injury by serving it too warm, and in a terrible glass. Take charge of the situation. You're paying for it!

A less-expensive alternative to Champagne is a good California sparkling wine or, even less expensive, a decent French or Spanish sparkling wine.

We enjoy Champagne with all kinds of poultry, game birds, veal, and pork. For ham or lamb, a full-bodied rosé Champagne is excellent. Also, difficult-to-match spicy dishes, such as many Asian cuisines, are great with a non-vintage Champagne — thanks to the acidity and carbonation in the bubbly.

A great, old vintage Champagne is sublime with an aged hard cheese, such as Parmesan, aged Gouda, or aged Cheddar.

Be careful with desserts, however. Most Champagnes are too dry and acidic to accompany desserts. We'd suggest a *Demi-Sec* Champagne, which is fairly sweet, with desserts — and then only with a dessert that's not too sweet, such as pound cake, shortcake, or a lemon tart. For birthday cakes, wedding cake, and other sweet desserts, have a good Italian Asti, such as Fontanafredda or Martini & Rossi.

A French sparkling wine by any other name

Champagne is by no means the only French region that makes sparkling wines. Many of the other regions use the term *"crémant"* for their local bubbly — such as Crémant d'Alsace or Crémant de la Loire. This term originally applied to a certain style of Champagne, with lighter carbonation; when the French authorities decided that no other region could use the term *méthode champenoise* to describe the production method of their wines, they granted other regions the right to use *crémant* as a compromise. *Crémant* wines are always made by the Champagne method of second fermentation in the bottle — now called the traditional method, or the classic method.

Alsace, the Loire Valley, and Languedoc-Roussillon (covered in Chapters 11, 12, and 13) are three important French regions for sparkling wines.

Chapter 11

Alsace: White Wine Wonderland

· ·

In This Chapter

▶ France's most unique wine region

▶ White wines that even red wine lovers can love

▶ Stylistic extremes: bone dry to lusciously sweet

▶ France's most versatile wines for food

· ·

*T*he region of Alsace seems a world apart from the rest of
France. We get there by flying to Basel, Switzerland, where
the tiny airport deposits passengers into three different countries: Switzerland, France, or Germany, depending on which
door they exit! Alsace sits on the verge of France, with a culture, architecture, and cuisine uniquely its own.

Alsace's wines are also unique. The grape varieties that grow
there, for the most part, don't grow elsewhere in France. The
wines are varietals, named after these grapes — a nomenclature unheard of in France's other classic wine regions. And the
wines taste like nothing made anywhere else in France. Without
Alsace in its repertoire, France would still be a great wine
country, but Alsace ices the cake.

Location, Location

The location of the Alsace region has everything to do with
the type of wines the region makes. Besides dictating the *terroir*, Alsace's location also has cultural and historical implica-
tions that influence the style of the region's wines.

Alsace is situated in northeastern France, across the Rhine River from Germany. The Alsace region, along with the area northwest of Alsace called Lorraine, was formerly part of Germany, time and again. Most recently, France regained possession of Alsace in 1919, as a result of World War I.

Today, many of the French who live in Alsace have Germanic names, and the towns have Germanic names, but the region is French — no doubt about it. (Cross any bridge over the Rhine River from Germany to Alsace, and the dramatic change in scenery, from industrial highway on one side to quaint, flower-bedecked towns on the other side, tells you immediately that you have arrived at a new place.) And yet Alsace wines have been shaped by Germany. Like German wines, they are

- Predominantly white wines
- Predominantly unblended wines (each made from a single grape variety)
- Usually without oaky flavor

Also, their grape varieties are the same as some of those used in Germany. The winemakers of Alsace have even adopted the German practice of naming their wines according to the grape variety used to make the wine.

Despite these conceptual similarities, however, Alsace wines don't taste at all like German wines because growing conditions in Alsace are very particular.

Mountains' majesty

The most important factor in the Alsace landscape is actually not the Rhine River (and Germany on the other side of it) but the Vosges *(vohj)* Mountains, which flank Alsace's vineyard area on the west. The mountains are important because they block rain from the west. Their foothills also provide slopes that are ideal for vineyards, and a variety of soil types, which creates diversity in the wines.

Alsace is a long, narrow region (see Figure 1-1). The terrain rises gently from the Alsace Plain in the east, near the Rhine River, and becomes steeply hilly toward the Vosges Mountains in the west. Several small rivers cut through the region, creating valleys.

The vineyards themselves occupy 35,300 acres, stretching over an area that's approximately 70 miles long and barely more than one mile wide; this vineyard area begins about 12 miles west of the Rhine River. The best vineyards are situated in the hills; vineyards also occupy gentle slopes leading down to the plain.

Millions of years ago, geological upheavals formed the Rhine River and the Vosges Mountains. That geological activity created a patchwork of soils throughout what is now Alsace — here a granite soil, there a heavier schistous soil, and nearby, clay. Today, many winemakers delight in pointing out the different characteristics of their wines that result from the different vineyards' soils. Their best wines usually come from single vineyards that each have a particular type of soil; the soil differences make each wine different from the next, even when the grape variety is the same.

Forecast: sunny and dry

In terms of climate, the Vosges Mountains cut the Alsace region off from any Atlantic influence by blocking moisture and storms that blow eastward from the ocean. As a result, Alsace enjoys an unusually dry, sunny climate — the driest of any classic French wine region. (Colmar, the main city in the southern part of Alsace, is the second driest city in France, with an annual rainfall of only about 19 inches, compared to 37 inches in Bordeaux, for example.) Because the mountains are lower in the north, and less effective in blocking rain and clouds, the northern part of Alsace tends to be moister and less sunny than the south, although it still has a fairly dry climate.

September and October are the driest months — a particularly fortunate circumstance, because dry autumns enable the growers to leave the grapes ripening on the vine without fear of damaging rains. Thanks to the long, dry growing season, the grapes attain a good level of ripeness on a regular basis. The region's cool nights assure high levels of refreshing acidity. The combination of ripe fruit flavors and crisp acidity is a trademark of Alsace's wines.

When we first began learning about French wines, we took one look at Alsace's location on a map and decided that the region must have a very cool climate, because it's so northerly. But we didn't take into account the protective mountains, the slopes of the vineyards, the dry climate, and the sunshine. In fact, Alsace's wines have a richness, weight, and ripe fruity character that are unusual for cool climates, although their grape varieties are mainly those typical of cool climates. It's this paradox that makes Alsace wines so unique and so special.

The Grapes of Alsace

Compared to many other French wine regions, Alsace grows a real hodgepodge of grapes: Nearly a dozen varieties in all are permitted in the production of AOC wines. All but one grape variety is white.

Four white varieties enjoy special status: They are entitled to be used in the production of *grand cru* wines, a special, high-level category of Alsace wine. (Read more about *grand cru* Alsace wines in the section "Alsace *Grand Cru*" later in this chapter.) These four varieties are Riesling, Gewurztraminer, Pinot Gris, and Muscat.

Riesling *(rees ling)* is one of the two best white grape varieties in the world (along with Chardonnay), and, by general consensus, it's the finest variety grown in Alsace. It's also the single most planted grape variety in Alsace, populating slightly more than 23 percent of the vineyard acreage. Because it's the latest variety to ripen, it particularly benefits from the long, sunny Alsace autumns.

Gewurztraminer *(ga-VERZ-tra-mee-ner),* is Alsace's third most planted variety, covering nearly 18 percent of the vineyard land. Of all the wine regions of the world that grow this highly aromatic variety, Alsace undoubtedly is the most suitable, in view of how excellent Alsace's Gewurztraminer wines can be.

Pinot Gris represents about 10.5 percent of Alsace's grape plantings. Some people consider this grape number two after Riesling in terms of the quality of wine it makes in Alsace.

Although it's considered one of the four noble grapes of Alsace, Muscat is a minor variety quantitatively, covering less than 2.5 percent of the vineyard land. And that small amount of acreage is actually divided between two distinct varieties, Muscat d'Alsace (elsewhere known as the Muscat à Petits Grains, or small-berried Muscat) and Muscat Ottonel. Usually the two Muscats are blended together and the wines are labeled simply "Muscat."

Beyond these four white varieties, several others are important locally, for various reasons:

✔ Pinot Blanc is the second most planted variety after Riesling, covering 21 percent of the vineyards. Some of this quantity is actually not Pinot Blanc at all, however; it's another variety called Auxerrois, which looks similar to Pinot Blanc except that its grapes are more greenish when they're ripe. The two varieties are usually blended together and the wines are labelled as Pinot Blanc. Pinot Blanc is a fairly undistinguished variety, with shy aroma and flavor, but in the right vineyard, it can be very good.

✔ Pinot Noir is Alsace's only black variety, and it makes the region's only red wines. It covers nearly 9 percent of the vineyard land, an amount that's slowly rising.

✔ Sylvaner represents nearly 14 percent of Alsace's production, although wines bearing this name are rarely seen on the shelves of wine shops in the U.S.

 Other varieties grown in Alsace include Chardonnay (for the production of sparkling wines), Chasselas, and Klevener de Heiligenstein, a local variant of Traminer that's also called Savagnin Rosé.

The Range of Wines

Because of the varying terrain and soil types in the region, and the variability in the protection the Vosges Mountains offer, Alsace wines run the gamut of styles within the white wine category. The lower altitude vineyards, for example, tend to produce light-bodied, fresh white wines, while the hillside vineyards make intense, concentrated wines. As another example, the northern vineyards supply most of the grapes for sparkling wine because the rainier climate results in less-ripe grapes of the sort that are suitable for sparkling wine production.

Alsace's wine production encompasses the following styles:

- ✔ Sparkling white and rosé wines, ranging from dry to semi-dry
- ✔ Off-dry, light-bodied, fruity white wines
- ✔ Dry white wines, light-bodied to full-bodied, with varying degrees of richness
- ✔ Sweet dessert wines from late-harvested grapes
- ✔ Light-bodied red wines

Non-sparkling *(still)* whites are the largest category. (In fact, Alsace produces 18 percent of France's entire still white wine production.) Sparkling wines account for 14 percent of production. Dessert wine production generally represents only a tiny portion of Alsace's wines.

The dominant style

The majority of Alsace wines are dry, medium-bodied white wines with pronounced aromas and flavors that derive from the grapes and the land rather than from winemaking techniques. For example, Alsace whites do not have smoky, toasty aromas and flavors from oak barrels.

Picture-perfect travelling

If you like to visit wine regions, put Alsace at the top of your list. The region is dotted with beautiful medieval towns that are so charming, you might suspect they're not for real (but of course, they are). Each of the old towns has its own personality, as well as plenty of history. The vineyards come right to the edges of town. Apart from the region's beauty, the food (and of course the wine!) is terrific.

Since the 1990's, some producers have made some of their wines less dry. We first noticed this trend in Pinot Blanc wines. Many Alsace winemakers believe that Pinot Blanc is the wine that can convert wine drinkers to Alsace because it is light and easy to enjoy; making it ever so slightly sweet enhances the wine's softness and likeability, they believe. (Many producers still make classic, bone-dry Pinot Blanc, however.)

More recently, we've noticed a slight trend toward greater richness in Alsace Riesling, Gewurztraminer, and Pinot Gris: Some wines have very ripe fruit flavors and are not fully dry. This trend could be the result of global warming and riper vintages in recent years — but we believe that it's a reflection of producers' pushing the envelope to make extreme wines that will score well with critics who favor rich wines. The majority of Alsace's wines are dry, however.

Legally speaking

The laws governing the naming and labeling of Alsace wines are just about the easiest to understand of all French wine laws — but they do have a few particular wrinkles of their own.

Technically speaking, all the wines of Alsace can be divided into just three AOC names:

- ✔ Alsace AOC
- ✔ Alsace Grand Cru AOC
- ✔ Crémant d'Alsace AOC

Crémant d'Alsace

Cremant d'Alsace is the region's sparkling wine. Pinot Blanc usually forms the base of the wine, with various other grape varieties blended in. Only six varieties may be used to make Crémant d'Alsace: Pinot Blanc, Pinot Gris, Riesling, Auxerrois, Chardonnay, and Pinot Noir.

Appearances deceive

You might associate thin, elongated wine bottles with slightly sweet wine, because many off-dry (slightly sweet) German wines come in such bottles, and Riesling wines from many countries, which are often off-dry, have a similar package. In Alsace, however, that shape-taste association doesn't apply. All Alsace wines are sold in a special bottle called a *flûte d'Alsace,* which is a tall, thin green bottle that carries a raised seal of the region. Most of these wines are dry.

As for all French sparkling wines with the word *crémant* as part of their name, Crémant d'Alsace is made by the *méthode traditionelle* — the same general method used to make Champagne, which involves a second fermentation in the bottle to make the wine bubbly. Generally, the wine is light-bodied, somewhat fruity, delicate, and youthful — without the toasty flavors typical of Champagne, because of shorter aging. Some producers, such as Pierre Sparr, make several Crémant d'Alsace wines that range from delicate to intense, using different blends and different aging regimens.

Alsace AOC

Most of the wines made in Alsace carry the appellation Alsace AOC, which has existed since 1962. Each varietal wine must be made entirely from the grape whose name it carries.

Alsace AOC also covers blended white wines. Regulations provide for a specific blended wine called Edelzwicker (a German word meaning "noble blend"), made from any combination of Gewurztraminer, Riesling, Pinot Gris, Muscat, Pinot Blanc, Pinot Noir, Sylvaner, or Chasselas. It's generally a light, innocuous, inexpensive wine. Other blended wines, especially the better blends, have proprietary names instead. The best-selling Alsace wine in the U.S., Hugel's Gentil (pronounced *jahn tee),* is a blended wine.

Alsace Grand Cru

Over the centuries, the grape-growers in various parts of Alsace have come to know that certain hillsides produce better grapes than others. In 1975, the concept of the superiority of certain vineyard sites was codified into law with the creation of the Alsace Grand Cru appellation. After several years of study (and certainly politicking), 25 vineyard sites received *grand cru* status in 1983; another 23 slopes qualified in 1983, followed by more two sites in 1988, and one in 1990, for a total of 51 *grand cru* vineyards.

Varietal wines made from any of the four "noble" Alsace varieties — Riesling, Gewurztraminer, Pinot Gris, and Muscat — grown in a *grand cru* vineyard can carry on their label the name of that vineyard and the appellation Alsace Grand Cru. *Grand cru* wines are more expensive than basic Alsace AOC wines, are usually higher in quality, and have great aging potential. They represent about 5 percent of Alsace's production.

The Alsace Grand Cru appellation is somewhat controversial. Some producers believe that the sites selected as *grands crus* are too numerous, and the boundaries of some of the sites were drawn too large, to establish any integrity for the appellation. Therefore, some producers refuse to use *grand cru* vineyard names on their wines that actually come from *grand cru* vineyards. The most notable producers not using *grand cru* appellations are Trimbach, Hugel, and Léon Beyer — all of whom figure prominently in the U.S. market.

Conversely, some Alsace wines that carry a single-vineyard name are not *grand cru* wines because that vineyard was not given *grand cru* status. Reading the small print can tell you whether a wine is technically *grand cru* or not: If the label says *Appellation Alsace Contrôlée*, the wine is not *grand cru*. Figure 11-1 shows the label of a *grand cru* wine.

JOSMEYER

ALSACE GRAND CRU
APPELLATION ALSACE GRAND CRU CONTRÔLÉE

HENGST

1990

RIESLING

mis en bouteille par JOSMEYER à F 68920 WINTZENHEIM

ALC.12,5% BY VOL.   PRODUCT OF FRANCE   750 ml

Figure 11-1: The words *Appellation Alsace Grand Cru Contrôlée* on this label indicate that the wine is a *grand cru;* Hengst is the name of the vineyard.

VT and SGN: Measures of ripeness

Alsace has two more categories of wine that cut across both the Alsace and Alsace Grand Cru appellations. These categories are not based on where the grapes grow, but on how ripe the grapes are when they're harvested. Such distinctions are common in Germany, where grape ripeness (rather than vineyard location) is the principle behind the wine laws, but they're unheard of in France — outside Alsace, that is. (You can read about how Germany classifies its wines in Chapter 12 of *Wine For Dummies,* 2nd Edition, published by Hungry Minds.)

In Alsace, when the grapes attain an unusually high concentration of sugar, often with the help of *botrytis cinerea* (noble rot), the wine can be labeled as *"Vendange Tardive,"* (pronounced *ven dahnj tar deev),* which means "late harvest." (Turn to "Sweet White Bordeaux" in Chapter 6 for an explanation of

botrytis.) The extra sugar concentration in the grapes translates into extra richness in the wine; often VT wines — the
shorthand for *Vendange Tardive* — are sweet or medium
sweet, but not necessarily.

When the grapes are extraordinarily ripe and are infected
with botrytis, the wine can be labeled as *"Sélection de Grains
Nobles" (seh lec see ohn deh gran no bleh),* which roughly
means "choice berry harvest." The desiccated grape berries
make an extremely rich, concentrated, sweet dessert wine
that's as delicious as it is rare. Only the very finest vintages
give producers the opportunity to make SGN wines, as they
are known, and the wines are quite expensive — more than
$60 for a 375 ml "half bottle."

Only four grape varieties may make VT or SGN wines — the
same varieties that can be used for *grand cru* wines: Riesling,
Gewurztraminer, Pinot Gris, and Muscat.

Riesling, Above All

If we could drink only one type of Alsace wine for the rest of
our lives, that type would be Riesling. The Riesling grape is
one of the greatest white wine grapes in the world, and the
wines that this grape makes in Alsace are our very favorites.

In Alsace, the characteristics of Riesling wines are the
following:

- ✔ They tend to have aromas and flavors of citrus (especially grapefruit), citrus peel, apple, or peach, along with
  definite mineral accents, such as steeliness or flintiness;
  these characteristics vary according to the vineyard.

- ✔ They're generally medium-bodied, although some wines
  have such weight that they cross the line into full-bodied;
  they are fuller than most Rieslings from other regions.

- ✔ Alsace Rieslings that are not late-harvested range from
  bone-dry to sweet; the majority of them taste dry, either
  because they *are* dry (their sugar was completely fermented into alcohol), or because their high acidity coun-
  terbalances any sweetness in the wine and creates an
  impression of dryness.

- ✔ They have a firm backbone of acidity.

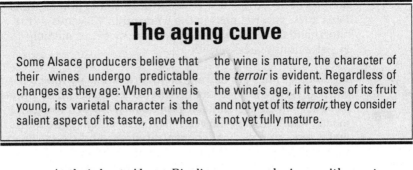

The aging curve

Some Alsace producers believe that their wines undergo predictable changes as they age: When a wine is young, its varietal character is the salient aspect of its taste, and when the wine is mature, the character of the *terroir* is evident. Regardless of the wine's age, if it tastes of its fruit and not yet of its *terroir,* they consider it not yet fully mature.

At their best, Alsace Rieslings are regal wines, with great depth, length, and complexity. They have so much to say, but so unobtrusively, that tasting them thoughtfully can stun you into reverent silence. (At least that's how they affect us.)

Now here's the catch: Alsace Rieslings need age. We like to drink them at least three years after the vintage date, but preferably eight to 15 years from the vintage. With age, their acidity is less noticeable, and they are therefore a bit softer and less austere than when they're young. They also develop fascinating, smoky, aged aromas that might remind you of diesel fuel (which sounds weird, but can be quite appealing), along with apricot flavors; if you don't like that character, drink your Alsace Rieslings in their first eight years or so of life, while their aromas are still youthful.

What if you need to drink them young? If you want to try a bottle this weekend, and your wine shop doesn't have any older vintages (which, unfortunately, is often the case), buy the least expensive Riesling from a good producer. Most Alsace wineries make two or more Rieslings:

- A "basic" Riesling, which is the softest and lightest

- A "special" Riesling, such as a reserve wine

- One or more *grand cru* Rieslings

- A VT or SGN, late-harvested wine, if the weather permits

The least expensive is the "basic" bottling. Drinking it young is less criminal than drinking a finer Riesling young, in the eyes of Alsace aficionados. Alsace Rieslings range from $12 to $75 a bottle, not counting the late-harvest wines. (Some of the most expensive SGN's can cost as much as $150.)

In the section, "Top Alsace Producers" later in this chapter, we mention our favorite Alsace wineries. But we can't leave this Riesling section without mentioning two wines from one of our favorite Riesling producers, Trimbach. One Trimbach wine — Riesling Clos Ste Hune — is the greatest of all Alsace Rieslings; its production is quite small (never more than 700 cases per year), and the wine is quite expensive (about $75 per bottle when it's first released; as much as $150 if you buy older vintages at auction).

The other Trimbach Riesling that we love is Cuvée Frédéric Emile, the winery's third Riesling up the quality ladder, after its basic Riesling and its Réserve Personnelle Riesling. In the typical Trimbach style, the wine is bone-dry; it has ripe apple and peach flavors that make a compelling contrast to the wine's dry, firm structure. Even with 15 years of age, this wine is fantastic. Cuvée Frédéric Emile costs about $30 when it's first released.

Alsace's Other Wine Gems

One of the virtues of Alsace is that the region makes so many terrific wines, each suitable for different tastes or different levels of experience. Although we love Riesling above all, you might very well prefer one of Alsace's other gems.

Gewurztraminer

Apart from dessert wines, Gewurztraminer gets our votes as the most exotic wine on earth — and nowhere is Gewurztraminer as rich and exotic as it is in Alsace.

Close your eyes and imagine the fragrant aromas of lychee fruit, roses, and spice: that's Gewurztraminer. You might expect a wine that smells so floral and fruity to be sweet — but when you taste it, you find it surprisingly dry. The wine's rather full body and slight undercurrent of earthy bitterness provide yet more contrast to the heady aromas and flavors. Fascinating!

Gewurztraminers have a touch of sweetness more frequently than Rieslings do, in our experience — similar to the sweetness of many California Chardonnays, for example, which everyone classifies as a dry wine; the low acidity of Gewurztraminer reinforces this impression of sweetness. We judge Gewurztraminer by how rich its aromas and flavors are, and how well balanced it is; if the wine is quite dry, all the better for our tastes, but we've found some sweet ones that we've liked very much.

Gewurz — a nickname that's widely used in wine circles — doesn't age as remarkably as Riesling, but it lasts surprisingly long for such a fruit-driven wine. As a general recommendation, we suggest that you drink Gewurztraminer when it is three to ten years old.

To capture the full Gewurztraminer experience, try one from an Alsace producer who favors a rich style of wines, such as Hugel. (Hugel's Jubilee Gewurztraminer, his top bottling, is a great example.) A basic Gewurz from most producers will cost you about $13 a bottle; reserve-level wines are $20 to $30, and the top bottlings, such as *grand cru* wines, run from $40 to $60.

Pinot Blanc

The Pinot Blanc grape is the personality opposite of Gewurztraminer: Its aromas and flavors are so mild that they're often described as "neutral." In Alsace, though, Pinot Blanc wines do have some character, generally a minerally and delicately floral aroma and delicate flavors of pear and citrus.

Of the Alsace wines that are usually available on export markets, Pinot Blanc is the lightest-bodied, the mildest, and the least expensive (about $10 to $15 a bottle). Which is not to say that it can't be a very good wine: Producers such as Paul Blanck, Josmeyer, and Mark Kreydenweiss make stunning Pinot Blancs.

Alsace Pinot Blanc often contains some Auxerrois, which is perfectly legal despite Alsace's 100 percent varietal rule. (Some producers make a separate Auxerrois wine, although the AOC laws don't technically permit it.) Other than asking the producer, there's really no way of knowing whether a Pinot Blanc contains Auxerrois or not, and what percentage. We do ask, when we have the opportunity, but frankly, the two wines are so similar — Auxerrois is a bit lower in acid, and tastes slightly buttery and spicy — that we don't lose sleep over the issue.

If you visit Alsace, you might see wines labeled Clevner or Klevner; these are local synonyms for Pinot Blanc, and they are rarely used on bottles for export markets. (Klevner, with only two "e's," is not the same as Klevener de Heiligenstein, a Gewurztraminer-like wine.)

If you've never had an Alsace wine, try a Pinot Blanc as an introduction to the area. And drink it as young as you like; most Pinot Blancs are best from when you buy them to about four years of age.

Tokay-Pinot Gris

Fifteen years ago, we heard that the producers of Alsace would be required to drop the word "Tokay" from the name of this wine to prevent confusion with Hungary's classic Tokaji wines — but the hyphenated name is still in use by some companies (until about 2006).

Whatever they call it, the Pinot Gris wines of Alsace are the most unique expression of this grape variety in the world. They have concentrated flavors of peach — more precisely, the part of a cling peach that surrounds the pit — and sometimes citrus (lime, lemon, tangerine, and orange peel) or even tropical fruit such as mango; some typical Alsace minerally character usually accompanies this fruitiness. (In general, these wines are less interesting aromatically than Rieslings, however.) They are rich but solid wines with good firmness. Alsace Pinot Gris wines are dry — with the usual caveat that some producers make them in a very rich style.

If your experience of the Pinot Gris grape is limited to Italy's inexpensive Pinot Grigio or Oregon's Pinot Gris wines, brace yourself for a completely different experience when you taste Alsace Pinot Gris. The wine's concentration, flavor intensity, and character (as in "a man of character") are impressive. And, as always in Alsace, the wines have a striking combination of vivid fruity flavor and firmness — although in the balance, Tokay-Pinot Gris is richer, fatter, and less firm than Riesling. They're Alsace's fullest-bodied wines.

You can find Alsace Pinot Gris wines at $14 to $18 for a producer's basic quality tier, up to $70 for *grand cru* wines; these wines are best from about four years of age to ten years.

Because Pinot Gris is relatively susceptible to noble rot, VT and SGN styles of Pinot Gris are more common than similar styles of Riesling. These cost about $30 to $60 for a half bottle.

Other Alsace wines

Alsace Sylvaner exists on the North American market, but it's not common. The wines are dry, crisp, and lean with a some-what oily mouthfeel and mineral flavors. When you do find them, they're usually inexpensive (about $9 to $14) because they're not in strong demand. Drink them very young.

Muscat d'Alsace is also uncommon, which is fine with us. Although Muscat is one of Alsace's Favored Four grapes, we've never been big fans of these wines; we much prefer Italy's light, sprightly floral style of Muscat wine to the full-bodied, dry, slightly clumsy Alsace versions. Where available, Alsace Muscats cost about $15, with some *grand cru* Muscats as high as $35.

Alsace's blended wines can be delightful, provided that they are fresh and young. Wines such as Hugel's or Willm's Gentil or Josmeyer's L'Isabelle are tasty wines with fruity and floral flavors and crisp acidity — and superior in quality to many an inexpensive Chardonnay. They run about $10 to $12.

Pinot Noir, Alsace's only red wine, traditionally really wasn't so red, because the grapes didn't ripen sufficiently to produce deeply pigmented skins. The progress in recent years, how-ever, has been amazing. Changes in how the grapes are grown and how the juice is vinified have resulted in red wines that look and taste like self-respecting Pinot Noir. One of our favorites is Hugel's, which costs $18 at the basic level, or $30 for the reserve. Despite our admiration for the new style, how-ever, we consider Alsace Pinot Noir a novelty. If you want Pinot Noir, go southwest, young wine drinker, to Burgundy (see Chapter 7).

Enjoying Alsace Wines

At a recent wine-and-food seminar in Stratton, Vermont, a pan-elist insisted that no white wine in the world could go well with duck. We responded with one word: Alsace. Alsace wines are among the world's most versatile wines for food.

The only trick to matching Alsace wines with food is to choose the lighter and more delicate wines — such as Pinot Blanc, Sylvaner, or a light, blended wine — with light foods such as delicate fish, and to choose the richer Gewurztraminer and Tokay-Pinot Gris wines for heartier foods. What about Riesling? That depends on the style, because Riesling can range from fairly delicate to powerful.

Some classic wine-unfriendly foods actually are friendly to Alsace wines. Take asparagus, for example. They taste great with Muscat or Pinot Blanc. Tomatoes and Gewurztraminer are surprisingly good together. Sauerkraut is no problem for Tokay-Pinot Gris (nor are caramelized onions — from the completely opposite end of the flavor spectrum!).

Alsace cuisine features delicate dishes, such as river fish, as well as hearty fare such as onion tarts, sausages with sauerkraut, and bean dishes. The wines accommodate the whole spectrum of flavors and richnesses.

We suggest that you not chill Alsace wines very much, because you'll lose the wines' nuances; cool cellar temperature (about 58°F, 14°C) is fine. We also suggest that you pour the wines into decanters to aerate them for 30 minutes or so before drinking them — if you have the time. And don't forget that Rieslings, in particular, become more interesting with age, and with aeration.

Our strongest advice on enjoying Alsace wines is to experiment with the various types of wines and with producers. The Alsace region boasts a wealth of fine wines that's just begging for you to discover it!

Top Alsace Producers

The average quality of winemaking in Alsace is among the highest in France. The finest wines are magnificent, but even the ordinary quality wines are well made and worth drinking.

As in most other wine regions, Alsace wine producers vary in nature:

> ✔ Some sell only the wine they make from their own vine-yards; these are the smallest producers.
>
> ✔ Others are grower-*négociants,* who own vineyards but also purchase grapes and wines.
>
> ✔ Others are cooperative wineries, where dozens of grow-ers pool their grapes.

Our list of recommended producers features growers and grower-*négociants.* Some of these brands are widely available outside France, while others are hard to find, but worth the search. We list these producers alphabetically, and provide a few comments for some of them:

Jean-Baptiste Adam
Domaine Lucien Albrecht
Jean Becker
Léon Beyer (true varietal character and very good quality)
Paul Blanck (high quality dry wines with strong *terroir* character)
Bott-Geyl
Albert Boxler
Ernest Burn
Marcel Deiss (a top-quality producer in all categories)
Dopff & Irion
Dopff au Moulin
Hugel (impressively rich wines, especially the "Jubilee" tier)
Josmeyer (fine-tuned, elegant wines of very high quality)
Roger Jung
André Kientzler
Domaine Klipfel
Marc Kreydenweiss (a fine, small producer making dry but rich wines)
Kuentz-Bas

Gustave Lorentz (makes terrific Gewurztraminer)
Domaine Julien Meyer
Mittnacht-Klack
Muré/Clos St.-Landelin (reliable wines, and a very good Pinot Noir*)*
Domaine Ostertag
Preiss-Henny
Rolly Gassmann
Charles Schleret
Albert Seltz
Domaine Schlumberger (great *grand cru* wines)
Pierre Sparr (very good *crémant,* and a full line of fairly rich wines)
Trimbach (very dry, sleek, well-concentrated wines)
Domaine Weinbach (rich wines with ripe fruit character)
Willm (particularly good Gewurztraminer)
Domaine Zind-Humbrecht (a celebrated producer making some of the richest of all Alsace wines)

Chapter 12

The Loire Valley's Hidden Gems

. . . .

In This Chapter

▶ Mouthwatering white wines from Sauvignon Blanc

▶ The Pouilly that's not Fuissé

▶ Chenin Blanc's finest moments

▶ Summertime red

▶ Muscadet — underappreciated and undervalued

. . . .

*F*rance has so many great wine regions that sometimes the Loire Valley gets overlooked. That's a pity because it's one of France's most beautiful regions, as well as the home of unique wines. You can appreciate the region's beauty by taking a leisurely auto trip west from Paris on local roads following the Loire River — through the historic towns of Orléans and Tours, past beautiful 15th-, 16th-, and 17th-century castles that were once the summer homes of French nobility. Savor the region's wines by sipping a crisp Sancerre with fresh goat cheese, tasting a Muscadet with briney oysters, or inhaling the incomparable aroma of a Chinon.

The Rambling Loire Valley

The Loire *(l'wahr)* Valley is the longest and most rural wine region in France. It follows the path of the Loire River, France's greatest waterway. The region begins in north-central France, a little to the south of Paris, and stretches about 250 miles across northwest France to the port city of Nantes, where the Loire empties into the Atlantic. The region has tremendous beauty, and yet it's still unspoiled, and not overrun by tourists. The Loire Valley is the secret gem of France.

The Loire Valley makes white, rosé, red, sparkling, and dessert wines, but white wines, both dry and sweet, are the main story. White wine represents 55 percent of the region's production, compared to 24 percent red wine, 14 percent rosé wine, and 7 percent sparkling wine. A total of 40 AOC wines are produced across the Loire Valley; in a typical vintage, they account for about 32 million cases of wine.

The Loire's climate and soil

As you might expect in such a large area (see Figure 12-1), climate and soils vary across the width of the Loire Valley. The climate is well suited for most types of wines, with the exception of full-bodied, high-alcohol reds, which require more heat than the Loire Valley can offer.

Influenced by both the Atlantic Ocean and the Loire River, the climate is generally temperate throughout the Valley, with fairly warm but not hot summers, and winters that are never intensely cold. Summers have some rain, but most rain falls in the autumn and winter. As wine regions go, it's a rather cool area — and the closer to the ocean, the cooler and damper the growing season is.

The cool weather dictates the types of wines that the region makes. The region specializes in crisp, white wines because white wine grapes need less heat and sun than red wine grapes. The red wines from the Loire Valley tend to be light-bodied and fairly low in alcohol, reflecting their struggle to ripen in the northerly Loire latitude.

Of the Loire Valley's various soils, the most significant soil is chalky limestone, especially in the Upper Loire (the eastern part of the region, near Paris), around the towns of Sancerre and Pouilly-sur-Loire. The slopes of Vouvray in the Central Loire are rich in limestone and tuffeau (a calcareous rock, like soft limestone), soil extremely favorable for the Chenin Blanc grape, the dominant variety of the Vouvray district. In the Lower Loire (the western part, near the Atlantic Ocean), the hills are mainly sand and gravel — soils that exist throughout the rest of the Valley, as well.

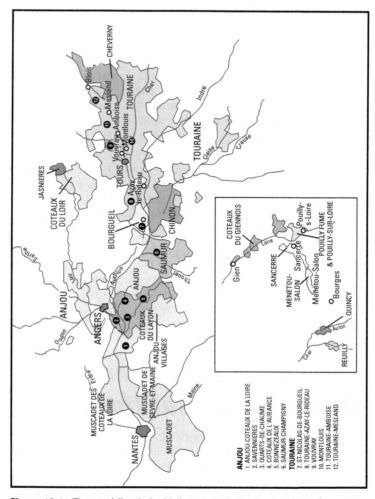

Figure 12-1: The rambling Loire Valley spreads across northern France.

The major wine districts

The Loire Valley has three very different areas, encompassing four major wine districts. Each district specializes in different grape varieties and makes wines that are unlike those of the other districts. The three main areas are the following:

- ✔ **The Upper Loire:** This is the eastern part, about 120 miles south of Paris, and east of Orléans, called the Upper Loire because it is the area closest to the river's source in the Massif Central, the high plateau of eastern France. Here the Sauvignon Blanc grape variety rules; the main wines are Sancerre and Pouilly-Fumé. There's also some Pinot Noir for reds and rosés.

- ✔ **The Central Loire:** This is the largest part of the Loire wine region, containing the cities of Tours *(tor)* and Angers *(ahn jhay)*. It has two major wine districts: the Touraine and Anjou-Saumur. The leading white grape variety is Chenin Blanc, and the leading red variety is Cabernet Franc.

- ✔ **The Lower Loire (Pays Nantais):** The western part, near the Atlantic Ocean, is known as the Pays Nantais *(peh yee nahn tay)*, the "Nantes countryside," after its principal city, Nantes. This area has one major white grape variety, Muscadet *(moos cah day)*, which is also the name of the local wine.

The Upper Loire: Sauvignon Blanc's Spiritual Home

The Upper Loire district is the extreme eastern part of the region, situated roughly in the center of France. This area is much closer to parts of Burgundy — it's only about 60 miles from Chablis — than it is to the opposite end of its own region. In fact, it shares a grape variety with Burgundy: the red Pinot Noir. But it doesn't grow Chardonnay, the grape of Chablis; the white wines of the Upper Loire come mainly from Sauvignon Blanc.

Because the Upper Loire district is the most interior part of the Loire Valley, its climate is dryer and more continental than that of the rest of the region — but it's still a cool climate. Dry white wines dominate, although a fair amount of red and rosé wines also come from here.

Sancerre and Pouilly-Fumé

We believe that five places in the world make really fine wines from Sauvignon Blanc: Bordeaux (see Chapter 6), the Loire Valley, New Zealand, Northeastern Italy (Alto Adige and Friuli), and South Africa.

Of these regions' wines, we suspect that those of the Upper Loire, primarily Sancerre *(sahn sair)* and Pouilly-Fumé *(poo yee foo may),* are the world's finest interpretations of the Sauvignon Blanc variety. They're less intensely herbaceous than New Zealand and Italian Sauvignon Blancs, but more assertive than most South African versions. They're more concentrated than Bordeaux's Sauvignon Blanc-based whites, and racier than Bordeaux's richer whites, which are often blended with Sémillon. The Loire Valley's versions are also the most food-friendly.

Sancerre, the wine, comes from vineyards around the town of Sancerre, on the western bank of the Loire. It has by far the largest production of all wines in the Upper Loire, and it's the district's most well-known wine. In fact, it's one of the most popular white wines in France; Sancerre is especially fashionable in bistros and restaurants in Paris.

Of the one million-plus cases of Sancerre produced annually, about 80 percent is white, made entirely from Sauvignon Blanc. The other 20 percent is dry rosé and red Sancerre, from Pinot Noir; both are pleasant enough, but not of the quality of white Sancerre.

The Sancerre zone covers 14 communities; besides the town of Sancerre itself, the villages of Bué, Chavignol, and Verdigny contain the most renowned vineyards; when the grapes come from these areas, the village name often appears on the wine's label.

Across the river from the Sancerre vineyards, the town of Pouilly-sur-Loire *(poo ee sir l'wahr)* is the center of another vineyard area, for a similar white wine. Called Pouilly-Fumé, this wine is also 100 percent Sauvignon Blanc, but its production is only about half of Sancerre's. The Pouilly-sur-Loire vineyards also produce another white, simply called Pouilly-sur-Loire (a VDQS wine; see Chapter 3). It's made from Chasselas, the principal variety of Swiss white wines. Unfortunately, Chasselas makes less distinguished wines in the Upper Loire than in Switzerland; Pouilly-sur-Loire is decent enough and inexpensive, but it's not of the quality of Pouilly-Fumé.

Sancerre and Pouilly-Fumé wines are more similar than different. They are both light- to medium-bodied, crisp, and lively, with spicy, herbaceous, green-grass, mineral, and citrus aromas and flavors, and they are both usually un-oaked. The herbaceous aromas are usually more pronounced in Sancerre, while Pouilly-Fumé wines often have a distinct flinty, minerally aroma. Also, Pouilly-Fumés are slightly fuller, rounder, and less spicy than Sancerres — which tend to be livelier and a bit lighter-bodied.

Price-wise, Sancerre and Pouilly-Fumé wines are both good values. Most of them retail in the $15 to $25 range — but a few of the best examples of Pouilly-Fumé can cost more than $50.

Sancerre and Pouilly-Fumé, typical of most wines made entirely from Sauvignon Blanc, are best when they're consumed within one to four years of the vintage — with two or three years being their optimum age. In some cases, they can live longer, but they begin to lose their freshness and liveliness, two of their most endearing characteristics.

Two "Pouillys," two different wines

It's easy to confuse the two "Pouilly" wines. Pouilly-Fuissé, made around the villages of Pouilly and Fuissé in the Mâcon district of southern Burgundy (see Chapter 7), is a wine made completely from Chardonnay; it's a rather full-bodied, rich white wine. Pouilly-Fumé, 100 percent Sauvignon Blanc, is far lighter and crisper. Another difference: Most Pouilly-Fuissés undergo some oak aging and therefore have smoky, toasty aromas of oak; only the most expensive Pouilly-Fumés age in oak.

Other wines of the Upper Loire

The Upper Loire Valley is the home of three other fairly important AOC vineyard areas. They are

- Quincy (*can see*)
- Reuilly (*reuh yee*)
- Ménétou-Salon (*meh neh too sah lohn*)

In terms of white wines, all three produce dry, crisp whites based entirely on Sauvignon Blanc that are stylistically fairly similar to Sancerre and Pouilly-Fumé.

Of the three, Ménétou-Salon — from an area southwest of the town of Sancerre and near the ancient city of Bourges — is the most available in the U.S. and the most comparable to Sancerre and Pouilly-Fumé in style, flavor, and overall quality. Since none of these are well-known wines, they tend to be good values; some white Ménétou-Salon wines retail for less than $15, despite the fact that production is only about 40,000 cases annually.

Although the white wines of Quincy and Reuilly (*reuh yee*) — not to be confused with Rully (*rouh yee*), a Burgundian wine made from Chardonnay (see Chapter 7) — are also well-priced, they tend to be lighter-bodied and more herbaceous than Sancerre and Pouilly-Fumé.

Whereas Quincy makes only white wine, Reuilly and Ménétou-Salon also make red and rosé wines. In Reuilly, half the production is red or rosé wine, the red made from Pinot Noir and the rosé made from Pinot Gris, a white variety with fairly dark skin. About 40 percent of the production of Ménétou-Salon is rosé or red, from Pinot Noir. Most of the dry rosé and light-bodied red wines of Ménétou-Salon and Reuilly are also light in flavor and color. These wines are pleasant enough to accompany a warm-weather lunch, but they have no aging capacity; you should drink them within two or three years of their vintage date — the younger, the better. Nevertheless, Ménétou-Salon's rosés and reds tend to be more interesting than those of Sancerre.

Another AOC area of the Upper Loire is **Coteaux du Giennois** *(coh toh dew jhee en wah),* the newest AOC zone of the district. Thirty percent of its production is white wine from Sauvignon Blanc; the balance is mainly light red wine from Gamay or Pinot Noir, as well as some rosé. These wines are even more obscure than Quincy, Reuilly, and Ménétou-Salon.

Leading Upper Loire producers

Sancerre producers to look for include the following (listed in our rough order of preference):

Domaine Henri Bourgeois	Domaine Roger Neveu
Domaine Lucien Crochet	Domaine de Montigny
Cotat Frères	Bernard Reverdy
Domaine Alphonse Mellot	Domaine Vacheron
Domaine Vincent Pinard	Jean-Max Roger
Pascal Jolivet (also, Château du Nozay)	Gitton Père et Fils
Domaine Vincent Delaporte	Comte Lafond (also spelled "Lafon")
Domaine Paul Millerioux	Bailly-Reverdy et Fils
Château de Maimbray	

Top Pouilly-Fumé producers are listed here in our rough order of preference (the first two producers' best Pouilly-Fumés are over $50):

Didier Dagueneau	Masson-Blondelet
De Ladoucette (especially Baron de L)	Michel Redde (best wine, "La Moynerie")
Domaine Cailbourdin	Château de Tracy
Jean-Claude Chatelain	Domaine Guy Saget
Domaine Serge Dagueneau	Tinel- Blondelet

The Baron de L of de Ladoucette, and Didier Dagueneau's Pouilly-Fumé, both partially fermented and aged in new oak barrels, are the exception to the rule that Upper Loire wines should be consumed very young; they are fine with even five or six years of age.

Two good Ménétou-Salon producers are Domaine de Chatenoy and Henri Pelle. Few Quincy, Reuilly, or Coteaux du Giennois wines are imported into the U.S., but they make for interesting discoveries when you visit the Loire Valley. Look for Domaine Sorbe for both Quincy and Reuilly wines, Domaine Mardon for Quincy, and Claude Lafond for Reuilly.

The Diverse Central Loire

The Central Loire is by far the largest and most diversified wine area of the Loire Valley. All kinds of wines are made in the Central Loire: dry white, sweet white, rosé, red, and sparkling.

The Central Loire area has two main districts:

- ✔ The Touraine
- ✔ Anjou-Saumur *(ahn jhoo saw muhr)*

These two districts share the same grape varieties — mainly Chenin Blanc for white wine and Cabernet Franc for the reds — but each district encompasses numerous wine zones.

Touraine's (too) many AOCs

The historic city of Tours is the focal point of the Touraine district, and gives its name to the district. The Touraine is a large area producing red, white, rosé, and sparkling wines, dry wines, off-dry wines, and sweet wines (in other words, everything under the sun). The climate varies from the eastern part, which is warmer and dryer, to the western part, which has more maritime influence. Soils also vary across the breadth of the Touraine.

The Touraine is a confusing district because it makes so many different wines (many of which are fairly minor and are seldom seen in wine shops). Some of the vineyards grow wines with the district-wide AOC, Touraine. Other vineyards are in smaller, more precise AOC zones named for specific communities such as Vouvray and Chinon. Still other vineyards grow grapes for wines that share their AOC name with vineyards from the Anjou district, such as Rosé de la Loire.

Even the simple, district-wide appellation of Touraine is perplexing. It includes a Sauvignon de Touraine, a dry, crisp white from Sauvignon Blanc grapes, and Gamay de Touraine, a light, fruity red. (So far so good.) But it also includes blended wines that are called simply Touraine Blanc, Touraine Rouge, or Touraine Rosé. And it includes a lightly sparkling wine (Touraine Pétillant) and a sparkling wine (Touraine Mousseux, pronounced *moo suh*). Table 12-1 lists the grape varieties that may be used for each of these wines. The Touraine AOC also includes three sub-district appellations, for wines whose grapes come from specific areas: Touraine-Mesland (red and rosé wines), Touraine-Amboise (all three colors), and Touraine-Azay-le-Rideau (rosé and dry whites); the permitted varieties for these wines are the same as listed in Table 12-1 for wines of similar color.

Table 12-1   Permitted Varieties in Touraine AOC Wines

Wine	Permitted Grape Varieties
Touraine Blanc	Chenin Blanc, Arbois, Sauvignon Blanc, Chardonnay (maximum 20 percent of the blend)
Touraine Rouge	Cabernet Franc, Cabernet Sauvignon or Malbec, Pinot Noir, Pinot Meunier, Pinot Gris, Gamay, Pineau d'Aunis
Touraine Rosé	Same varieties as Touraine Rouge, with the addition of Grolleau and, as minor varieties, three variants of Gamay
Touraine Mousseux (sparkling white)	Chenin Blanc, Arbois, and, as minor varieties, Chardonnay, Cabernet Franc, Cabernet Sauvignon, Pinot Noir, Pinot Meunier, Pinot Gris, Pineau d'Aunis, Malbec, and Grolleau
Touraine Mousseux (sparkling red)	Cabernet Franc
Touraine Mousseux (sparkling rosé)	Cabernet Franc, Malbec, Pinot Noir, Pinot Meunier, Pinot Gris, Gamay, Grolleau

Other fairly obscure AOC zones within the Touraine district or in its vicinity include the following:

✔ **Coteaux du Loir:** Vineyards along the Loir River, a tributary of the Loire, to the north; whites from Chenin Blanc; reds and rosés from Pineau d'Aunis, Cabernet Franc, Cabernet Sauvignon, Gamay, Malbec, and Grolleau

- ✔ **Jasnières** *(jah n'yair):* Also to the north; whites from Chenin Blanc

- ✔ **Cheverny** *(sheh vehr nee):* To the east; whites mainly from Sauvignon Blanc; reds mainly from Pinot Noir and Gamay; rosé mainly from Pinot Noir

Despite all the breath we've expended on the Touraine district, we haven't yet touched on the really important Touraine wines: the wines that come from specific, smaller AOC zones. We discuss those wines in the sections that follow.

The many faces of Vouvray

What is clearly the most famous wine of the Touraine — Vouvray — comes from a vineyard area just east of Tours. The AOC zone includes the village of Vouvray *(voo vray)* and seven other villages; the grape variety is Chenin Blanc. Along with areas within the Anjou district, the Vouvray area produces the world's best Chenin Blanc wines. Wines made from Chenin Blanc hail from California, South Africa, and other places, but it is only in Vouvray, and in the Anjou district, that Chenin Blanc rises to noble heights.

Vouvray's production is more than a million cases a year — but that million cases represents several styles of wine. Vouvray can be still or sparkling. The still versions of Vouvray can be dry, semi-dry, or fairly sweet. (The sweet style is called *moelleux,* pronounced *m'wah leuh.*)

The style of a particular Vouvray depends on the nature of the vintage: A very warm vintage with very ripe grapes can produce sweeter, richer wines, for example, while a very cool year can produce relatively under-ripe grapes suitable for sparkling wine. Grapes for the *moelleux* style are generally affected with noble rot and are late-harvested, for additional richness. (See "Sauternes/Barsac" in Chapter 6 for a discussion of *botrytis cinerea,* the so-called noble rot.)

The *moelleux* style of Vouvray is considered the best, and certainly it's the most long-lived; these rich, mellow wines can develop for 50 years or more, taking on flavors of apples and honey and becoming more unctuous and complex with age.

You can't always see what you get

Vouvray does have a small, cult following among wine lovers for its rich, intensely flavored *moelleux* wines. But for most wine drinkers, Vouvray is an unknown quantity as a wine, because it comes in so many styles. If you ask your wine merchant what a Vouvray is like, he or she might just answer (with a straight face), "That depends."

Most Vouvray producers help out by putting words on the label to describe the style: *Sec, Sec-tendre* (off-dry), *Demi-sec* (semi-dry), or *Moelleux* (rich and fairly sweet). Some don't use the "dry," "off-dry," or "semi-dry" terms — although just about everyone uses *moelleux*. At any rate, you know *moelleux* Vouvrays by their price alone: They're the ones that are over $30!

(We tasted a delicious 1919 Vouvray *moelleux* recently that showed no signs of deterioration.) The dry and semi-dry styles of Vouvray often have floral and/or nutty flavors along with fruity character; they can be quite rich in texture, and yet they have refreshing, high acidity. They need four or five years to soften, and can live far longer; even the dry Vouvray wines can age and improve for 15 to 20 years or more.

Among sparkling Vouvray wines, two different versions exist: *pétillant (peh tee yahn;* slightly sparkling), or *mousseux (moo suh;* fully sparkling). Both are made by the classic method of second fermentation in the bottle. Drink bubbly Vouvrays within three years of the vintage if they are vintage dated, or soon after you buy them, if they are non-vintage wines.

 Most dry and semi-dry styles of still Vouvray retail from $8 to $15 a bottle, but wines from a few of the best producers (Gaston Huët-Pinguet and Domaine du Clos Naudin, to name two) are in the $20 to $25 range. Most of the sweet *(moelleux)* Vouvrays are in the $20 to $50 price range (often for a 500 ml bottle, rather than the standard 750 ml size); a few of the finest sweet Vouvrays cost $75 to $90. Sparkling Vouvrays run about $15 to $20. Good recent vintages of Vouvray and

Montlouis (discussed in the next section) have been the 1997, 1996 (especially good), 1995, 1990, and 1989 (especially good).

Vouvray's little brother

Montlouis *(mohn loo wee)* is a wine village across the Loire from Vouvray, on the south bank of the River. The wines of Montlouis, also 100 percent Chenin Blanc, are similar in most ways to those of Vouvray; you can find all of the same styles: dry, semi-dry, sweet, and sparkling. Montlouis wines tend to be softer, a bit lighter-bodied, and less concentrated than those of Vouvray. They are also ready sooner, and not as long-lasting. Montlouis is a bit less expensive — especially the sweet *(moelleux)* Montlouis wines — which are about $20 to $45. Montlouis production is roughly 200,000 cases annually — only about 20 percent that of Vouvray. About half of Montlouis wines are sparkling wines.

Many Vouvrays labelled "dry" are the least interesting wines, especially when they're very inexpensive. A good dry or semi-dry Vouvray or Montlouis wine should be fruity, sometimes with a hint of peaches or honey, and have a decent amount of acidity so that it doesn't taste too soft. Your safest bet is to buy Vouvray or Montlouis from a good producer; check out the following section for our recommended producers.

Recommended Vouvray and Montlouis producers

Some of the best producers of Vouvray wines, listed in our rough order of preference, are the following:

Class One

Domaine Le Haut Lieu, of Huët-Pinguet

Domaine du Clos Naudin, of Philippe Foreau

Didier and Catherine Champalou

Domaine des Aubuisières

Class Two

Domaine Allias (also known as Clos du Petit Mont)

Château Gaudrelle, of Monmousseau

François Pinon

Marc Brédif

Clos Baudoin, of Prince Poniatowski

Domaine de la Fontainerie

Domaine Bourillon-D'Orléans

Five good Montlouis producers, in our rough order of preference, are the following:

Domaine Olivier Délétang   Alain Lelarge
Domaine François Chidaine   Claude Levasseurr
Dominique Moyer

The Touraine's best red wines

About 25 miles west of Tours is the one area in the Loire Valley that is known for its *red* wine. This area encompasses three AOC zones whose wines are all named after their villages:

- ✔ Chinon *(shee nohn)*, south of the Loire River
- ✔ Bourgueil *(boor guh'y)*, north of the river
- ✔ Saint-Nicolas-de-Bourgueil *(san nee co lah deh boor guh'y)*, also north of the Loire

Cabernet Franc is the main grape variety for all three of these wines. This variety ripens earlier than Cabernet Sauvignon, and is therefore more suited to cool climates. Nevertheless, in 1996, French wine authorities allowed up to 10 percent Cabernet Sauvignon in these wines, and in 2000, the maximum amount rose to 25 percent. Apparently, this law was introduced in an effort to beef up these frequently light-bodied wines.

The Chinon vineyards produce about 700,000 cases a year, more than those of the other two red wines combined. Chinon is light- to medium-bodied, fruity, and lively, and often has aromas and flavors of raspberries and/or wild strawberries. It is the most elegant and generally the finest of the three red wines. Chinon can be good when it's young and exuberant, but some Chinons can age quite well in the best vintages. You can find it in two styles:

- ✔ The light-cherry red, light-bodied (and inexpensive) style for immediate enjoyment
- ✔ The dark red, medium-bodied style, with some tannin; this style will age for a decade or so in good vintages (see the vintage chart in Appendix C)

Despite its occasional aroma of violets, Bourgueil is more rustic and earthy than Chinon, and needs about four or five years of aging. Saint-Nicolas-de-Bourgueil, lighter-bodied than Bourgueil, is ready to drink sooner.

All three of these wines have fairly high acidity, which makes them refreshing, especially in warm weather. None of the three is a particularly long-term wine. With the possible exception of the fuller-styled Chinons, enjoy their fruitiness and berry-like flavors in their adolescence.

You can also find some decent dry rosé wines in Chinon, Bourgueil, and Saint-Nicolas-de-Bourgueil — all made from Cabernet Franc. Chinon also produces a very small quantity of Chinon Blanc, made from Chenin Blanc.

Like Sancerre, these three red wines, especially Chinon, are quite popular in France; you can find them in most of Paris' wine bars and bistros. These three reds are also good values. Retail prices for Chinon, Bourgueil, and Saint-Nicolas-de-Bourgueil range between $12 and $20. Good vintages for all three of the red Touraine wines have been 1996, 1995, 1990, and 1989.

Chinon producers to look for, listed in our rough order of preference, are the following (the first two Chinon producers are especially fine):

Olga Raffault	Domaine Bernard Baudry
Charles Joguet	Château de la Grille
Couly-Dutheil	Philippe Alliet

Bourgueil producers that we recommend are Pierre-Jacques Druet, Domaine de la Lande, and Domaine des Ouches. Saint-Nicolas-de-Bourgueil producers to look for are Domaine Joël Taluau and Cognard-Taluau.

The dry and the sweet of Anjou-Saumur

You cannot categorize Anjou-Saumur. Every type of wine — dry white, semi-dry white, sweet white (of varying types), rosé (both dry and semi-dry), dry red, and sparkling — has a strong presence in this wine district.

Cabernet Franc, front and center

The Loire Valley might be the only wine region in the world where the Cabernet Franc variety emerges from the shadow of Cabernet Sauvignon and gets the respect it deserves. It's a pity that this variety has been relegated to an understudy role because it has a lot to offer. Drink a good Chinon, for instance; that delicious hint of raspberry or the taste of bell peppers (which can be bracing, when not overdone) is due to Cabernet Franc.

Ironically, quite a few ampelographers (grapevine specialists) believe that Cabernet Sauvignon came into the world as a mutation, or variant, of Cabernet Franc. We do know that Cabernet Franc preceded Cabernet Sauvignon in Bordeaux.

The Anjou-Saumur district lies east of the Touraine. Anjou and Saumur are each towns within the district; Saumur is nearly on the eastern edge of the district, and Anjou is about 20 miles to the west (see Figure 12-1). This district is close enough to the Atlantic Ocean that its climate is maritime, reflecting the cool and rainy influence of the ocean.

Although Anjou-Saumur is traditionally linked together as one district, we treat Anjou and Saumur as separate areas here, because they really are quite different in the type of wine they each produce. The Saumur appellation zone, in fact, is closer in miles to Bourgueil, in the Touraine district, than it is to Anjou.

The wines of Saumur

The town of Saumur *(saw muhr)* is surrounded by vineyards, and the major business of the town is sparkling wine production. Saumur, in fact, is the leading sparkling wine producer of the Loire Valley. It produces up to 3 million cases of mainly traditional-method sparkling wine (made by second fermentation in the bottle) annually, primarily from Chenin Blanc, with some Cabernet Franc. A rosé version also exists.

Saumur AOC sparkling wine comes from grapes grown in 93 communities. Another sparkling wine, Crémant de Loire (white and rosé), is also made in Saumur, but the grapes for that wine can originate anywhere within the Anjou-Saumur or

Touraine districts. Permitted varieties for Crémant de la Loire are Chenin Blanc, Cabernet Franc, Cabernet Sauvignon, Grolleau, Pinot d'Aunis, Pinot Noir, Chardonnay, and Arbois.

Both Saumur and Crémant de la Loire sparkling wines are a good deal, retailing for $10 to $15.

Sparkling Saumur producers that we recommend, listed in our rough order of preference, are the following:

Langlois-Château	Gratien & Meyer (of the
Bouvet-Ladubay	Champagne Alfred Gratien)
Château de Passavant	Domaine de Gabillière
Ackerman-Laurance	Veuve Amiot

Saumur also makes a small amount of still white wine, mainly from Chenin Blanc; rosé wine, called Cabernet de Saumur; and Saumur Rouge, a fairly light red wine based on Cabernet Franc, Cabernet Sauvignon, and Pineau d'Aunis grapes.

But Saumur's best still wine is clearly the red called Saumur-Champigny. Saumur-Champigny is, in fact, the best red wine in the entire Anjou-Saumur district, and a great value in the $10 to $18 range. It derives from Cabernet Franc grapes grown in the vineyards around Saumur and the nearby village of Champigny *(shahm pee n'yee)*. At its best, the wine is quite dark in color, fairly low in tannin, and easy to drink — without any aging needed. Saumur-Champigny resembles the wines of nearby Chinon, but is also similar to a light-bodied Bordeaux. Saumur-Champigny producers that we recommend, in our rough order of preference, are the following:

Clos Rougéard	Château de Targé
Domaine Filliatreau	Domaine des Roches Neuves
Château de Villeneuve	

The Anjou district

Most of the Anjou *(ahn joo)* district is on the southern banks of the Loire River, south of the city of Angers. Anjou produces more different kinds of wine than any other Loire Valley district, but its largest production is its rosé wines, and its rosés are the wines that wine drinkers associate with "Anjou."

Anjou producers make three different kinds of rosé wines:

- **Rosé d'Anjou:** The highest production; a semi-dry wine made from Gamay, Malbec, and a local variety called Grolleau, or Groslot.

- **Cabernet d'Anjou:** Also semi-dry; a more serious rosé made from Cabernet Franc and Cabernet Sauvignon; unusually for a rosé, it's capable of aging for several years.

- **Rosé de la Loire:** A dry rosé that's mainly Cabernet Franc.

Rosé d'Anjou and Cabernet d'Anjou fall into the broad appellation, Anjou, which includes red and white wines as well as these two rosés. Other Anjou AOC wines include the following:

- **Anjou Rouge:** Made mainly from Cabernet Franc, along with Cabernet Sauvignon, Pineau d'Aunis, and Malbec; a simple, fruity wine.

- **Anjou Gamay:** Made entirely from Gamay.

- **Anjou Blanc:** White wines made from Chenin Blanc, with Chardonnay and Sauvignon Blanc also permitted; mainly dry, but can be sweet.

- **Anjou-Coteaux de la Loire:** Off-dry and *moelleux* white wines made from Chenin Blanc.

Another AOC wine is Anjou-Villages, a red wine from Cabernet Franc and Cabernet Sauvignon grapes grown in 46 communities within the Anjou district. All Anjou wines are excellent values (in the $10 to $18 price range), and are fine choices as everyday wines — when you choose a good producer.

Producers of Anjou AOC and Anjou-Villages AOC that we recommend, listed in our rough order of preference, are the following:

Château Pierre-Bise	Domaine Ogereau
Domaine de Montgilet	Château de la Genaiserie
Domaine Richou	Château de Fesles
Domaine des Rochelles	

Anjou's best wines

The best wines of Anjou are white wines — both dry and sweet — from two limited AOC zones.

Arguably the greatest *dry* Chenin Blanc wines in the world come from the Savennières *(sah ven yair)* area, on the northern banks of the Loire. Savennieres wines are concentrated and intensely flavored, with intriguing mineral notes to their aroma and flavor that give them more character than other dry Chenin Blanc wines. Despite their wonderful floral, honeyed aromas, they are totally dry.

Two special vineyards within the Savennières AOC hold *cru* status: Coulée de Serrant *(cool ay deh seh rahn)* and Roche aux Moines *(rohsh oh m'wan)*. Nicolas Joly, the sole owner of Coulée de Serrant vineyard and part owner of Roche aux Moines, is a standout producer in the Savennières area. The wines from these two Savennières *crus* can age and improve for 20 years or more in good vintages. Vintages to buy Savennières include 1997, 1996, 1995, 1990, 1989, and 1985.

Considering its quality, Savennières is very reasonably priced, because it hasn't truly been discovered yet. Savennières starts in the $18 to $20 range, and can go up to about $60 for the finest examples. Savennières producers that we recommend, in our rough order of preference, are the following:

Clos de la Coulée de Serrant,
   of Nicolas Joly
Domaine des Baumard
Domaine du Closel

Château d'Epiré
Clos de Coulaine
Clos des Perrières
Domaine Laffourcade

The other great white wine of the Anjou, on the southern banks of the Loire, and also made from Chenin Blanc, is Coteaux du Layon *(coat toe doo lay awn)*. The wines of the Coteaux du Layon area are naturally sweet, made from overripe Chenin Blanc grapes that are often affected by noble rot, as in Sauternes (see Chapter 6). Like Sauternes, the Coteaux du Layon wines have that wonderful balance between sweetness and acidity that prevents them from being cloying. And like Sauternes, these wines really improve with at least ten years of aging. As they mature, Coteaux du Layon wines take on aromas of apricots, peaches, honey, and spice.

Coteaux du Layon is a rather large zone, and within it are two areas so special that they have separate AOC status:

  ✔ **Quarts de Chaume** *(cahr deh show'm)*

  ✔ **Bonnezeaux** *(bon zoe)*

Like Coteaux du Layon, these are sweet wines from nobly-rotted grapes. They need *at least* five or six years to develop — better yet, ten — but then they can age and improve for 20 years or more in good vintages. Prices range from about $20 up to $75, with a few extraordinary bottles over $100. Many of these wines come in a 500 ml bottle.

Coteaux du Layon, Quarts de Chaume, and Bonnezeaux producers that we recommend, in our rough order of preference, are the following (the first producer is particularly fine):

Château de Fesles	Domaine des Forges
Domaine de la Sansonnière	Domaine Cady
Domaine des Baumard	Moulin-Touchais
Domaine du Petit Val	Patrick Baudouin
Domaine de Terrebrune, of	Château Pierre-Bise
René Renou	Château de Plaisance
Château de Bellerive	Château du Breuil
Château Soucherie	Château des Rochettes
Domaine Ogereau	Domaine Delesvaux
Domaine Laffourcade	Domaine Pithon
Château de la Genaiserie	

Another appellation making good sweet white wine is the small **Coteaux de l'Aubance** *(coh toh deh low bahntz)* area, named for the Aubance River; it's just south of Angers and close to Coteaux de Layon.

Good vintages for these sweet Anjou wines are 1997, 1996 (especially), 1995, 1990, 1989, and 1985.

Muscadet: The Value White

Brittany, the French province that faces the Atlantic Ocean and is known for its fishing, is the home of the Pays Nantais *(peh yee nahn tae)* wine district. The Pays Nantais is the western end of the Loire Valley. Because it's close to the Atlantic Ocean, the weather is cooler and damper than in other parts of the Loire Valley wine region.

This district, named for the city of Nantes, is the home of Muscadet *(mus cah day)*, a dry, light-bodied white wine made from the Melon de Bourgogne grape variety — also known as Muscadet. A long time ago, French wine authorities blacklisted this variety in Burgundy, where it did not perform well, but it thrives in the cool but mild climate of the Pays Nantais, where it produces a light, dry, pleasant white wine that is always well-priced.

The simplest form of Muscadet is simply Muscadet AOC. Three other AOC's must come from lower-yielding vineyards, and therefore are generally higher in quality:

- ✔ **Muscadet de Sèvre-et-Maine:** Named for two local rivers; this is the largest production area, and usually makes the best wines.

- ✔ **Muscadet des Coteaux de la Loire:** An area in the North producing only one-fifth as much as the Muscadet de Sèvre-et-Maine AOC, and therefore more difficult to find.

- ✔ **Muscadet Côtes de Grand Lieu:** In the Southwest, the newest AOC area, having gained that status only in 1996.

If you pick up a bottle of Muscadet at your wine shop, chances are that it will be Muscadet de Sèvre-et-Maine, and that the label will also say "Sur Lie." These two words refer to a production process whereby the wine is held in its fermentation tank along with the deposits of fermentation — the *lees* — until it is bottled. The lees are mainly dead yeast cells. They enrich the flavor of the wine, and they retain some carbon dioxide within the wine, giving it a slightly prickly taste.

Muscadet is one of the great bargains in the wine world. We don't recommend this wine if it's older than three years — in fact, the younger, the better. When it's properly fresh and crisp, Muscadet is a perfect warm-weather white wine, especially with shellfish. Retail prices for Muscadet range from $6 to $12.

Recommended Muscadet producers, in our rough order of preference, include the following:

Louis Métaireau	Domaine de la Fruitière
Domaine de l'Ecu, of Guy Bossard	Domaine de la Haute-Févrie
	Domaine de la Louvetrie
Chérau-Carré	Château de la Mercredière
Château du Cléray, of Sauvion	Domaine Les Hautes Noëlles
Château de la Ragotière	Domaine Pierre Luneau-Papin
Domaine des Herbauges	Domaine de la Tourmaline
Domaine la Quilla	D. Bahuaud
Domaine Chiron	Marquis de Goulaine
Domaine des Dorices	Château de la Preuille

Enjoying Loire Valley Wines

Serve the light-bodied dry white Loire wines, such as Muscadet, and the rosé wines, such as those from Anjou, fairly cold — in the 50°F to 53°F (10°C to 12°C) range. Dry and semi-dry Vouvray, Sancerre, and Pouilly-Fumé are best when they're cool, but not cold — about 55°F to 58°F (13°C to 15°C). The more complex dry wines from Savennières should not be too cool, so that you can appreciate their aromas and flavors; 58°F to 62°F (15°C to 17°C) is a good range for these wines.

Serve red Loire wines slightly cool to appreciate their light-bodied, low-tannin freshness; 58°F to 62°F (15°C to 17°C) is ideal. The sweet white Loire wines are best at cellar temperature, cool, but not cold — about 54°F to 56°F (13°C to 14°C).

We recommend these food combinations with Loire wines:

- **Sancerre, Pouilly-Fumé, Ménétou-Salon:** Fish and seafood; goat cheese (warm or cold)

- **Muscadet:** Oysters; other shellfish

- **Vouvray and Montlouis (dry or semi-dry):** Chicken; fish in butter sauce

- **Sparkling Saumur (and other Loire Valley sparkling wines):** With apéritif foods, such as almonds, stuffed mushrooms, or smoked oysters; fish or seafood

- **Anjou white and rosé:** River fish; apéritif foods

- **Red Loire wines:** Veal; poultry; meaty fish, such as salmon; earthy vegetables such as spinach, escarole, or portobello mushrooms

- **Sweet Loire wines:** Foie gras, with or without truffles; desserts that are not too sweet, such as apple tarts or lemon cake

Chapter 13

The South of France

- -

In This Chapter

▶ The hot, "new" wine region of France

▶ Tradition side-by-side with progress

▶ Talk about "value" wines!

▶ The most beautiful corner of France

- -

*T*he south of France claims two superlatives among French wine regions: It's the country's oldest wine-producing area, as well as the area that produces the most wine. The Greeks made wine in Provence — one of the wine regions of the South — as long ago as the 6th century B.C., well before the Romans conquered Gaul. And Languedoc-Roussillon, a dual wine region, boasts 38 percent of France's vineyards and over 40 percent of its wine production! Yet, the world didn't pay much attention to these wines until recently. Now, ironically, these old wine regions are hot — especially Languedoc-Roussillon. Much of the experimental work in France's vineyards is taking place here. This warm south of France is mainly red wine country, but these regions also produce rosés, sparkling wine, and some interesting whites, as well as dessert wines. The best part is that prices for the wines from southern France are still very affordable.

Languedoc-Roussillon: The Mother Vineyard of France

The south of France is teeming with wine. To put the quantity into perspective, Languedoc-Roussillon, this *one* part of France, produces more wine than the entire United States!

For a long time, quantity was about all that Languedoc-Roussillon had. The quality of the wines was only adequate, at best; most wines from the region stayed in France and were consumed locally. But in the past two decades, the story has changed. Modern technology and increased knowledge have improved both grape-growing and winemaking in Languedoc-Roussillon and throughout southern France. What were once just inexpensive wines are now — at about $8 to $15 — real values, because their quality is higher than ever. This new quality has opened world markets to the wines.

Languedoc-Roussillon *(lahn guh doc roo see yohn),* also known as the Midi *(mee dee),* is the most prolific wine region not only in France, but also in the world — making more than three times as much wine as Bordeaux. One of every ten bottles of the world's wine comes from Languedoc-Roussillon.

The lay of the land

Roussillon and Languedoc are two adjoining ancient regions that stretch along the Mediterranean shores of south-central France, from the Pyrénées Mountains — France's border with Spain — eastward to the Rhône River (see Figure 13-1). Languedoc, the eastern region, is by far the larger of the two. Although Roussillon and Languedoc are each technically separate wine regions, with their own traditions and culture, people generally treat them as a single region — as we do here.

Languedoc covers three French *départements,* or counties: (from west to east) the Aude, Hérault, and a small part of the Gard. It's a region of sunny, fertile plains — especially in the eastern and south-central parts — where grapevines flourish. The western part of the region is hilly, especially in the interior, away from the Mediterranean. The Cévennes Mountains form a northern barrier in the central part of the region. Montpellier is Languedoc's largest city and one of its oldest.

Roussillon is a much smaller and more mountainous region, directly north of Spain. In fact, the main language of most of the rural inhabitants is not French, but Catalan (which is also spoken in northern Spain). The old Roman city of Carcassonne is in the northern part of Roussillon, and Perpignan lies in the heart of the region.

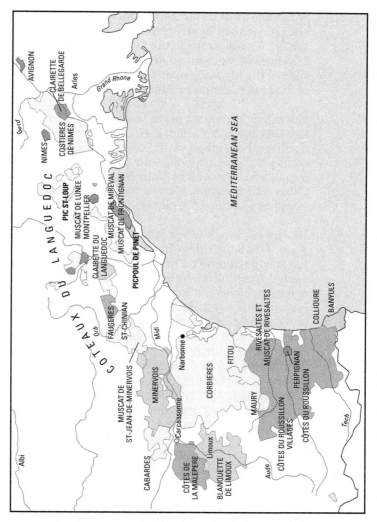

Figure 13-1: Languedoc-Roussillon, France's most prolific wine region.

Almost all of Languedoc-Roussillon — with the exception of a few areas in the northern foothills — has a Mediterranean climate: dry, sunny, and warm. Rain seldom falls during the vines' growing season, but winds from mountains often bring refreshing, cool weather. Roussillon is the sunniest and driest part of France (with Languedoc close behind). The area is so dry and sunny that drought can occur.

Soils vary throughout the region, ranging from fertile, alluvial soils (deposited by rivers or seas) on the plains, to gravel, schist, and limestone in the foothills of the Pyrénées and Cévennes Mountains, south of the Massif Central. The schist soils of the highest slopes make intense wines, while the soils of the lower hills make lighter, more approachable wines.

More than 90 percent of the wine grown in Languedoc-Roussillon is red. Carignan, Grenache, and Cinsault are the traditional red grape varieties of the area, but as the quest for quality has grown among wine producers, so have the plantings of Syrah, as well as Mourvèdre. In recent decades, even Cabernet Sauvignon, Merlot, and other popular grape varieties have become big players in Languedoc-Roussillon.

Like other French wine regions, Languedoc-Roussillon has many AOC wine zones. But unlike most other regions, Languedoc-Roussillon has a significant production of commercially successful wines in the *vins de pays*, or country wine, category; 85 percent of French *vins de pays* come from this region. (Chapter 3 explains the difference between the AOC and *vins de pays* categories of French wine.) These wines are mainly varietal wines from well known French grape varieties, such as Chardonnay, Cabernet Sauvignon, Syrah, and so forth. The largest *vins de pays* district is Vins de Pays d'Oc, an area that covers the entire Languedoc-Roussillon territory. The name "Languedoc" is believed to be a reference to the Occitan language that was once the tongue of the land in that area and, in fact, is still spoken by the older generation. "Languedoc" derives from the phrase, "langue d'oc," meaning "Oc tongue." Interestingly, some scholars believe that Occitan is the same language as a dialect spoken by the Piedmontese of northwestern Italy.

The seeds of change

The current wave of progress for Languedoc-Roussillon wines began about two decades ago. Two forces combined to forge a radical change in the types and quality of wines produced in the region:

- ✔ The French, who had always been the region's main consumers, started drinking less wine; decreased consumption created a huge oversupply of wine in the Midi.

✔ Modern winemaking and grape-growing technology came to the region, as did innovative wine producers from other parts of France and from other countries. These winemakers had a common goal — to make less, but better, wine — and their tools were the noble grape varieties: Syrah, Mourvèdre, Cabernet Sauvignon, Merlot, and Chardonnay.

A few large wineries marketed these new wines and gave the region a new image, both at home and abroad. In 1982, for example, a leading French agricultural industrialist, Robert Skalli, began large-scale production of Languedoc-Roussillon wines under the brand name of Fortant de France. His company specialized in producing varietally-labeled wines from the noble varieties: Cabernet Sauvignon, Merlot, Syrah, Chardonnay, Sauvignon Blanc, and Viognier. These new-fangled wines didn't carry any traditional AOC name, but simply the designation *Vins de Pays d'Oc*. Together with Réserve St. Martin, another popular brand of Languedoc-Roussillon varietals, Fortant de France wines are now ubiquitous in U.S. wine shops.

The Languedoc-Roussillon quality movement began on a smaller scale a few years earlier, when Aimé Guibert founded a wine estate in a cool microclimate in the northern Languedoc in the 1970s; he called his estate Mas de Daumas Gassac. ("Mas" is the local name for "domaine.") Guibert was convinced that "foreign" varieties, such as Cabernet Sauvignon, could make successful wines in certain parts of southern France, and he set out to prove his point. He released his first wines in 1978, and over the years won critical acclaim for his efforts. Mas de Daumas Gassac became the forerunner of many other serious, small Languedoc-Roussillon wine estates that make fine wines from non-native varieties. (Mas de Daumas Gassac's red wine is a long-lived Bordeaux-type blend, made mainly from Cabernet Sauvignon. The property also has a dry rosé, as well as an aromatic white wine from the Viognier grape variety. All three wines bear the humble designation, *Vin de Pays de l'Hérault*.)

These two movements established Languedoc-Roussillon as a suitable region for wines from France's classic grape varieties — both on a mass market and on a boutique level.

Classical wines: better than ever

The progressive movement in Languedoc-Roussillon wines went a long way towards improving the traditional wines of the region as well. Syrah has become a more important variety in the blends of the region's AOC wines, and Carignan, a lower quality variety, has diminished in importance. Winemaking know-how has also improved for the classical wines.

The largest AOC zone of Languedoc is Coteaux du Languedoc, an area that covers most of the Hérault *département* from the town of Narbonne in the west, extending almost to the Roman town of Nîmes in the east. Much of the area is plains, but it also includes some foothills. The wines include good-value blended reds from Grenache, Lladoner Pelut (a local variety similar to Grenache), Syrah, and Mourvèdre, with Carignan and Cinsault now limited to 40 percent of the blend. There are also light, dry rosés, and some interesting dry white wines — made mainly from Grenache Blanc, Bourboulenc, Picpoul, and Clairette (all Southern Rhône varieties).

The large Coteaux du Languedoc zone encompasses three freestanding AOC zones — Faugères, Saint-Chinian, and Clairette du Languedoc — that we describe later in this section. It also encompasses several individual vineyard areas that may append their names to the Coteaux du Languedoc name. (Figure 13-2 depicts such a label.) In time, many of these areas will earn a separate AOC.

Two areas of Coteaux du Languedoc are noteworthy:

- ✓ **Picpoul de Pinet** *(peek pool deh pee nay)*: This area near the Mediterranean coast is unusual in that it produces only white wines (from the Picpoul Blanc variety) in the heart of red wine country. The wines are very fruity, but dry.

- ✓ **Pic St.-Loup** *(peek san loo'p)*: Twelve villages make up this zone, producing mainly red wines, similar in style to Southern Rhône wines. Grenache, Syrah, and Mourvèdre must constitute 90 percent of the red wine blends. Pic St.-Loup holds potential to be a high quality wine area.

MORTIÈS

1 9 9 9

PIC SAINT-LOUP

Coteaux du Languedoc
Appellation Coteaux du Languedoc Contrôlée

750 ML
ALC. 13.5% BY VOL.
PRODUCT OF FRANCE

RED LANGUEDOC WINE
Mis en bouteille au Mas de Mortiès
Duchemin-Jorcin vignerons
34270 St-Jean-de-Cuculles

SYMAPS

Figure 13-2: This wine hails from Pic Saint-Loup, one of the specific vine-yard areas within the Coteaux du Languedoc zone.

Two other zones within Coteaux du Languedoc making better than average wine are La Clape and Montpeyroux. The remaining zones are St.-Saturnin, La Méjanelle, Cabrières, Quatourze, St.-Christol, St.-Drézéry, Vérargues, and St.-Georges d'Orques.

Besides Coteaux du Languedoc, the Languedoc-Roussillon region has numerous other AOC areas. The following is a round-up of the region's principal AOC wine districts and their important wines:

- **Corbières** *(cor bee air):* This large area in the Pyrénées foothills of southwestern Languedoc, comprised of 11 sub-districts, is perhaps the region's most well-known and most important red wine area. Dense, dark, full-bodied, spicy, dry red wines are the specialty. Carignan is the dominant grape variety, but Syrah and Mourvèdre are increasingly being planted, and Cinsault is also used. White Corbières derives from ten local varieties.

- **Minervois** *(mee ner vwah):* This old Roman wine area is in western Languedoc, north of Corbières. Its red wines are generally softer and more supple than those of Corbières, but capable of aging for several years. In an effort to upgrade the wine, AOC regulations have reduced Carignan to no more than 40 percent of the blend, with

Grenache, Syrah, Mourvèdre, and other local varieties making up the balance. White Minervois, from six local varieties, also exists.

✔ **Fitou** *(fee too):* This entirely red wine district is situated on the Mediterranean coast of Languedoc between Corbières and the Roussillon sub-region. The best wines come from the slopes of the Pyrénées, farther inland. Fitou is dominated by wine cooperatives, not private estates. Carignan and Grenache are the main varieties in the medium- to full-bodied, rustic, dry red wines, but more and more Syrah and Mourvèdre are being used.

✔ **Faugères** *(foh jhair):* The mainly red wines of this Languedoc district come from the slopes of the Cévennes Mountains northeast of the Minervois area. They are full-bodied, spicy, rustic, dry, but fruity wines; the previously omnipresent Carignan is now limited to 40 percent in Faugères' red wine blends, with Syrah, Grenache, and Mourvèdre becoming more important; Cinsault and Lladoner Pelut are also allowed.

✔ **St.-Chinian** *(san shin ee an):* This area located between Minervois and Faugères, in the foothills of the Cévennes, makes very full-bodied, dry red wines as well as some dry rosés. Carignan and Cinsault are gradually being replaced with Syrah, Grenache, and Mourvèdre.

✔ **Clairette du Languedoc** *(clair et doo lahn guh doc):* This tiny but longstanding AOC area makes only white wines from the Clairette Blanche variety.

✔ **Clairette de Bellegarde** *(clair et deh bel gahr):* Another tiny AOC area making whites entirely from Clairette; it's southeast of Costières de Nîmes.

✔ **Costières de Nîmes** *(cos t'yair deh neem):* This is the easternmost district of the Languedoc, separated from the southern Côtes-du-Rhône vineyards by the Rhône River. It shares the soil (including the stones) and climate of the Côtes-du-Rhône, and the major variety of the Southern Rhône, Grenache, is also dominant here. But Syrah is slowly replacing Carignan in the blend, and becoming a major factor in the wines. About 75 percent of the wines are medium-bodied reds — but some powerful, dry rosés and a small amount of white wines also exist. The whites are based on Clairette, Grenache Blanc, Bourboulenc, and Ugni Blanc.

✔ **Côtes du Roussillon:** This is the most southerly appellation zone in France, in the Pyrénées, next to the Spanish border; it covers the lower two-thirds of the Roussillon region. Naturally, the district has a strong Spanish influence. The wines are mainly big, spicy red wines, made primarily from Carignan with at least 40 percent from a blend of varieties in which Syrah and Mourvèdre must make up half; Grenache, Lladoner Pelut, and Cinsault are also permitted. This area also makes some fruity dry rosés, as well as floral, robust, dry whites made from the Spanish Maccabéo variety, Grenache Blanc, and other grapes. Château de Jau is a major producer.

✔ **Côtes du Roussillon-Villages:** This appellation area makes up the northern part of the Côtes du Roussillon zone (the upper-third of Roussillon), and is south of Corbières and Fitou. It's an all-red wine zone consisting of 28 villages. The wines derive from basically the same varieties as the red wines of the Côtes du Roussillon, but production requirements are more stringent, and the wines are generally higher in quality.

Four villages can append their names to the Côtes du Roussillon Villages appellation. They are Caramany, Latour de France, Lesquerde, and Tautavel. Production is limited, but the wines are powerful and of high quality.

✔ **Banyuls** *(bahn yule):* Named after the picturesque town of Banyuls, this area of terraced hillside vineyards sits on the Mediterranean coast, north of the Spanish border, and at the southeast corner of Roussillon. It's France's leading district for production of *vins doux naturels* (sweet, fortified wines known, in short, as VDNs). Banyuls can be red, rosé, tawny, or white; the red is the richest and most acclaimed, but the white, which turns old-gold in color with aging, is the most commonly produced. Grenache is the dominant grape variety in Banyuls. Dr. Parcé is *the* renowned producer of Banyuls wines; his wines are in the $55 to $60 price range.

✔ **Collioure** *(coh lee or):* This seaside village in the Banyuls district has a separate appellation; from this area comes a rich, spicy, high-alcohol (up to 15 percent) red wine made from overripe grapes. Mourvèdre, Syrah, and Grenache are the main varieties. Collioure wines are technically dry, but the very ripe flavors give the impression of sweetness. Look for Dr. Parcé's Collioure wines, in the $35 to $40 price range.

- **Muscat de Frontignan** *(moos cah deh fron tee nyahn):* Frontignan is a village on the Mediterranean coast, just northeast of the port town of Sète, in the Languedoc region. Of various fortified, sweet, spicy Muscats made in the region, Muscat de Frontignan is the most-renowned; it's a VDN made solely from the Muscat Blanc à Petit Grains (also known as Muscat of Frontignan), the most popular Muscat variety. (See "Unnatural process, natural sweetness" in this chapter for more info on the fortified dessert wines of Languedoc-Rousillon.)

- **Blanquette de Limoux** *(blahn ket deh lee moo):* The zone for this sparkling wine is in southwest Languedoc, west of Corbières; the small town of Limoux is in the heart of the zone. This area has a distinctly cool microclimate, high in the Pyrénées foothills and away from any Mediterranean influence (for which reason it is sometimes classified as part of southwest, rather than southern, France). Natives of the area maintain that the world's first sparkling wine was made in 1531 at the Abbey of St.-Hilaire in Limoux. Blanquette de Limoux is a good-value, white sparkling wine made from a minimum of 90 percent Mauzac (known locally as Blanquette), sometimes with Chardonnay and Chenin Blanc.

Languedoc fringe dwellers

Two wine districts of Languedoc can easily be classified as part of either Southwest France or Languedoc-Roussillon, depending on the criteria being used. They are part of Languedoc-Roussillon, but their climate is more similar to that of wine zones in the Southwest. These two areas are the following:

- **Cabardès** *(cah bar dez):* This sizeable area is north of the city of Carcassonne. The climate is somewhat maritime, from Atlantic influences, and also Mediterranean. The grape varieties, for red and rosé wines, are also of two minds: They include the Cabernets, Merlot, and Malbec of Bordeaux, as well as Syrah, Grenache, Fer Servadou, Cinsault, and a declining amount of Carignan. This area has attracted innovative winemakers such as the Australian Nerida Abbott, who blends Syrah and Grenache with Bordeaux varieties to make a rich, flavorful wine more typical of the New World.

Unnatural process, natural sweetness

The wines called *Vins Doux Natural,* or VDNs (translated as "naturally sweet wines"), have an ironic name. They're made by adding alcohol to grape juice that has barely begun fermenting; the high alcohol (about 15 percent) blocks any further fermentation. Doesn't sound very natural, does it? On the other hand, this process preserves the grapes' natural sweetness, by preventing it from being converted into alcohol. It also preserves the flavors of the juice in their most primary form.

France's VDN wines — made from Grenache, Macabeu, Torbato, Muscat à Petits Grains, or Muscat of Alexandria, depending on the wine — are a big specialty of Languedoc-Roussillon. The Roussillon versions include Banyuls, Maury, Rivesaltes, and Muscat de Rivesaltes. Languedoc produces four Muscat-based VDNs: Muscat de Frontignan, Muscat de Lunel, Muscat de Mireval and Muscat de St. Jean de Minervois.

↙ **Côtes de la Malepère** *(coat deh lah mahl pair):* This area south of Cabardès and north of the Blanquette de Limoux vineyards has a more distinctly maritime climate because mountains near Corbières block it from Mediterranean influence. Merlot and Malbec, along with Cinsault in some parts of the area, are the main thrust here, but both Cabernets, Grenache, and Syrah are also allowed. Carignan is not allowed. The wines are mainly red.

Beautiful Provence

Provence *(pro vahn's)* is perhaps France's most beautiful region — and it's certainly its most fashionable and touristic. Provence is in southeastern France, east of Languedoc-Roussillon, southeast of the Southern Rhône, just south of the Alps, and west of Northern Italy (see Figure 13-3). The region's southern border is the Mediterranean Sea. Provence is the playground of France, the home of the Riviera (the *Côte d'Azur),* Nice, Cannes, and the bustling seaport of Marseilles, France's second-largest city.

In many ways, Provence is timeless. The old capital of the once-independent region, the town of Aix-en-Provence, is still an important wine area. And the ancient language, Provençal, continues to be spoken by the older natives of Provence, just as it was when Vincent Van Gogh was painting all those brilliant landscapes here. The excellent light and climate of Provence have always attracted great artists, who painted some of their best works there.

Today, wine remains an integral part of Provence's culture and economy. The region makes about 40 million cases of red, white, and rosé wine annually.

Figure 13-3: Provence has several AOC zones, small and large.

Climate and soil

The climate of Provence is classic Mediterranean: very warm summers, mild winters, and little rainfall. The famous wind that sweeps down from the north, the *mistral,* minimizes the threat of diseases to the vineyards; on the other hand, vines must be planted in protected areas to avoid destruction by the fierce wind. Many of the best vineyards are near the sea-coast, where cool breezes minimize the effects of sometimes harsh and brutally hot weather.

The soil is so variable throughout Provence that generalizations are difficult. One significant pattern is pockets of limestone and shale in the hillsides; in the Cassis AOC zone on the Mediterranean, for example, the calcareous clay of the hillside vineyards is perfect for the cultivation of white grape varieties.

The wines of Provence

Provence has always been known for its rosé wines (all the rave among tourists at beachside cafés), which still dominate production — despite the fact that many Provençal rosés are quite innocuous. But more producers are now making good red wine, for which the climate is well suited. Over one-third of Provençal wines are now red, and there's a small amount of white wine, including some interesting ones.

Provence has eight AOC wine zones, which are responsible for most of its wines. They are the following:

- ✔ **Côtes de Provence:** This huge area of 85 communes and 400 producers is the largest in Provence, accounting for about 75 percent of the region's wine production. Eighty percent of Côtes de Provence's wines are rosé, with 15 percent red and 5 percent white; red wine production, however, is increasing. To improve quality, no more than 40 percent of the prolific Carignan variety is now allowed in Côtes de Provence's red wines; 60 percent of the blend must be Grenache, Cinsault, Mourvèdre, and Tibouren (a local variety). Joining these varieties, more and more Syrah and Cabernet Sauvignon are going into the district's red and rosé wines. A favorite producer of ours is Domaine Richeaume, for its red and excellent rosé wines.

- ✔ **Coteaux d'Aix-en-Provence** *(coh toh dex on pro vahn's):* This AOC zone, the second-largest in Provence, occupies the western and northwestern part of the region; it covers about 50 villages, including the historic town of Aix-en-Provence. The wines are generally of a higher level than Côtes de Provence wines, and the emphasis on red wines is greater: 60 percent of the production is red, 35 percent is rosé, and 5 percent is white. Grenache, Cinsault, and Mourvèdre are the dominant varieties in the red and rosé wines, but Cabernet Sauvignon is making inroads; in fact, the reds are permitted to be as much as 60 percent Cabernet. A top producer is Château Vignelaure, which makes a Bordeaux-style red wine based on Cabernet Sauvignon. Château Calissane and Château Revelette make excellent wines, with *prestige cuvees* produced from Syrah and Cabernet Sauvignon.

- **Les Baux-de-Provence** *(lay boh deh pro vahn's):* This district, in the northwest corner of Provence, was until recently a part of Coteaux d'Aix-en-Provence, but now is an independent AOC zone. At its center is the renowned, scenic, hilltop village, Les Baux-de-Provence, with many starred restaurants. Red wines dominate production (80 percent), most of which are deeply-colored and full-bodied; the remaining 20 percent of production is dry, mainly full-bodied rosés. Grenache, Mourvèdre, and Syrah, which must make up at least 60 percent of the AOC red wine blends, are the primary red varieties. The best and most-renowned wine estate here is Domaine de Trévallon, which makes a non-AOC wine of the same name composed of 60 percent Cabernet Sauvignon and 40 percent Syrah. Two other top wine estates in the Les Baux-de-Provence district are Mas de la Dame (Figure 13-4 depicts a label) and Domaine des Terres Blanches.

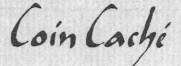

Coin Caché

N° 1997

Figure 13-4: This Grenache–Syrah blend comes from Mas de la Dame, one of the great wine estates in Provence.

✔ **Coteaux Varois** *(coh toh var whah):* This district is named after the Var *département,* in which the main part of Provence lies. The Coteaux Varois AOC zone is situated in hilly central Provence, between Côtes de Provence and Coteaux d'Aix-en-Provence. Rosés dominate the district's production, along with one-third red and a little bit of white wine. Grenache, Syrah, Cinsault, Mourvèdre, Cabernet Sauvignon, and Carignan are all used in varying proportions for red and rosé wines. From Coteaux Varois, look for the good-value wines of Château Routas.

✔ **Bandol:** This AOC district has the greatest reputation of all Provence's appellations for its wines — especially its red wines. Located in southwest Provence, bordering the Mediterranean Sea, it encompasses the town of Bandol, an old fishing village right on the coast that's a popular holiday resort. Eight communities make up the Bandol AOC zone, with the best vineyards on the hillsides a couple of miles in from the coast. The stony, silico-limestone soil and the warm climate are perfect for the late-ripening Mourvèdre variety, which thrives here.

Red Bandol AOC wines must be at least half Mourvèdre; Grenache and Cinsault are two other important components, for both red and rosé wines. Bandol is mainly red, but rosés represent about a third of the wines, and a little bit of white wine also exists. The reds are dark, rich, intense, and complex, with black fruit flavors; they require at least ten years to fully develop. The leading producer of red Bandol is the renowned Domaine Tempier, clearly one of Provence's finest wine estates. Mas de la Rivière and Domaine de Pibarnon are two other fine red wine producers. Bandol is also home for Domaines Ott, famous for its rosés and earthy whites.

✔ **Cassis** *(cahs seese):* This wine has no relation to the black currant liqueur of the same name. Cassis is the one AOC district in Provence where white wines dominate, with over 75 percent of the production. Cassis is a small district on the coast, and also the name of a small, pretty fishing village, ten miles west of Bandol and close to the city of Marseilles. Its vineyards are now being protected by law from further encroachment by land developers from Marseilles. The white wines, grown in limestone soil, are made mainly from Clairette and Marsanne, with some Ugni Blanc and Sauvignon Blanc; they are full-bodied, dry, low-acid, herbal-scented wines that are great with the local specialty, *bouillabaisse*. The wine is so popular locally (especially in summer) that the rest of the world sees little of it. Domaine de La Ferme Blanche is a major producer. Red and rosé wines from Cassis are less distinguished; the whites are the stars.

✔ **Bellet** *(behl lay):* This small AOC district is in southeastern Provence, in the hills above the city of Nice, where urban sprawl threatens the vineyards. Equal parts of red, white, and rosé wines are made, but the fresh, fragrant whites, made from Rolle (Italy's Vermentino), Roussanne, Chardonnay, and Clairette, are Bellet's best wines. Sadly, most Bellet wines never leave the *Côte d'Azur.*

✔ **Palette** *(pah let):* East of the town of Aix-en-Provence, Palette is Provence's smallest AOC district; in fact, most of its vineyards, which are on limestone soil, are owned by one wine estate, Château Simone. This estate produces rich, long-lived reds, rosés, and white wines. The red and rosé — made mainly from Grenache, Mourvèdre, and Cinsault — resemble Southern Rhône wines, as does the white, which is made chiefly from Ugni Blanc.

Chapter 14

Other French Wine Regions

*T*his is the chapter in which we put together four wine regions that just didn't seem to fit into other chapters. They are very diverse. The largest of the four, Southwest France, is actually a group of smaller regions which we combine for convenience's sake. What the Southwest France subregions do have in common is one big climatic influence — the Atlantic Ocean.

Two other regions, the Jura and Savoie, do have something in common: geography. Both are in the foothills and/or slopes of the Alps, tucked away in eastern France, next to Switzerland. And both specialize in white wines. (But the Jura has a couple of "white" wines of its own that are quite unique.)

Corsica, the birthplace of Napoleon, is a large island that's closer to Sardinia and to mainland Italy than to France. And perhaps closer in wine styles and in temperament as well. Some writers, when discussing French wine regions, attempt to link Corsica with Provence, its nearest neighbor in France. But the only thing the two regions have in common is their Italian influence. Rugged Corsica stands alone.

Southwest France

Southwest France, with its main city, Toulouse, at its center, includes wine regions next to Bordeaux (such as Bergerac and Monbazillac), and Cahors (its most famous region), right down to the tiny Basque area of Irouléguy in the Pyrénées, on the Spanish border (see Figure 1-1).

The entire Southwest France region mainly has a maritime (temperate) climate, influenced by the Atlantic Ocean to its west. Many of the red wines of the region are made from Cabernet Sauvignon, Cabernet Franc, and Merlot, with Malbec the main variety in Cahors; a local red variety, Tannat, is also used in Cahors and in other southwest regions. Some good white wines, both dry and sweet, are made throughout Southwest France from local varieties.

The wines of Southwest France are still fairly obscure because historically, they didn't have the opportunity to gain the international recognition of Bordeaux wines. The entire region — especially the areas close to Bordeaux, such as Bergerac and Cahors — suffered discrimination at the hands of the Bordeaux merchants and shippers during the centuries following the Middle Ages. Their wines were over-taxed and shipped abroad late, always after all the Bordeaux wines were shipped; these factors hindered their commercial success abroad. The wine producers of the inland, southwest areas depended on Bordeaux to sell and ship their wines, however, and had no recourse.

Bergerac

The Bergerac *(ber jhe rak)* region is the largest wine-producing area in Southwest France. It's situated in the province of Périgord, directly east of Bordeaux. The town of Bergerac, on the Dordogne River, is the winemaking center. It's a famous prehistoric area, with ancient cave drawings; its more modern works of art include *foie gras* and black truffles.

The Bergerac region makes very Bordeaux-like red wines under the Bergerac AOC designation — using all the Bordeaux varieties, especially Merlot — but without Bordeaux prices. The best Bergerac reds are barrel-aged wines from lower-yielding vineyards, and they carry the appellation Côtes de Bergerac.

Actually, almost half of Bergerac's wines are white, and a little dry rosé exists as well. The dry whites carry the AOC designation, Bergerac Sec, and derive mainly from Sémillon and Sauvignon Blanc; Muscadelle, Ondenc, and Chenin Blanc are other authorized varieties. They're similar to lighter-styled white Bordeaux wines, and are good values, often costing as little as $7 a bottle. We recommend them highly for parties, but with one caveat: They should be no more than three years old, or they won't be fresh.

About 25 percent of Bergerac's white wines are sweet wines made from Sémillon; they carry the appellation Côtes de Bergerac Moelleux.

The greater Bergerac area encompasses four other AOC zones: Monbazillac, Rosette, Montravel, and Pécharmant. We include three additional AOC areas, Côtes du Marmandais, Côtes de Duras, and Buzet, in our discussion of the Bergerac area, because they are close.

Monbazillac

The Monbazillac *(mon bah zee yak)* AOC area lies just south of the town of Bergerac. This area specializes in sweet, *botrytis*-affected dessert wines similar to Sauternes. (See Chapter 6 for an explanation of *botrytis*-affected wines.) In fact, Monbazillac wines are made from the same varieties as Sauternes — Sémillon, Sauvignon Blanc, and Muscadelle. They're less expensive than Sauternes, but they lack Sauternes' complexity and aging ability.

West of Monbazillac, **Saussignac** is a small, separate appellation for sweet whites based on Sémillon and Muscadelle, with Chenin Blanc and Sauvignon Blanc also permitted.

Pécharmant

The Pécharmant *(peh shar mahn)* AOC zone, just east of the town of Bergerac, specializes in medium- to full-bodied Bordeaux-like reds mainly from Merlot, with Cabernet Franc and Cabernet Sauvignon, and sometimes Malbec. These are the most long-lived red wines in the Bergerac region; most of the small production stays within the region.

Next to Pécharmant is the even smaller appellation of **Rosette**, which makes sweet white wines from the same varieties as Monbazillac.

Montravel

On the western edge of Bergerac region, next to the Bordeaux region, the Montravel AOC area specializes in crisp, white wines made mainly from Sémillon, Sauvignon Blanc, and Muscadelle. Two separate appellations, Côtes de Montravel and Haut-Montravel, apply to small quantities of semi-sweet and sweet wines from Sémillon, Sauvignon Blanc, and Muscadelle.

Côtes de Duras

The town of Duras centers this AOC district, southwest of Bergerac and adjacent to the Entre-Deux-Mers district of Bordeaux. The same grape varieties as in Bordeaux make up the Côtes de Duras dry red wines; dry and sweet white wines come from the white Bordeaux varieties. Both styles of its white wines are superior to its reds.

Côtes du Marmandais

This district, situated on the Garonne River and surrounding the town of Marmande, gained AOC status in 1990. It's just east of the Graves and Entre-Deux-Mers districts of Bordeaux, and south of the Côtes de Duras. The Garonne's cooling effect results in relatively light red wines. These reds derive up to 75 percent from the red Bordeaux varieties, with the remainder coming from the local Arbouriou variety, plus the Fer, Gamay, and Syrah varieties. Also, a small amount of dry whites is made mainly from Sauvignon Blanc.

Buzet

This almost exclusively red wine district is situated on the Garonne River, 60 miles southeast of the city of Bordeaux, and just north of the Armagnac region (where grapes for Armagnac, a spirit, grow). The town of Buzet *(boo zay)* and 26 other communes comprise the AOC zone. The wines are very Bordeaux-like, barrel-aged reds made from Merlot, Cabernet Sauvignon, Cabernet Franc, and Malbec, and are produced mainly by one modern cooperative. Buzet reds are very good values. This area also makes whites from white Bordeaux varieties.

Côtes de Brulhois wines come from an area to the southeast of Buzet. They are dark reds made from Tannat and the red Bordeaux varieties.

Cahors and Vicinity

Cahors *(cah or)* is the second-largest wine-producing district in Southwest France, after Bergerac. The town of Cahors, situated on the Lot River, is the capital of the Lot *département* and is about 120 miles southeast of the city of Bordeaux.

The Cahors area makes red wine only; in fact, it's the most prestigious red wine district in all of Southwest France, and has a wine history older than Bordeaux's. But history hasn't always been kind to Cahors. The *phylloxera* epidemic (a louse that wiped out European vineyards in the late 19th century) devastated the area to such an extent that the wine has made a comeback only in the last 40 years.

Cahors AOC wines come from the territory of 45 communes near the town of Cahors. They must derive at least 70 percent from Malbec (locally, called Auxerrois), with the remainder Tannat and/or Merlot. Two distinct styles of Cahors exist:

- The dark, tannic, traditional reds — mainly Malbec, coming from the hillsides — need about 10 years to soften, and can live for 20 or more years.

- The lighter, fruitier reds, mainly from the plains, use more Merlot and Tannat; they are drinkable within a few years of the vintage.

Cahors wines are arguably the finest expression of the Malbec grape variety in the world. We recommend traditional producers, such as Château Lagrezette (retail price, $18 to $24).

Two other AOC zones are close enough to Cahors that we describe them in the following sections.

Côtes du Frontonnais

This area takes its name from the town of Fronton, on the Garonne River south of Cahors and north of Toulouse. Côtes du Frontonnais is a red wine area, with some rosés; most of its wines are consumed in Toulouse.

Côtes du Frontonnais wines are unique in that they are made (50 to 70 percent) from a very aromatic, local red variety called Négrette; other varieties used are Fer, Syrah, and both

Cabernets. Frontonnais reds are fruity and supple; they are low in tannin and acidity, and are best when served cool. Drink them within two years of the vintage.

Gaillac

Gaillac *(gah yahk)* is one of the oldest wine-producing areas in France, dating back to Gallo-Roman times, in the 1st century A.D. The small town of Gaillac, 30 miles northeast of Toulouse, is on the Tarn River — as is the district's major city, Albi (one of the more beautiful cities in France). A total of 78 communities produce Gaillac AOC wines.

The wines of Gaillac are very diverse: Powerful, spicy dark reds, made mainly from local varieties such as Duras and Fer Servadou, as well as Syrah, make up 60 percent of the total production; rosés are made from the same varieties, plus Gamay; white wines come in both dry and sweet styles, with Mauzac the principal variety in the dry whites, and Sémillon and Muscadelle in the sweet whites. Sweet wines are often labeled Gaillac Doux, or the even better Gaillac Premières Côtes AOC — for wines made from grapes grown on special limestone slopes. Some dry whites also fall under the Gaillac Premières Côtes AOC.

But wait, there's more. Perhaps Gaillac's most renowned wines are its sparkling wines, carrying the Gaillac Mousseux AOC. Produced mainly from the Mauzac grape, these sparkling wines come in two styles: A dry, slightly *pétillant* wine sold as "Gaillac Perlé" and made by the usual *méthode champenoise* (see *Champagne For Dummies* by Ed McCarthy, published by Hungry Minds, for more info of this term); and a fruity, lightly sparkling wine made by the traditional local *méthode gaillaçoise* (the wine is bottled when it has only partially finished its first fermentation, leaving it semi-sweet).

Drink both styles while they are young; they don't age well.

Marcillac

This small, mountainous appellation zone is west of Cahors. It specializes in potent red wines (and some rosés) made mainly from the Fer Sevradou variety.

Béarn

Béarn is an area in extreme Southwest France, close to the Atlantic Ocean and to the Spanish border. The greater Béarn *(beh arn)* area, famous for Béarnaise sauce, includes the districts of Madiran and Jurançon, both individual AOC zones, as well as several anonymous wine areas. We include Irouléguy AOC in this section, because it's closer to Béarn than to any other wine region of France.

The Béarn AOC itself applies to strongly-flavored red wines as well as rosé wines deriving up to 60 percent from Tannat, along with both Cabernets and other local varieties. The Béarn AOC actually covers white wine as well, but production is miniscule.

Madiran

The AOC red wine district of Madiran *(mah dee rahn)* produces old-style, full-bodied, tannic reds, perfect for the hearty cuisine of the local Gascony province. The main grape in Madiran is the dark, tannic Tannat (40 to 60 percent of the blend); Cabernet Sauvignon and Cabernet Franc make up the remainder. Traditionally-made Madiran wines need about ten years to soften.

Dry and sweet white wines from Madiran are marketed under the Pacherenc du Vic-Bilh AOC *(pah sher onk doo veek beal)*. Local varieties such as Arrufiac, Courbu, and Petit Manseng are the main grapes.

Madiran has recently gained winelovers' attention thanks to the efforts of Alain Brumont of Château Montus and Château Bouscassé.

Jurançon

The Jurançon *(joo rahn sohn)* AOC district produces white wines only, both dry and sweet. A particularly beautiful area, Jurançon is located in the Pyrénées-Atlantiques *département,* near the Spanish border. Its major city is Pau, directly north of the town of Jurançon.

This district won its fame for its sweet wines, but it is the dry white, using the AOC Jurançon Sec, that dominates production today. Both wines use the same three local varieties: Petit Manseng, Gros Manseng, and Courbu. Gros Manseng is the chief variety in the floral, intensely-flavored Jurançon Sec; Petit

Manseng dominates the sweet, tangy, luscious AOC Jurançon, which is late-harvested, and which often comes from botrytized grapes, just as in Sauternes (see Chapter 6). Jurançon is a good-value wine, but not so complex as Sauternes.

Irouléguy

Just before you cross the Spanish border, in the heart of Basque country, you come across the last French AOC district, Irouléguy *(ee roo leh ghee)*, where terraced vineyards hug the slopes of the Pyrénées. The language is not French nor Spanish here; it is Basque, and so you'll see a lot of "Xs," common in the difficult-to-read Basque tongue, on the wine labels. A village called Irouléguy does exist, but the main town in this small, isolated district is St.-Jean-Pied-de-Port. Tannat is the principal grape variety in the rich, spicy, tannic reds and fragrant, powerful rosés, but both Cabernet varieties go into the wines as well. White Irouléguy derives from Courbu and Manseng varieties. Look for the wines of Domaine Brana.

Jura

The Jura *(joo rah)* wine region is in the mountain range of the same name (really the foothills of the Alps) in the extreme east-central part of France, not far from the Swiss border (see Figure 1-1). Jura is directly east of, and runs parallel to, Burgundy's Côte d'Or district. The Jura resembles the Côte d'Or in that it's long rather than wide, and its vineyards face south and southeast. From the town of Arbois in the north, the vineyards run along the Jura's western slopes 50 miles to the south — never more than four miles wide.

The Jura is a small region, wine-wise, producing only one percent of France's wine. More than half of its wine is white, and much of the rest is rosé. The climate is continental, with quite a bit of rain, and very cold winters.

Jura is chiefly renowned for its two distinct wines: Its "Yellow Wines" *(Vins Jaunes)* — made nowhere else in France — and its "Straw Wines" *(Vins de Paille)*, a little of which is also made in the Northern Rhône, but which is a specialty here. We describe these wines in sidebars in this section.

Jura has four AOC wine areas: Arbois, Côtes du Jura, Château-Chalon, and L'Etoile.

The Yellow Wines of Jura

Clearly the Jura's most distinctive and interesting wine is Vin Jaune *(van joh'n),* the so-called "Yellow Wine." It is made from the Savagnin grape variety in all of the region's AOC districts, but is the exclusive specialty of the village (and appellation) of Château-Chalon.

Vin Jaune is comparable to a light Spanish Fino Sherry, but it's not fortified. The wine is made from late-picked, but not botrytized, Savagnin grapes (see Chapter 6 for an explanation of botrytized grapes). The sweet juice undergoes a slow fermentation, and then ages for a minimum of six years in old oak barrels, in cool cellars. Because the barrels are never filled to the top, a powdery film of yeasts (similar to the *flor* that forms in Fino Sherry casks) eventually develops on the wine. Because of the oxidation that results from the wine's exposure to air, and the subsequent protective character of the yeast coating, the wine has both a nuttiness and a particular tangy character. The wines are deep golden yellow or amber in color, dry, powerful, and rich in extract. And they are practically ageless. Vin Jaune comes in unique, square 620 ml bottles called *clave-lins.* Unfortunately, Vin Jaune is difficult to find outside of France. But it's worth seeking out.

Arbois

The town of Arbois (*ahr bwah*) was the home of one of France's — and the world's — greatest scientists, Louis Pasteur. The Arbois AOC zone, in the northern part of Jura, produces about half of Jura's wines. Half of that is white — either Chardonnay, or more appealingly, blends in which the local Savagnin (*sah vah n'yan*) variety is used; Pinot Blanc is also allowed. Savagnin, a relative of Italy's Traminer variety, imparts an unusual nutty flavor, and is *the* variety in *Vin Jaune* (see "The Yellow Wines of Jura" sidebar in this chapter).

Arbois' red wines are really deep pink, and its rosés are even paler. Three varieties go into the reds and rosés: the local Poulsard and Trousseau — neither very distinguished — and Pinot Noir. These are wines to consume in their youth.

Yellow Wines and Straw Wines also come from Arbois, as well as sparkling wines labelled Arbois Mousseux AOC.

Arbois is the home base of Henri Maire, the Jura region's largest *négociant*-producer, who sells about half of Jura's wines.

The Straw Wines of Jura

Vin de Paille *(van deh pah'ee)*, commonly called "Straw Wine" — more for the traditional way that it's made than for its color — is a rich, deep golden or amber, sweet dessert wine made in small quantities by some producers throughout the Jura region, excepting Château-Chalon. (A particularly good version of Vin de Paille is also made occasionally by Hermitage producers such as Chave and Chapoutier in the Northern Rhône).

Vin de Paille is very much like Tuscany's Vin Santo (See *Italian Wine For Dummies*, also written by us and published by Hungry Minds, Inc.), both in appearance and flavor as well as in winemaking methods. Ripe but not botrytized grapes (in the Jura, it's usually Savagnin or Chardonnay) are harvested late (in especially ripe vintages), and then placed on straw mats or in baskets and/or hung from the rafters in dry attics for two months or more; the grapes shrivel up like raisins, and become very concentrated in grape sugar, and luscious. Then a very slow fermentation takes place, sometimes taking years to complete. The resulting wine is not only full, rich, and concentrated, but also very nutty and raisiny, with good natural acidity. Because producing Vin de Paille is such a laborious process, fewer and fewer producers in the Jura are making it nowadays.

Côtes du Jura

The Côtes du Jura district is south of Arbois and is the second-largest appellation in the region, spread over 12 communes. Its wines include white, red, rosé, sparkling, Yellow Wines, and Straw Wines; they're similar in style and grape varieties to those of Arbois, but generally a bit lighter. White wines are dominant in the Côtes du Jura, as reds and rosés make up only about 20 percent of the district's production. The town of Arlay, in the Côtes du Jura, is the home of the Jura's best producer, Château d'Arlay.

Château-Chalon

This AOC zone within the Côtes du Jura district makes only one wine — and then only in decent vintages — Jura's famous Vin Jaune. Château-Chalon is the most distinguished and renowned of all the Vins Jaunes.

Despite its name, Château-Chalon is not an individual wine estate; it's a hilltop village whose vineyards produce the white Savagnin grape variety, the only variety allowed in Vin Jaune.

Château-Chalon wine is deep golden brown in color, with a particularly nutty flavor, and can last for decades.

L'Etoile

L'Etoile _(leh t'wahl)_ is a small AOC zone in the southern Jura whose three communes, including the village of Etoile, produce small amounts of white wine, Vin Jaune, and Vin de Paille, as well as sparkling wines called L'Etoile Mousseux. The specialty of L'Etoile — indeed the specialty of all of Jura — is Vin Jaune.

Savoie

The French Alpine region of Savoie _(sah v'wah)_ vies with Corsica for the dubious title of least-known wine region in France. Even the Jura, whose wines we don't see often, is well-known compared to Savoie.

The Savoie region (sometimes anglicized as "Savoy"), like Jura, is in the extreme eastern part of France (see Figure 1-1). Jura is to the north, Switzerland and Northwest Italy directly east, with the city of Lyons and the Beaujolais region to the west. The nearest city to Savoie — and the best entry way if you're travelling there directly — is Geneva, Switzerland. Savoie is close to the huge Lake Geneva (Lac Léman), which undoubtedly has a moderating influence on the climate of this mountainous region.

Savoie is a winter sports area (Annecy, Aprémont, and other French ski areas are nearby, and Grenoble is just south) and a summer recreation center — which is the main reason that not much of the wine leaves the region. Savoie produces some light red and rosé wine, and some decent sparkling wines, but — as you might expect in this cool, mountainous region — most of its production is crisp, dry white wine. The Savoie region has two distinct sub-regions:

- ✔ The vineyard area to the north, around the shores of the French side of Lake Geneva (in the Haute-Savoie _département_)

- ✔ The larger region to the south (in the Savoie _département_), where the villages of Seyssel and Aprémont and the towns of Aix-les-Bains and Chambéry are located.

Many of the southern Savoie vineyards are on the banks of the Rhône River, flowing down from Lake Geneva towards the Rhône Valley.

Savoie has one region-wide AOC (called Vin de Savoie) and three other AOCs within that appellation. What follows is a brief description of the wines in these AOC zones:

- ✔ **Vin de Savoie:** Most (about 85 percent) of the region's wines carry this general appellation, about 70 percent of which are delicate white wines. Local varieties, such as Jacquère, Roussette, Malvoisie, and Mondeuse Blanche, along with Chardonnay and Aligoté, are the dominant white varieties. Gamay, Mondeuse (a red variety called Refosco in Italy's Friuli region), and/or Pinot Noir go into the light red and rosé wines.

- ✔ **Roussette de Savoie:** A separate appellation within the Vin de Savoie AOC zone for white wines made primarily or entirely from Roussette, Savoie's best variety. If one of four villages (Frangy, Marestel, Monteminod, or Monthoux) is appended to the Roussette de Savoie appellation, the wine must be 100 percent Roussette. Otherwise, Chardonnay can be added, too.

- ✔ **Crépy** *(creh pee):* A small white wine AOC for vineyards along the south shore of Lake Geneva in Haute-Savoie. The grape variety for Crépy is Chasselas (often called Fendant in Switzerland's Valais area). The dry, light wines of Crépy in fact resemble Swiss wines.

- ✔ **Seyssel** *(say sell):* Perhaps Savoie's best-known appellation. The village of Seyssel is located on the banks of the Rhône River, just north of Lac du Bourget, France's largest lake. Seyssel AOC wines are dry, light whites made mainly from Roussette. Seyssel often has delicate, herbal and floral aromas, and is one of the region's best wines. Less than a third of the AOC production of Seyssel is light sparkling wine under the name Seyssel Mousseux AOC; it uses mainly Chasselas. Although much Seyssel Mousseux is consumed locally, some is exported.

The Savoie region also has two region-wide appellations for sparkling wines: Vin de Savoie Mousseux, made from the Molette variety, and Vin de Savoie Pétillant (for slightly sparkling wines), made from the same varieties as the local still white wine, with the addition of Molette.

To the west of Savoie is another wine zone called **Bugey** (*boo jhay*). The Vin de Bugey wines are very similar to those of Savoie. They include white, red, and rosé wines from grape varieties similar to those used in Savoie. Wines made entirely from one variety are labelled with that variety's name.

Corsica

Corsica is a large, mountainous island 100 miles southeast of the mainland region of Provence. It is, of course, a French *département,* but it's only a few miles north of the Italian island of Sardinia, and only 50 miles from the Italian mainland. In fact, Corsica was part of the city-state of Genoa for over four centuries (from 1347 to 1768), but Genoa, tired of dealing with unrest on the island, sold Corsica to France. To this day, Corsica is fiercely independent.

Corsica's proximity to Italy and its history have brought many Italian grape varieties to this birthplace of Napoleon. In fact, Corsican wines *do* resemble Italian wines more than French.

Most of the wine made in Corsica — mainly by cooperatives — is strictly *vin ordinaire.* But the island has three AOCs, all located around the temperate coastal areas. AOC wines, in fact, are now 24 percent of total Corsican production.

Well over 50 percent of Corsica's wines are red — mainly medium- to full-bodied, dry, fruity wines — with 30 percent rosés, 10 percent dry white wines, and a small amount of dessert and sparkling wines. The rosés and the whites are dry and quite full-bodied.

The three AOC areas and their wines are the following:

✔ **Vin de Corse** *(van deh corse):* This is the region-wide appellation, and it covers about 45 percent of Corsica's AOC wines; sometimes, a particular sub-district, such as "Calvi" or "Figari" is appended to *Vin de Corse* on the label. The main varieties for red and rosé wines here are Nielluccio (thought to be related to the Tuscan Sangiovese), the local Sciacarello, and Grenache; these three varieties must constitute at least 50 percent of all AOC red and rosé Vin de Corse wines. The white wines must be at least 75 percent Vermentino — the leading variety in nearby Sardinia. In terms of quality, Vin de Corse wines are the least of Corsica's three AOC wines.

- ✔ **Patrimonio** *(pah treh mo nee oh):* This zone on the northern tip of the island was Corsica's first AOC wine area, and is still its best. The chalk and clay soils in Patrimonio are well suited to the Nielluccio variety, which makes up at least 95 percent of the AOC red wines; its white AOC wines are 100 percent Vermentino.

- ✔ **Ajaccio** *(ah jahk see oh):* In the western part of Corsica; the vineyards surround the town of Ajaccio, Corsica's capital. Medium-bodied red and rosé wines, primarily from the Sciacarello variety, are the main wines of Ajaccio. A little white wine comes from Ugni Blanc and Vermentino.

Corsica's *vin de pays*-level wines carry the enticing name, Vin de Pays de l'Ile de Beauté — country wines of the Isle of Beauty.

Other French Regions

A few of France's wine zones refuse to fall neatly into any of the larger regions. Four such examples are the following:

- ✔ **Côte Roannaise** *(coat ro ahn naze):* An obscure area on the Loire River, near the river's source in central France, and west of Beaujolais. This appellation takes its name from the town of Roanne where the famous Troisgros restaurant is situated. The wines are light reds based on Gamay. The area has had AOC status only since 1996.

- ✔ **Côtes du Forez** *(coat doo for ay):* South of the Roannaise area, producing red and rosé wines from Gamay.

- ✔ **Côtes d'Auvergne** *(coat doh vair n'yeh):* West of Côtes du Forez, this area makes light reds and rosé from Gamay and Pinot Noir, and whites from Chardonnay.

- ✔ **St.-Pourçain** *(san por saan):* North of Côtes d'Auvergne, this area makes red wines from Gamay and Pinot Noir and crisp, light-bodied whites from two local varieties, Tressallier and St. Pierre-Doré, as well as Aligoté, Chardonnay, and Sauvignon Blanc.

Part IV
The Part of Tens

In this part . . .

Are all Burgundies expensive? Are Rosé Champagnes dry? We tackle these and other common questions about French wines in this part. Here we also debunk ten common myths that somehow still survive, such as the Myth of the Sweet Riesling and the Myth of Champagne, the Celebration-Only Wine.

Chapter 15

Answers to Ten Common Questions about French Wines

*W*hen we teach wine courses, we find that we keep answering the same questions about French wines. We've chosen ten of those frequently asked questions to answer here.

Why Are French Wines so Expensive?

We have to answer this question by saying, "They're not! At least not necessarily." Only a small percentage (less than 5 percent) of French wines are very expensive. They include:

✔ The most prestigious, sought-after Bordeaux (see Chapter 4)

✔ The best red and white Burgundies (see Chapter 7)

✔ A handful of the top Rhône wines (see Chapter 9)

✔ Prestige Cuvée Champagnes (see Chapter 10)

In general, Burgundy wines are the most expensive as a category, and the reason is simple: Demand far exceeds the limited supply.

So many French wines are under $15, and quite a few under $10 retail, that we simply can't categorize them as "expensive." For example, search out inexpensive red Bordeaux, Beaujolais, most Rhône wines, Alsace and Loire Valley wines, plus all the wines of the southern part of France — those from Languedoc-Roussillon, Provence, and Southwest France. Just about all of these wines are great values.

How Are French Wines Different from American Wines?

French wines are more nearly similar to other European wines than to the wines of the "New World" (such as the U.S., Chile, or Australia). French wines differ from American wines in three major ways:

✔ How the wines are named. Most French wines are named after the place they come from, such as "Bordeaux" or "Burgundy." American wines are named after their primary grape varieties, such as "Chardonnay" or "Merlot."

✔ Many French wines are made in cool or temperate-climate regions — such as Bordeaux, Burgundy, the Loire Valley, and Champagne — while very little American wine, volume-wise, is made in such cool climates. As cool-climate wines, French wines are lighter-bodied, lower in alcohol, and higher in acidity than warm-climate wines, such as many of California's wines. These characteristics enable many French wines to accompany food more graciously than do the fuller-bodied, high-alcohol American wines.

> ✔ French wines generally very much reflect their *terroir;* in other words, they speak the characteristics of the particular location where their grapes grew. Many American wines, especially the less expensive ones, speak the language of their grape variety: Trueness to varietal character is their main goal.

Are Rosé Champagnes Really Dry?

Yes, they are; moreover, they are as high in quality as any other Champagnes. Rosé Champagnes have an "image problem" with some people, especially in the U.S. Americans have been conditioned to believe that any wine that's pink must be sweet and ordinary, or even low in quality — partially because most American pink wines are sweet — and not very good. This is certainly *not* the case with rosé Champagne — or, in fact, with most European rosé wines.

Rosé Champagnes, which come in all beautiful shades, ranging from pale onion skin to rosy pink, are a particularly apt choice on romantic occasions. For Valentine's Day, a rosé Champagne is *de rigueur!* (See Chapter 10 for more information on rosé Champagne.)

Are French Wines the Best Wines?

Certain French wines do stand at the top of their class — they *are* the best wines of their type. This group includes the top red Bordeaux wines, the best red and white Burgundies and Rhônes, Champagne, Sauternes, and the Loire Valley's Chenin Blanc-based sweet wines. These wines are the standard against which producers of similar wines all over the world measure their own quality.

But plenty of French wines are ordinary, simple wines that make a good drink with the right food. Nowadays, many countries make wines at every level of quality from good to superb. France's wines run the same gamut, with a substantial edge in certain prestigious categories.

Do French Wines Age Long?

It really depends on the type of French wine. Certainly red Bordeaux wines can age extremely well, as can Sauternes, and, in fact, all French dessert wines. Also, the better Burgundies, both red and white, and Northern Rhône red wines can age for 20 years or more. In general, inexpensive (under $20) French wines are not made for aging. Enjoy them in their youth.

Are Prestige Cuvée Champagnes Really Better? Or Are They Just a Rip-Off?

Prestige cuvées — such as Dom Pérignon and Cristal — are really the best Champagnes; whether they're worth the extra money is something you have to decide for yourself. They are — as a category — the finest Champagnes for the following reasons:

- ✔ Their aromas and flavors are more elegant, more concentrated, and more complex.

- ✔ Their bubbles are typically finer — more tiny and delicate — and more profuse than those of other Champagnes.

- ✔ The finish (duration of the flavor on the palate) of prestige cuvées is longer than that of other Champagnes.

- ✔ When stored in a cool place, they can age longer than other types of Champagnes — often, 20 years or more.

(See Chapter 10 for more information on prestige cuvée Champagnes.)

Can I Keep My Wines in the Refrigerator?

You can certainly keep any wines or Champagnes in the fridge for a few days, or even a week. But we do *not* recommend storing wines and Champagne in the refrigerator for indefinite periods of time. Most refrigerators are set too cold (about 35°F; 2°C) for wine storage. Extended periods of cold temperatures numb your wines, leaving them flat and tasteless; they need more moderate temperatures (ideally, between 50 and 60°F; 10 to 15°C) to develop at a proper pace.

Also, wines and Champagnes kept in the fridge too long can pick up off-odors from foods (which permeate through the corks). And the turning on and off of the refrigerator motor creates vibrations, which could be harmful to your wines.

 If you have a refrigerator that you're not using for food storage, set it at its *highest* temperature, which probably will bring it up to between 45 and 50°F (7 to 10°C). It's not ideal (you'll still have the motor cycling problem), but it's still much better than a cold fridge, or storing your wines at high (over 65°F; 19°C) temperatures.

The French Make a Big Deal about "Terroir." Isn't This Concept Overrated?

We believe that *terroir,* which comprises all the growing conditions in the vineyard — not only soil and climate, but slope of the hill where vines are planted, amount of exposure to the sun, and so forth — definitely affects the characteristics of whatever grapes are grown in the vineyard. And what affects the grapes affects the wines.

But *terroir* is a more important issue for fine wines than it is for simple beverage wines. If the point of the wine is just to taste good and be inexpensive, it might be blended from so many *terroirs* that it doesn't particularly express any of them — and, for that type of wine, that's not a bad thing. But fine wines have intriguing nuances, due partly to *terroir*.

The French make a big deal about *terroir* because they've got their various *terroirs* pretty much figured out, thanks to centuries of experience. Newer wine regions might disparage the concept, but maybe the reason is that they just haven't experienced the true impact of their own fine wine *terroirs* yet. (See Chapter 1 for more information on *terroir*.)

Is AOC (Appellation d'Origine Contrôlée) Status a Guarantee of Quality for French Wines?

Frankly, no. Nowadays, a high percentage of French wines are AOC wines. The AOC merely assures that the wine is made in the specific location stated on the label, that certain specified grape varieties are used for the wine, that the amount of alcohol is appropriate, and so forth. AOC wines must meet certain minimum quality standards, of course, but we're not talking excellence; many AOC wines are mediocre. And some *vin de pays* (non-AOC, country wines) are quite decent. The best way to look at AOC is as a badge of authenticity more than quality. (See Chapter 3 for more information on the AOC.)

Are All Burgundy Wines Expensive?

No, only the best ones! You can buy regional Burgundies — with the simple AOC "Bourgogne" — for under $20; most district-level Burgundies, such as "Côte de Beaune Villages," are under $30. And you can buy some white Burgundies, such as "Mâcon" and "Mâcon-Villages" wines, for under $15, many for about $10. Even white Burgundies with the better "St.-Véran" appellation cost only $15 to $16. (Chapter 7 tells you more about the wines of Burgundy.)

Chapter 16

Ten French Wine Myths Exposed

*W*ine myths are difficult to debunk. They've been repeated so often that people readily believe them. The French, who have been making wine for such a long time, have more than their share of wine myths. For instance, that one about Dom Pérignon first tasting Champagne and uttering, "Come, brothers, hurry! I am drinking stars!" Pure poppycock. That line first appeared in print in the 20th century (written, no doubt, by an early Champagne publicist), more than 200 years after the good Dom passed away. In this chapter, we expose ten other common myths about French wine.

Champagne Isn't For Dinner

Stuff and nonsense! Champagnes go extremely well with most foods — *except* tomato-based dishes (too acidic), full-flavored meat dishes — such as beef stew or venison — and most sweet desserts. Champagne is a fine accompaniment to egg dishes, many pastas, vegetables (particularly mushrooms), fish and seafood (definitely!), spicy Asian cuisine, poultry, and many different kinds of meat, such as pork or veal.

Red Bordeaux Takes Forever to Mature

The way that red Bordeaux wines — and most wines — are being made today is very different from the old days (about 30 to 35 years ago). Grapes are harvested later than they once were, and are therefore fully ripened, with lower acidity and softer tannins; these characteristics translate into fuller-bodied, softer, less lean wines than previously. The upshot? Most red Bordeaux nowadays — with a few exceptions — are ready to drink within ten to 15 years. And, of course, lots of inexpensive red Bordeaux wines (see Chapter 5) are drinkable and enjoyable as soon as they're released, or certainly within five or six years of their vintage date.

Sauternes Are Delicious Young

Frankly, for us, Sauternes and Barsacs are just too overpoweringly rich and sweet in their first ten to 15 years. As they start to turn to the color of an old gold coin with age, they lose some of their sweetness and start to develop incredible aromas and flavors reminiscent of orange rind, apricots, toffee, and honey. The better the vintage, the longer it takes to reach this plateau of complexity, and the longer your Sauternes or Barsac will age. The great Château d'Yquem, for example, usually needs 20 years or more before it really begins to develop, and can live for 100 years or more in good vintages.

Chablis Is Too Dry and Acidic

That's the way Chablis often was in the past. Two factors have changed the picture in Chablis:

 ✔ Modern viticultural methods now favor picking the Chardonnay grapes late in Chablis' vineyards; the fully-ripened grapes make wines that are lower in acidity, with richer, fruitier flavors than the Chablis wines of the past.

✔ Whether it's thanks to global warming or not, vintages in Chablis during the past two decades definitely have been warmer than in the past — another reason that modern Chablis wines are richer and fuller.

Champagne Is Too Expensive

Considering how labor-intensive Champagne is to make, and the fact that it's the world's best sparkling wine, Champagne is really not that expensive at all! Sure, you can't buy the *prestige cuvées* — such as Cuvée Dom Pérignon, Louis Roederer Cristal, and Veuve Clicquot La Grande Dame — with pocket change, but most Champagnes (85 to 90 percent) fall into the non-vintage brut category, and sell for $20 to $45 retail — hardly expensive for such a quality wine.

You Must Drink Beaujolais Nouveau before Spring

Classic myth. We don't know who started this one, or why. It's possible that some of the early Beaujolais Nouveau wines (back in the 1960's, for example) didn't last very long, but the idea that you *must* drink today's Beaujolais Nouveau within two or three months of its birth simply is not true.

Beaujolais Nouveau will last at least a year without any problem. However, if you let your Beaujolais Nouveau age for a year or more, it will no longer taste like Beaujolais Nouveau, as mature flavors will start to develop. (See Chapter 8 for more information about Beaujolais Nouveau.)

Châteauneuf-du-Pape Is Full-Bodied and Long-Lasting

We presume that you haven't tasted many Châteauneuf-du-Papes lately. Full-bodied, long-lasting, red Châteauneuf-du-Pape — with the exception of the wines of a handful of traditional producers, such as Château Rayas and Château de Beaucastel — has almost become a thing of the past. Most of today's Châteauneuf-du-Papes are medium-bodied wines made to drink within a few years of the vintage. If you want the real thing, make sure that you buy a Châteauneuf-du-Pape from a traditional producer. It will be deep in color and will cost $40 or more a bottle.

All Rieslings Are Too Sweet

Not the ones made in Alsace, France! Most Alsace Rieslings are dry, minerally, complex wines (unlike many German Rieslings, which are often slightly sweet, or most American Rieslings, which are insipid as well as sweet). Alsace Rieslings have more body and alcohol than the Rieslings of Germany. They're known for their fragrant, citrusy aromas, their crisp acidity, their concentration, and their great longevity, especially in good vintage years. Trimbach, Josmeyer, and Léon Beyer are three Alsace producers who specialize in dry Rieslings.

Wines of Southern France are Rustic and Mediocre

Not any more! Modern grape-growing and winemaking methods have come to the South of France, especially to Languedoc-Roussillon (France's largest wine-producing region). Some of France's best red wines — and certainly best-value wines — are now being made in this area.

Champagnes Don't Age Well

Not only do Champagnes age well (when stored in a cool place, of course), but they also improve with age. Even the least expensive type, non-vintage, tastes better if you keep it for two or three years. The extra time gives all the components of the Champagne (wines from different grape varieties and different villages — and for non-vintage — different years) a chance to blend together, to "marry," so to speak. The added maturity also brings complexity to the Champagne.

Part V
Appendixes

In this part . . .

Let's face it: French can be a very intimidating language. Our French wine pronunciation guide will help you out when you're ordering a Pauillac or a Puligny in a restaurant, or buying French wines in your local wine shop. And in either situation, you might wonder, "How good is 1994 Bordeaux or 1988 Champagne?" Appendix C — our updated French wine vintage chart — has those answers.

On the other hand, if you're trying to figure out how a particular Bordeaux is classified, or are someone's lifeline when the question of *grand cru* Burgundy comes up on a television quiz show, Appendix B is the only place to turn.

Appendix A

Pronunciation Guide to French Wine Terms

French words do not have stressed syllables. Any non-French terms have their stressed syllables indicated in capital letters.

Name	Pronunciation
Aligoté	*ah lee go tay*
Aloxe-Corton	*ah luss cor ton*
Alsace	*ahl zass*
Anjou-Saumur	*ahn jhoo saw muhr*
Appellation d'Origine Contrôlée	*ah pel lah see ohn daw ree jheen con troh lay*
Auxerrois	*aus ser wah*
Auxey-Duresses	*awe see duh ress*
Aÿ	*eye ee*
Banyuls	*bahn yule*
Bâtard-Montrachet	*bah tar mohn rah shay*
Beaujolais-Villages	*bo jho lay vee lahj*
Beaune	*bone*
Bergerac	*ber jhe rak*
Blanc de Blancs	*blahn deh blahn*
Blanquette de Limoux	*blahn ket deh lee moo*

(continued)

Name	Pronunciation
Blaye	*bly*
Bonnezeaux	*bonh zoe*
Bordeaux Blanc	*bor doh blahn*
botrytis cinerea	*boh TRY tis sin eh RAY ah*
Bourgogne	*boor guh nyeh*
Bourgueil	*boor guhy*
Brouilly	*broo yee*
Cabernet Sauvignon	*cab er nay soh vee nyon*
Cahors	*cah or*
Carignan	*cah ree nyahn*
Chablis	*shah blee*
Chambolle-Musigny	*shom bowl moo sih nyee*
Champagne	*sham pah nyah*
Chassagne-Montrachet	*shah sahn nyah mohn rah shay*
Château d'Yquem	*sha toh dee kem*
Château Grillet	*sha toh gree yay*
Château Lynch-Bages	*sha toh lansh bahj*
Château Pape-Clément	*sha toh pahp cleh mahn*
Château Trotanoy	*sha toh troh tahn wah*
Châteauneuf-du-Pape	*sha toe nuff dew pahp*
Chénas	*shay nahs*
Chevalier-Montrachet	*sheh vah lyay mohn rah shay*
Chinon	*shee nohn*
Chiroubles	*sheh roob leh*
Cinsault, or Cinsaut	*san soh*
Condrieu	*con dree uh*
Corbières	*cor bee yair*

Name	Pronunciation
Corton-Charlemagne	*cor tohn shar leh mahn*
Côte Chalonnaise	*coat shal oh nayse*
Côte de Nuits	*coat deh nwee*
Côte Rôtie	*coat ro tee*
Coteaux d'Aix-en-Provence	*coh toh dex on pro vahns*
Coteaux du Layon	*coat toe doo lay awn*
Coteaux Varois	*coh toh var whah*
Côtes du Luberon	*coat dew loo bear on*
Côtes du Rhône-Villages	*coat dew rone vee lahj*
Côtes du Ventoux	*coat dew vahn too*
Coulée de Serrant	*coo lay deh seh rahn*
Cramant	*crah mahn*
crémant	*cray mahn*
Crozes-Hermitage	*crows er mee tahj*
Cru Bourgeois	*crew boor jwah*
cuvée	*coo vay*
dégorgement	*day gorj mahnt*
Domaine Leroy	*doh main le rwah*
département	*day par mahn*
dosage	*doh sahj*
Échézeaux	*esh eh zoh*
Entre-Deux-Mers	*ahn treh douh mare*
Faugères	*foh jhair*
Fitou	*fee too*
Fixin	*fee san*
Fleurie	*flehr ee*

(continued)

Name	Pronunciation
Fourchaume	*for shohm*
Gaillac	*gah yahk*
Gevrey-Chambertin	*jehv ray sham ber tan*
Gewurztraminer	*ga VERZ tra mee ner*
Gigondas	*gee gohn dahs*
Givry	*jee vree*
Gosset	*go say*
grand cru classé	*grahn crew clahs say*
grand vin	*grahn van*
Graves	*grahv*
Grenache	*gren ahsh*
Grenouilles	*greh nwee*
Haut-Brion	*oh bree ohn*
Haut-Médoc	*oh meh dock*
Hermitage	*er mee tahj*
Irouléguy	*ee roo leh ghee*
Juliénas	*jool yay nahs*
Jura	*jhoo rah*
Jurançon	*jhoo rahn sohn*
La Mission-Haut-Brion	*lah mees yohn oh bree ohn*
Languedoc-Roussillon	*lahn guh doc roo see yohn*
Les Baux-de-Provence	*lay boh de pro vahns*
Les Clos	*lay cloe*
Les Forêts	*lay for ay*
Les Genevrières	*lay jhen ev ree air*
Les Perrières	*lay per ee air*
Les Preuses	*lay pruhz*

Name	Pronunciation
Lirac	*lee rak*
Loire	*lwahr*
Mâcon-Villages	*mah con vil lahj*
Mâconnais	*mah cawn nay*
Madiran	*mah dee rahn*
Médoc	*may doc*
Melon de Bourgogne	*meh lohn deh boor guh nyeh*
Ménétou-Salon	*meh neh too sah lohn*
Mercurey	*mair coo ray*
méthode champenoise	*meh tode sham peh nwahs*
Meursault	*muhr so*
millésime	*mill eh seem*
Minervois	*mee ner vwah*
mis en bouteille au château	*mees ahn boo tay oh sha toh*
moelleux	*mwah leuh*
Moët	*moh eT*
Monbazillac	*mon bah zee yak*
Montagne de Reims	*mohn tahn yeh deh rhaams*
Montagny	*mohn tah nyee*
Monthélie	*mon tel lee*
Montmains	*mohn man*
Montrachet	*mohn rah shay*
Morey-Saint Denis	*maw ree san dnee*
Morgon	*mor gohn*
Moulin-à-Vent	*moo lahn ah vahn*
Moulis	*moo lees*

(continued)

Name	Pronunciation
Mourvèdre	*moore vedr*
mousseux	*moos seuh*
Muscadet	*moos cah day*
Muscat de Beaumes-de-Venise	*moos cah deh bohm deh veh nees*
négociant	*neh goh see ant*
Nuits-Saint-Georges	*nwee san johrj*
Pauillac	*poy yac*
Pernand-Vergelesses	*per nahn ver jeh less*
Perrier-Jouët	*pehr ree yay jhoo eT*
Pessac-Léognan	*peh sack lay oh nyan*
pétillant	*peh tee yahn*
petits châteaux	*peh tee shah toh*
phylloxera	*feh LOX er ah*
Pinot Gris	*pee noh gree*
Pinot Noir	*pee noh nwahr*
Pol Roger	*pole ro jhay*
Pommard	*pohm mahr*
Pouilly-Fuissé	*poo yee fwee say*
Pouilly-Fumé	*poo yee foo may*
Pouilly-Vinzelles	*poo ee van zell*
premier cru	*prem yay crew*
Provence	*pro vahns*
Puligny-Montrachet	*poo lee nyee mohn rah shay*
Quarts de Chaume	*cahr deh showm*
Quincy	*can see*
Régnié	*ray nyay*

Name	Pronunciation
remuage	*reh moo ahj*
Reuilly	*reuh yee*
Riesling	*rees ling*
Roche aux Moines	*rohsh oh mwan*
Rully	*rouh yee*
Saint-Amour	*sant ah more*
Saint-Aubin	*sant oh ban*
Saint-Nicolas-de-Bourgueil	*san nee co lah deh boor guhy*
Saint-Romain	*san roh man*
Saint-Véran	*san veh rahn*
Sancerre	*sahn sair*
Santenay	*sahnt nay*
Saumur Champigny	*saw muhr shahm pee nyee*
Savennières	*sah ven nyair*
Savigny-lès-Beaune	*sah vee nyee lay bone*
Savoie	*sah vwah*
Sélection de Grains Nobles	*seh lec see ohn deh gran no bleh*
Sémillon	*seh mee yohn*
Seyssel	*say sell*
St.-Chinian	*san shin ee an*
St.-Emilion	*sant eh mee lyon*
St.-Estèphe	*sant eh steff*
St.-Joseph	*san jhoe sef*
St.-Julien	*san jhoo lee ehn*
supérieure	*soo per ee uhr*
Syrah	*see rah*

(continued)

Name	Pronunciation
Tavel	*tah vell*
terroir	*ter wahr*
tête de cuvée	*tet deh coo vay*
Tokay-Pinot Gris	*toh kay pee noh gree*
Ugni Blanc	*oo nyee blahnk*
Vacqueyras	*vac keh rahs*
Vaillons	*vye yohn*
Vaudésir	*voh deh zeer*
Vendange Tardive	*ven dahnj tar deev*
vieilles vignes	*vee ay veen*
Vieux-Château-Certan	*vyuh shah toe sair tan*
vigneron	*vee nyer ohn*
vin de paille	*van deh pahee*
vin de pays	*van deh pay ee*
vin jaune	*van john*
vins doux natural	*van doo nah too rahl*
Viognier	*vee oh nyay*
Vosne-Romanée	*vone roh mah nay*
Vougeot	*voo jhoe*

Appendix B

Bordeaux and Burgundy Classifications

*W*e present three classifications of Bordeaux wines:

- ✔ The 1855 Classification, done by the Bordeaux wine merchants, listed according to their ranking within each class (all the red Bordeaux are from Haut-Médoc except one; Sauternes/Barsac are also part of the classification)

- ✔ The 1959 Classification of red and white Graves (Pessac-Léognan) wines by the French appellation board (INAO), listed alphabetically

- ✔ The 1955 Classification (re-classified in 1996) of St.-Emilion wines, by the French appellation board (INAO), listed alphabetically

(See Chapters 4 to 6 for further information on Bordeaux wines.)

We also list the *grand cru* Burgundy wines, red and white, geographically, from north to south. (See Chapter 7 for further info on Burgundy wines.)

The 1855 Classification of Bordeaux

Table B-1	Haut-Médoc Wines: First Growths	
Estate	*Commune*	*Annual Production (Cases*)*
Château Lafite-Rothschild	Pauillac	20,000
Château Latour	Pauillac	34,000
Château Margaux	Margaux	33,000
Château Haut-Brion	Pessac-Léognan**	16,000
Château Mouton-Rothschild	Pauillac	32,500

* A case is 12 750 ml bottles or 6 1.5 l bottles. Case totals reflect the entire Château production, including second-label Bordeaux. Case total is an average figure; production totals vary from year to year.

** Château Haut-Brion is the only red Bordeaux in the 1855 Classification that is not in the Haut-Médoc district; see Chapter 4 for further information.

Table B-2	Haut-Médoc Wines: Second Growths	
Estate	*Commune*	*Annual Production*
Château Rausan-Ségla	Margaux	23,500
Château Rauzan-Gassies	Margaux	12,500
Château Léoville-Las Cases	St.-Julien	45,000
Château Léoville-Poyferré	St.-Julien	38,000
Château Léoville-Barton	St.-Julien	25,000
Château Durfort-Vivens	Margaux	13,000
Château Lascombes	Margaux	40,000
Château Gruaud-Larose	St.-Julien	45,800

Estate	Commune	Annual Production
Château Brane-Cantenac	Cantenac-Margaux	38,000
Château Pichon-Longueville-Baron	Pauillac	24,500
Château Pichon-Lalande	Pauillac	36,000
Château Ducru-Beaucaillou	St.-Julien	19,000
Château Cos d'Estournel	St.-Estèphe	36,000
Château Montrose	St.-Estèphe	27,000

Table B-3   Haut-Médoc Wines: Third Growths

Estate	Commune	Annual Production
Château Giscours	Labarde-Margaux	42,000
Château Kirwan	Cantenac-Margaux	15,500
Château d'Issan	Cantenac-Margaux	27,000
Château Lagrange	St.-Julien	52,000
Château Langoa-Barton	St.-Julien	8,300
Château Malescot St. Exupéry	Margaux	18,500
Château Cantenac-Brown	Cantenac-Margaux	26,000
Château Palmer	Cantenac-Margaux	20,000
Château La Lagune	Ludon (Haut-Médoc)	37,000
Château Desmirail	Margaux	13,000
Château Calon-Ségur	St.-Estèphe	30,000
Château Ferrière	Margaux	5,000
Château Marquis d'Alesme-Becker	Margaux	5,250
Château Boyd-Cantenac	Cantenac-Margaux	8,000

Table B-4 Haut-Médoc Wines: Fourth Growths

Estate	Commune	Annual Production
Château St.-Pierre	St.-Julien	9,000
Château Branaire-Ducru	St.-Julien	27,000
Château Talbot	St.-Julien	56,000
Château Duhart-Milon	Pauillac	28,000
Château Pouget	Cantenac-Margaux	4,500
Château La Tour Carnet	St.-Laurent (Haut-Médoc)	19,000
Château Lafon-Rochet	St.-Estèphe	22,500
Château Beychevelle	St.-Julien	46,500
Château Prieuré-Lichine	Cantenac-Margaux	35,000
Château Marquis-de-Terme	Margaux	13,000

Table B-5 Haut-Médoc Wines: Fifth Growths

Estate	Commune	Annual Production
Château Pontet-Canet	Pauillac	45,000
Château Batailley	Pauillac	22,000
Château Grand-Puy-Lacoste	Pauillac	18,000
Château Grand-Puy-Ducasse	Pauillac	14,700
Château Haut-Batailley	Pauillac	10,000
Château Lynch-Bages	Pauillac	46,000
Château Lynch-Moussas	Pauillac	15,000
Château Dauzac	Labarde-Margaux	22,700
Château d'Armailhac	Pauillac	22,000
Château du Tertre	Arsac-Margaux	20,000

Estate	Commune	Annual Production
Château Haut-Bages-Libéral	Pauillac	14,000
Château Pédesclaux	Pauillac	9,000
Château Belgrave	St.Laurent (Haut-Médoc)	29,000
Château Camensac	St.Laurent (Haut-Médoc)	29,500
Château Cos Labory	St.-Estèphe	8,500
Château Clerc-Milon	Pauillac	16,000
Château Croizet-Bages	Pauillac	11,000
Château Cantemerle	Macau (Haut-Médoc)	35,000

Table B-6   Sauternes and Barsac: First Great Growth

Estate	Annual Production
Château d'Yquem	7,920

Table B-7   Sauternes and Barsac: First Growths

Estate	Annual Production
Château Guiraud	16,000
Château La Tour Blanche	6,250
Château Lafaurie-Peyraguey	7,500
Château de Rayne-Vigneau	20,000
Château Sigalas-Rabaud	2,800
Château Rabaud-Promis	5,000
Clos Haut-Peyraguey	3,500
Château Coutet	5,500

(continued)

Table B-7 *(continued)*

Estate	Annual Production
Château Climens	3,900
Château Suduiraut	8,500
Château Rieussec	10,000

Table B-8   Sauternes and Barsac: Second Growths

Estate	Annual Production
Château d'Arche	3,000
Château Filhot	12,000
Château Lamothe-Despujols*	1,250
Château Lamothe-Guignard*	2,700
Château de Myrat	4,000
Château Doisy-Daëne	6,500
Château Doisy-Dubroca	600
Château Doisy-Védrines	2,200
Château Suau	1,580
Château Broustet	2,000
Château Caillou	4,500
Château Nairac	1,800
Château de Malle	5,200
Château Romer du Hayot	4,200

The original Château Lamothe is now two estates.

Graves (Pessac-Léognan): 1959 Official Classification

Table B-9	Classified Red Wines of Graves (Pessac-Léognan)
Wine	*Commune*
Château Bouscaut	Cadaujac
Château Carbonnieux	Léognan
Domaine de Chevalier	Léognan
Château de Fieuzal	Léognan
Château Haut-Bailly	Léognan
Château Haut-Brion	Pessac
Château Latour-Haut-Brion	Talence
Château Malartic-Lagravière	Léognan
Château La Mission-Haut-Brion	Talence
Château d'Olivier	Léognan
Château Pape-Clément	Pessac
Château Smith-Haut-Lafitte	Martillac
Château La Tour-Martillac	Martillac

Table B-10	Classified White Wines of Graves (Pessac-Léognan)
Wine	*Commune*
Château Bouscaut	Cadaujac
Château Carbonnieux	Léognan
Domaine de Chevalier	Léognan

(continued)

Table B-10 *(continued)*

Wine	Commune
Château Couhins	Villenave d'Ornon
Château Couhins-Lurton	Villenave d'Ornon
Château Haut-Brion	Pessac*
Château Laville-Haut-Brion	Talence
Château Malartic-Lagravière	Léognan
Château d'Olivier	Léognan
Château La Tour-Martillac	Martillac

* Château Haut-Brion Blanc added to list in 1960

St.-Émilion 1955 Official Classification (Re-Classified 1996)

Premiers Grands Crus Classés (A)
Château Ausone
Château Cheval Blanc

Prem Grands Crus Classés (B)
Château L'Angélus
Château Beau-Séjour Bécot
Château Beauséjour (Duffau Lagarrosse)
Château Belair
Château Canon
Château Figeac
Clos Fourtet
Château La Gaffelière
Château Magdelaine
Château Pavie
Château Trotte Vieille

Grands Crus Classés
Château L'Arrosée
Château Balestard la Tonnelle
Château Bellevue
Château Bergat
Château Berliquet
Château Cadet-Bon
Château Cadet-Piola
Château Canon-La-Gaffelière
Château Cap de Mourlin
Château Chauvin
Château La Clotte
Château La Clusière
Château Corbin
Château Corbin-Michotte
Château La Couspade
Château Couvent des Jacobins
Château Curé-Bon
Château Dassault

Château La Dominique
Château Faurie de Souchard
Château Fonplégade
Château Fonroque
Château Franc-Mayne
Château Grand Mayne
Château Grand-Pontet
Château Grandes Murailles
Château Guadet-Saint-Julien
Château Haut-Corbin
Château Haut-Sarpe
Clos des Jacobins
Château Lamarzelle
Château Laniote
Château Larcis-Ducasse
Château Larmande
Château Laroque
Château Laroze
Château Matras
Château Moulin du Cadet
Clos de L'Oratoire

Château Pavie-Decesse
Château Pavie-Macquin
Château Petit-Faurie-de-
 Soutard
Château Le Prieuré
Château Ripeau
Château St.-Georges-Côte-
 Pavie
Clos St.-Martin
Château La Serre
Château Soutard
Château Tertre Daugay
Château La Tour-Figeac
Château a Tour-du-Pin-Figeac
 (Giraud-Bélivier)
Château la Tour-du-Pin-Figeac
 (Moueix)
Château Troplong-Mondot
Château Villemaurine
Château Yon-Figeac

Burgundy Grands Crus

All Côte d'Or *Grand Cru* Burgundies are listed, from north to south.

Table B-11	Côte de Nuits *Grands Crus*
Village	*Grand Cru*
(24 Grands Crus; all red wine)	
Gevrey-Chambertin	
	Mazis-Chambertin
	Ruchottes-Chambertin
	Chambertin Clos-de-Bèze
	Chapelle-Chambertin
	Griotte-Chambertin

(continued)

Table B-11 *(continued)*

Village	Grand Cru
	Le Chambertin
	Latricières-Chambertin
	Charmes-Chambertin
	Mazoyères-Chambertin
Morey-St.-Denis	
	Clos de la Roche
	Clos St.-Denis
	Clos des Lambrays
	Clos des Tart
	Bonnes Mares (small part)
Chambolle-Musigny	
	Bonnes Mares (larger part)
	Le Musigny
Vougeot	
	Clos de Vougeot
Flagey-Echézeaux	
	Grands Echézeaux
	Echézeaux
Vosne-Romanée	
	Richebourg
	Romanée-St.-Vivant
	La Romanée
	Romanée-Conti
	La Grande Rue
	La Tâche

Table B-12	Côte de Beaune *Grands Crus*
Village	*Grand Cru*
(*7 grands crus;* mainly white wines; one red *grand cru* indicated.)	
Aloxe-Corton	Corton (one mainly red *grand cru,* but 22 different vineyards — such as Clos du Roi, Renardes or Bressandes — can affix their names to Corton; also Corton Blanc)
	Corton-Charlemagne (25 percent of this vineyard is in Pernand-Vergelesses, and a small part is in Ladoix-Serrigny)
Puligny-Montrachet	Chevalier-Montrachet
	Bienvenues-Bâtard-Montrachet
	Le Montrachet (50 percent in Chassagne-Montrachet)
	Bâtard-Montrachet (½ in Chassagne-Montrachet)
Chassagne-Montrachet	Criots- Bâtard-Montrache

Appendix C

French Wine Vintage Chart: 1979 to 1998

• •

*H*ere is our 20-year French wine vintage chart. Any vintage chart must be regarded as a rough guide — a general, average rating of the vintage year in a particular wine region. Keep in mind that many wines will be exceptions to the vintage's rating; some wine producers always manage to find a way to make a decent — even fine wine — in a so-called poor vintage.

Wine Region	1979	1980	1981	1982	1983	1984	1985	1986	1987
Bordeaux:									
Médoc, Graves	80c	70d	80c	95c	85c	70d	90c	90b	75c
Pomerol, St.-Emil	80c	65d	80c	95c	85c	65d	85c	85b	75d
Burgundy:									
Côte de Nuits-Red	80c	85c	55d	75d	75c	75c	85c	70d	85c
Côte Beaune-Red	80d	80c	70d	75d	80d	70d	85c	70d	80d
Burgundy, White	85d	75d	80d	80d	80d	75d	85c	90c	80c
Rhône Valley:									
Northern Rhône	85c	80c	75d	85c	90b	75c	90c	80b	80c
Southern Rhône	85c	70d	85c	70d	85c	70d	80c	75d	60d
Alsace	80c	75d	85c	75d	95c	70d	90c	85c	75c
Champagne	90c	NV	85c	90c	80c	NV	95c	80c	NV
Sauternes	375c	80c	80c	70c	90b	70c	80c	90a	70c

Wine Region	1988	1989	1990	1991	1992	1993	1994	1995	1996	1997	1998
Bordeaux:											
Médoc, Graves	85b	90b	95a	75c	75c	80b	85b	90a	90a	85b	85a
Pomerol, St.-Emil	85b	90b	95a	60d	75c	80b	85b	90a	85a	85b	95a
Burgundy:											
Côte de Nuits-Red	80c	85c	95b	85b	75c	85a	80c	90a	90a	85b	85b
Côte Beaune-Red	85c	85c	90b	70c	80c	85a	80c	90a	90a	85b	85b
Burgundy, White	80c	90c	85c	70d	85c	75d	85c	90b	90a	85c	85b
Rhône Valley:											
Northern Rhône	90c	95b	90a	90b	75c	60d	85b	90a	85a	90b	90a
Southern Rhône	85c	95a	95b	65d	75c	80b	85a	90a	80c	80c	95b
Alsace	85c	95b	95b	75c	85c	85c	90b	85b	85b	85b	90b
Champagne	90b	85c	90b	NV	NV	80b	NV	90a	95a	?	?
Sauternes	95a	90b	95a	70c	70c	65c	75b	85a	85a	85a	85a

Key:

100	= Outstanding	c	= Ready to drink
95	= Excellent	d	= May be too old
90	= Very Good	NV	= Non-vintage year
85	= Good	?	= Too early to tell
80	= Fairly Good		
75	= Average		
70	= Below Average		
65	= Poor		
50-60	= Very Poor		
a	= Too young to drink		
b	= Can be consumed now, but will improve with time		

Wine Region	Recent Past Great Vintages
Bordeaux:	
Médoc, Graves	1959, 1961, 1970
Pomerol, St.-Emil	1961, 1964, 1970, 1975
Burgundy:	
Côte de Nuits-Red	1959, 1964, 1969, 1978
Côte Beaune-Red	1959, 1969
Burgundy, White	1962, 1966, 1969, 1973, 1978
Rhône Valley:	
Northern Rhône	1959, 1961, 1966, 1969, 1970, 1972 (Hermitage), 1978
Southern Rhône	1961, 1967, 1978
Alsace	1959, 1961, 1967, 1976
Champagne	1961, 1964, 1969, 1971, 1975
Sauternes	1959, 1962, 1967, 1975

Index

FOR DUMMIES®

A world of resources to help you grow

TRAVEL

Italy
0-7645-5453-0

Hawaii
0-7645-5438-7

Walt Disney World & Orlando
0-7645-5444-1

Also available:

America's National Parks For Dummies (0-7645-6204-5)

Caribbean For Dummies (0-7645-5445-X)

Cruise Vacations For Dummies 2003 (0-7645-5459-X)

Europe For Dummies (0-7645-5456-5)

Ireland For Dummies (0-7645-6199-5)

France For Dummies (0-7645-6292-4)

Las Vegas For Dummies (0-7645-5448-4)

London For Dummies (0-7645-5416-6)

Mexico's Beach Resorts For Dummies (0-7645-6262-2)

Paris For Dummies (0-7645-5494-8)

RV Vacations For Dummies (0-7645-5443-3)

EDUCATION & TEST PREPARATION

Spanish
0-7645-5194-9

Algebra
0-7645-5325-9

U.S. History
0-7645-5249-X

Also available:

The ACT For Dummies (0-7645-5210-4)

Chemistry For Dummies (0-7645-5430-1)

English Grammar For Dummies (0-7645-5322-4)

French For Dummies (0-7645-5193-0)

GMAT For Dummies (0-7645-5251-1)

Inglés Para Dummies (0-7645-5427-1)

Italian For Dummies (0-7645-5196-5)

Research Papers For Dummies (0-7645-5426-3)

SAT I For Dummies (0-7645-5472-7)

U.S. History For Dummies (0-7645-5249-X)

World History For Dummies (0-7645-5242-2)

HEALTH, SELF-HELP & SPIRITUALITY

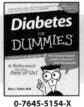

Diabetes
0-7645-5154-X

Sex
0-7645-5302-X

Parenting
0-7645-5418-2

Also available:

The Bible For Dummies (0-7645-5296-1)

Controlling Cholesterol For Dummies (0-7645-5440-9)

Dating For Dummies (0-7645-5072-1)

Dieting For Dummies (0-7645-5126-4)

High Blood Pressure For Dummies (0-7645-5424-7)

Judaism For Dummies (0-7645-5299-6)

Menopause For Dummie (0-7645-5458-1)

Nutrition For Dummies (0-7645-5180-9)

Potty Training For Dummies (0-7645-5417-4)

Pregnancy For Dummies (0-7645-5074-8)

Rekindling Romance For Dummies (0-7645-5303-8)

Religion For Dummies (0-7645-5264-3)

Available wherever books are sold. Go to www.dummies.com or call 1-877-762-2974 to order direct

CPSIA information can be obtained
at www.ICGtesting.com
Printed in the USA
BVOW06n0936260617
487517BV00002B/2/P